Chronicles of Darkness

Chronicles of Darkness

David Ward

ROUTLEDGE
London and New York

First published 1989
by Routledge
11 New Fetter Lane, London EC4P 4EE
29 West 35th Street, New York, NY 10001

Printed in Great Britain by T.J. Press Ltd., Padstow, Cornwall

British Library Cataloguing in Publication Data

Ward, David
  Chronicles of darkness
  1. English literature. Special subjects. South
  Africa. Critical studies
  I. Title
  820.9'3268

  ISBN 0 415 02995 3

Library of Congress Cataloguing in Publication Data

Ward, David
  Chronicles of darkness.

  Bibliography: p.
  1. South African fiction (English) – 20th century –
History and criticism. 2. South African fiction
(English) – White authors – History and criticism.
3. English fiction – 20th century – History and
criticism. 4. Africa in literature. 5. African
fiction – White authors – History and criticism.
I. Title.
PR9362.5.W37   1989   823   88-26413

ISBN 0 415 02995 3   68102

To Gillian
and to my mother and father

Contents

Acknowledgements

My thanks are due to Dr K. M. Newton and Mr J. C. Q. Stewart for reading parts of this book and making many valuable suggestions, and to Mr R. J. C. Watt for reading the whole of the first print-out, for his meticulous attention to detail and for his constructive criticism of many aspects of the book. My wife, Gillian, has read and corrected my work at many stages, and I have benefited greatly from her knowledge and acumen. I must thank Hilda Bernstein for her kindness in discussing aspects of South African literature and politics with me. An encounter with Nadine Gordimer was important in stimulating my thoughts about the subject. It would be impossible, though, to list all the African friends and acquaintances who have helped me in one way or another, and I beg their forgiveness for any inadequacies.

Author and publisher gratefully acknowledge permission granted by the following publishers and agents to reproduce excerpts from these works:

Karen Blixen ('Isak Dinesen'), *Out of Africa*, by permission of the estate of Karen Blixen, The Bodley Head Ltd, and Random House, Inc.

André Brink, *Looking on Darkness*, *A Dry White Season*, *An Instant in the Wind*, *Rumours of Rain*, by permission of the author, Faber & Faber Ltd, and William Morrow & Co. Inc.; *The Ambassador, The Wall of the Plague*, by permission of the author, Faber & Faber Ltd, and Simon & Schuster, Inc. *A Chain of Voices*, the author and Faber & Faber.

Joyce Cary, *Mister Johnson*, by permission of the estate of the author.

J. M. Coetzee, *Dusklands*, Copyright © J. M. Coetzee, 1974, 1982; *Foe*, Copyright © J. M. Coetzee, 1986; *In the Heart of the Country*, Copyright © J. M. Coetzee, 1976, 1977; *Life & Times of Michael K*, Copyright © J. M. Coetzee, 1983; *Waiting for the Barbarians*, Copyright J. M. Coetzee, 1980, by permission of Martin Secker & Warburg Ltd.

Nadine Gordimer, *Burger's Daughter*, Copyright © 1979 Nadine Gordimer; *July's People*, Copyright © 1981 Nadine Gordimer; *The Late Bourgeois World*, Copyright © 1966 Nadine Gordimer; *No Place Like: Selected Stories*, Copyright © 1971 Nadine Gordimer; *Occasion for Loving*, Copyright © 1960, 1963 Nadine Gordimer; *A Soldier's Embrace*, Copyright © 1975, 1977, 1980 Nadine Gordimer; *The Soft Voice of the*

Serpent, Copyright © 1950, 1951, 1952, renewed 1978, 1979, 1980 Nadine Gordimer; by permission of the author, Jonathan Cape Ltd, and Viking Penguin, Inc; *Something Out There, The Conservationist,* by permission of the author, Jonathan Cape, and Felix Licensing BP, *The Lying Days,* by permission of the author, Jonathan Cape Ltd, and Sidney Satenstein; *A World of Strangers,* the author, Jonathan Cape, and Russell & Volkening; *A Sport of Nature,* by permission of the author, Jonathan Cape, Felix Licensing BP and Alfred Knopf, Inc.

Graham Greene, *A Burnt-out Case,* Copyright © 1960, 1961 Graham Greene; *The Heart of the Matter,* Copyright © 1948, renewed © 1976 by Graham Greene. All rights reserved, both reprinted by permission of the author, William Heinemann Ltd, The Bodley Head Ltd, and Viking Penguin.

Elspeth Huxley, *The Flame Trees of Thika, The Mottled Lizard,* by permission of the author, Chatto & Windus, and Viking Penguin.

Doris Lessing, *Going Home,* by permission of Michael Joseph and Ballantine; *The Golden Notebook,* by permission of Michael Joseph and Curtis Brown Ltd; *The Grass is Singing,* by permission of Michael Joseph and Harper & Row.

Alan Paton, *Cry, the Beloved Country,* Copyright © 1948 Alan Paton; copyright renewed by the author 1976. By permission of the estate of the author, Chatto & Windus, and Charles Scribner's Sons.

William Plomer, *Turbott Wolfe,* by permission of the estate of the author and The Hogarth Press.

Laurens van der Post, *In a Province,* by permission of the author and The Hogarth Press.

Evelyn Waugh, *Scoop,* by permission of the estate of the author and Little, Brown, & Co.

Abbreviations of principal works discussed and editions cited

KAREN BLIXEN ('ISAK DINESEN')
OA   *Out of Africa* (1937), Penguin Books, Harmondsworth, 1954.

ANDRE BRINK
CV   *A Chain of Voices* (1982), Fontana, London, 1983.
DWS *A Dry White Season* (1979), Fontana, London, 1979.
IW   *An Instant in the Wind* (1976), Fontana, London, 1983.
LD   *Looking on Darkness* (Afrikaans, 1973, English, 1974), Fontana, London, 1984.
RR   *Rumours of Rain* (1978), Fontana, London, 1978.
WP   *The Wall of the Plague* (1984), Fontana, London, 1985.

JOYCE CARY
MJ   *Mister Johnson* (1939), Penguin Books, Harmondsworth, 1962.

J. M. COETZEE
D   *Dusklands (The Vietnam Project* and *The Narrative of Jacobus Coetzee)* (1974), Penguin Books, Harmondsworth, 1983.
F   *Foe* (1986), Secker & Warburg, London, 1986.
HC   *In the Heart of the Country* (1977), Penguin Books, Harmondsworth, 1982.
MK   *Life & Times of Michael K* (1983), Secker & Warburg, London, 1983.
WB   *Waiting for the Barbarians* (1980), Penguin Books, Harmondsworth, 1982.

JOSEPH CONRAD
HD   *Heart of Darkness* (1902), in *Youth: a Narrative, and Two Other Stories*, Uniform Edition of the Works of Joseph Conrad, Dent, London, 1923.

NADINE GORDIMER
BD   *Burger's Daughter* (1979), Penguin Books, Harmondsworth, 1982.

JP *July's People* (1981), Penguin Books, Harmondsworth, 1982.

LBW *The Late Bourgeois World* (1966), Penguin Books, Harmondsworth, 1982.

LD *The Lying Days* (1953), Virago, London, 1983.

NPL *No Place Like: Selected Stories* (1978), Penguin Books, Harmondsworth, 1978. (Later editions published with the title *Selected Stories*.)

OL *Occasion for Loving* (1963), Virago, London, 1983.

SE *A Soldier's Embrace* (1980), Penguin Books, Harmondsworth, 1982.

SN *A Sport of Nature* (1987), Jonathan Cape, London, 1987.

SOT *Something Out There* (1984), Penguin Books, Harmondsworth, 1985.

SVS *The Soft Voice of the Serpent* (1953), Penguin Books, Harmondsworth, 1962.

TC *The Conservationist* (1974), Penguin Books, Harmondsworth, 1982.

WS *A World of Strangers* (1958), Penguin Books, Harmondsworth, 1962.

GRAHAM GREENE

BOC *A Burnt-Out Case* (1960), Penguin Books, Harmondsworth, 1963.

HM *The Heart of the Matter* (1948), Penguin Books, Harmondsworth, 1962.

ELSPETH HUXLEY

FTT *The Flame Trees of Thika* (1959), Penguin Books, Harmondsworth, 1962.

DORIS LESSING

GH *Going Home* (1957), Triad/Granada, London, 1980.

GN *The Golden Notebook* (1962), Penguin Books, Harmondsworth, 1964.

GS *The Grass is Singing* (1950), Triad/Granada, London, 1980.

OCC *This was the Old Chief's Country* (1973), vol. 1 of *Collected African Stories*, Triad/Granada, 1979.

SBF *The Sun Between their Feet* (1973), vol. 2 of *Collected African Stories*, Triad/Granada, London, 1979.

ALAN PATON

CBC *Cry, the Beloved Country* (1948), Penguin Books, Harmondsworth, 1958.

WILLIAM PLOMER
TW   *Turbott Wolfe* (1926), Oxford University Press, London, 1985.

OLIVE SCHREINER
AF   *The Story of an African Farm* (1883), Penguin Books, Harmondsworth, 1982.
FMM *From Man to Man* (1927), Virago, London, 1982.

LAURENS VAN DER POST
IP   *In a Province* (1934), Penguin Books, Harmondsworth, 1984.

EVELYN WAUGH
S   *Scoop* (1938), Penguin Books, Harmondsworth, 1954.

1

Chronicles of darkness

i

This book is about the way in which Africa is treated by writers of fiction; white writers of fiction. When I set out, I intended to consider both black and white writers, but this caused problems which I could not immediately solve. Writers like Achebe, Soyinka, Ngũgĩ, have very different perspectives from each other. So do writers like Sarah Gertrude Millin, H. Rider Haggard, Doris Lessing, and Joseph Conrad. That was not the problem. I am a white myself – a white Briton – and many of the attitudes towards Africa with which I grew up were distorted. However much I wanted to write about black African writers, I had to negotiate my way through these distortions. And the more I read of the white writers, the more I realized that they, too, were either accepting a passive and distorted view, or confronting it. This seemed a subject that was worth writing about.

Doris Lessing wrote, in a review of *The Lost World of the Kalahari*:

> An African once said to me that beyond the white man's more obvious crimes in Africa there was an unforgivable one that 'Even the best of you use Africa as a peg to hang your egos on.' To this crime Mr. Van der Post is open. So are all of us.[1]

She goes on to identify a particular problem which faces the white who is born and brought up in Africa. Van der Post's book, she says,

> is mainly valuable because of its conscious crystallisation of the white man's malaise, an unappeasable hunger for what is out of reach. All white-African literature is the literature of exile: not from Europe, but from Africa.[2]

The two perceptions – a literature of egoism, a literature of exile – enclose a difficult and uncomfortable space. I decided taht, before I could look at black-African literature clearly, I had to explore and understand that space, that beam in my eye.

ii

> The world is like a Mask dancing. If you want to see it well you do not stand in one place.[3]

The speaker is Ezeulu, the Chief Priest in Chinua Achebe's splendid *Arrow of God*, and he is telling his son Oduche why he wants him to join the church, to find out more about the white man and the way he sees the world. Reading Achebe (and many other African writers) might be a way of liberating a European or white African from his egoism, even, eventually, from his exile. There's a long and difficult route there, and one which should be travelled. But it involves a realization of perspective like that of Stephen Gray, who refuses to separate literature written in English, Afrikaans, and in the various indigenous languages, and points to the interconnectedness of literatures in Southern Africa, to the syncretism of a polysystem.[4] Reading African literature written in English or French is like looking through a tunnel to try to understand the mountain round it.

Even confining oneself to the written literature is distortive. African culture remains firm in its foundation upon a complex of oral cultures: the supervention of the printed word gives the impression that African narrative is Anglophone, Francophone, Lusophone, with quaint ethnic outliers like Swahili. The decision of Ngugi to write in his first language, Kikuyu, is, to my mind, a wonderfully right decision, even if the majority of his readers have to wait for a translation into English. It's a return to the real foundations of discourse and intelligence, an opportunity for the vigour of the oral culture and the energy of the written word to refresh each other. But it increases our awareness of how big the mountain is around the tunnel.

iii

Achebe offers some tentative thoughts about what the African novel is:

> The first is that the African novel has to be about Africa. A pretty severe restriction, I am told. But Africa is not only a geographical expression; it is also a metaphysical landscape – it is in fact a view of the world and of the whole cosmos perceived from a particular position.[5]

If I understand Achebe, this means that a novel written about Europe or America by an African is also a novel about Africa: that a novel written about Africa by Joseph Conrad, Joyce Cary, or Graham Greene is also a novel about Europe. I believe that's true. In some cases Africa, even if it is merely a backdrop painted in crude and garish colours, becomes a way of revealing or admitting something about Europe which a writer might hold back when performing in a different theatre.

iv

Most readers outside Africa get most of their knowledge of the continent from white writers, whether journalists or novelists. We, the reading public outside Africa, are sure we know a great deal about South Africa, for instance, and it is true that an attentive reader in Britain or America will know more about some of the things which happen there than the majority of the white population of that country. But if we see Paton or Gordimer, Brink or Coetzee, as focuses for understanding the historical and political dilemma, we are tempted to concentrate on *their* conflicts. White-African writers are made more readily available to international readers because publishers judge them to be more accessible as discourse.[6] And so the novel-reading public begins to see the problem of *apartheid* as the problem of how a liberal-minded white African should react to it, and the conflicts it causes between his personal problems and his public duty.

v

> Conflict can provide a deep and powerful stimulus, but a culture as a whole cannot be made out of the groans and sparks that fly. And it is out of a culture, from which man's inner being is enriched as the substance in an integrated community grows fuller, that a literature draws its real substance in the long run. The thirst that comes from the salt of conflict will need some quenching.[7]

This is from an address by Gordimer to the National Union of South African Students's Winter School, published in 1960. My whole background and education draws me into a passive sympathy with the Arnoldian, Leavisian view of 'culture' she expresses. But its view of what is absent, its notion of the bounteous culture of 'an integrated community' nurturing 'man's inner being', affects profoundly Gordimer's earlier accounts of what was really there, around her.

It's a problem in time. To construct an imaginary future, one worth working towards, Gordimer implicitly evokes a past, a European past imbued with European values: the message is dissolved in the language she uses. In this view a literature thrives on values which are endangered by conflict, nourished by the harmony of integration, and which are imaginatively accessible to anybody who has located herself in a 'tradition', in a 'culture'. Dan Jacobson's argument is yet more provocative, but far from perfect:

> A Colonial culture has no memory. . . . A political entity which has been brought into existence by the actions of an external power; a population consisting of the descendants of conquerors, of slaves and indentured labourers, and of dispossessed aboriginals; a language in the courts and schools which has been imported like an item of heavy machinery; a prolonged economic and psychological subservience to a metropolitan centre a great distance away . . . such conditions make it extremely difficult for any section of the population to develop a vital, effective belief in the past as a present concern, and in the present as a consequence of the past's concerns.[8]

Elsewhere Jacobson extends the observation to cover all the cultural groupings of Southern Africa, in a remarkably cataracted view: 'We have no literature, we have no intellectual tradition . . . as a result of there having been so few people for so short a time in South Africa, the social fabric has a thinness, a simplicity.' And he laments *the absence of established and highly developed forms*.[9]

vi

So you either wait for a hundred years, for something which you call an 'integrated community' and something else you call 'established and highly developed forms', or you change the way you see 'community', and look elsewhere for 'forms' appropriate to it. It needed the rhetoric of Steve Biko, and perhaps his death, to force a re-examination of the idea of an 'integrated community'. Integration as a way of fighting *apartheid*, he asserts, is impossible in South Africa

> because it was being foisted on two parties whose entire unbringing had been to support the lie that one race was superior and others inferior.[10]

> If by integration you understand a breakthrough into white society by blacks, an assimilation and acceptance of blacks into an already established set of norms and codes of behaviour set up by whites, then YES I am against it.[11]

Literature written by blacks in Africa has frequently adopted the languages and the forms which have been imported from Europe. Now black writers are developing formal approaches not to be found in the alien repertoire. It might be the best way out of darkness for the white writers to try specifically African solutions. They needn't change their languages to Yoruba, Swahili, or Xhosa (though it would be interesting). But it may be that some of the assumptions behind the form of the novel and the short story, assumptions about identity and character, about realism and fantasy, about morality, ontology, and epistemology, conspire to make the chronicles dark. Lessing had to go to Europe to escape from some of the conventions of form and vision. Some white-Africans who remain are beginning to consider a similar leap, anticipating an integration of a new kind, looking for ways of writing appropriate to a new society.

vii

Every artefact carries with it an index – though an imperfect one – to the culture which produces it. Every potsherd, every arrowhead the archaeologist digs up may be used to construct a model of its society. Such artefacts can change, subvert, or destroy the cultures they are carried into – not just the arrowheads, the pots as well. Even trinkets can 'buy' Manhattan, introducing with them an alien concept of land ownership.

4

Literature can be the record and the defence of such purchases by an invading culture, not just in the sense that they tell how 'Kurtz' collected ivory, or Karen Blixen 'had a farm'. A language, a notion of education, a system of values, a variety of preferred cultural forms, in architecture, music, or literature, may be ways of following up the trinkets with more powerful ways of creating needs to exploit.

viii

But tales written by whites about Africa also express unease. In each case the unease, the egoism, and the sense of exile, are not simply existential anguish. In each case the work is the product of a moment of history.

Each is read in the present of the reader, in his own moment in history. Some of the books and authors I deal with have become influential because of the way in which they have been brought back into prominence by a change in the historical moment, as for instance Olive Schreiner, whose concern with the role of women has given her work a new lease of life. Others have been given new power as cultural artefacts by film, as in the case of *The Flame Trees of Thika* and *Out of Africa*. All of my subjects warrant their places because they have a widespread influence among international readers. I might have included many others on this same basis, but my space is limited: if the exclusions are arbitrary, the inclusions are not.

Joseph Conrad: *Heart of Darkness*

Marlow's narrative in *Heart of Darkness* (1902) is, formally, one of *statement*: Marlow recollects events happening in real time and real space, in historical sequence. But the whole thrust of the narrative is profoundly affected by the co-presence in the narrative of a parallel and competing mode. Marlow's narrative is, simultaneously, *performative*.[1] Not centrally as warning, promise, or bequest, though it might contain these as elements in its rhetoric, not even expiatory: hieratic is the best word I can discover.

This performative character is given it by the outer frame of narrative: Marlow does not simply address, he enacts before an audience, albeit a somnolent one. It isn't, however, a matter of a dramatic monologue wrapped in the framework of occasion, in which the occasion itself takes on the character of statement, to give the ensheathed performance credibility. The frame takes on *itself* the performative role. Not only Marlow, but his inter-mediary as well, the speaker in the frame, has the quality of metaphor, compounding the inward insecurity with a melancholy outward display. To match the outer window, the narrative of the first narrator, there is an inner spy-hole, through which abbreviation, in the form of Kurtz, speaks the diminished frame of horror. This inner view-line, in a topological paradox as queer as a Klein bottle, describes a surface round the outer text, a prolapse of the viscera now enclosing a terrible internal space of its own.

If Odysseus, Dante, or any other hero, wishes to find what space he occupies, he does not unroll a map, consult a compass, does not even take bearings on the stars. He has two options, both of which involve going elsewhere, and taking the space he wants to find with him. He can make the right libations to call a friend out from the inside, who can tell him (the Teiresias option). Or he can go with a friend inside the outside (the Vergil route). Either way invagination leads to uterine inversion, and, through the primary narrator, Marlow and Kurtz, Conrad (himself flickering in two forms which constantly cover each other, Korzeniowski/Conrad, dipolar apparitions speaking inner and outer languages) leads us into a heart where black and white unbind the contracts of conventional meaning.

The invader brings his own meaning with him. Geographically, histori-cally, in this continent which isn't called Africa and around this river which isn't called the Congo or Zaire, there have to be humans who call the place home, but in *Heart of Darkness* we are merely given peripheral glimpses of human histories beyond the range of a beleaguered vision. A darkness which the intruder brings with him shadows everything in the book, re-creating the world it perceives. The Africans at the margins of Marlow's vision are there as victims, but also as registers of something lost, a natural human-ness. What 'natural' really means is another matter: the role of the Africans is determined by a bitter sense of the profound moral and human failure of the colonial invader. The Africans, therefore, take a negative role – they suffer, they are different, they are *unlike*, outside, in a world in which it is still possible for humanity to participate.

There are those who detect a failure in an unresolved confusion at the heart of the work itself – an indecision (which is seen as distorting Conrad's intention) as to how far we are meant to trust Marlow's responses. McClure points to moments in the text where Marlow carries with him the defensive prejudices and terrors of the intruder, most pointedly in 'No, they were not inhuman. Well, you know, that was the worst of it – this suspicion of their not being inhuman' (*HD* 96).[2] A 'nightmare vision of "horned shapes" and the equation of the Congolese with a "conquering darkness" haunt Marlow long after his return to Europe, and they seem intended to haunt the reader as well'.[3]

Marlow gives conflicting signals, the signals of the ignorant invader who returns from a journey with sufficient understanding of himself to locate, though not to dissipate, the real source of the nightmare. The residual conflicts of Marlow are part of the integrity of the book. What may disturb any reader is that there is apparently no effort on the part of the shadowy Conrad who lies behind the apparatus of multiple narrators to settle the conflict, to discriminate for us. This reservation, too, is part of a narrative integrity, identifying areas in which minds fail to resolve the problems of telling the self. Or, ways in which writing or speech may point to their own elusiveness: Derrida's '*L'écriture en abîme*' might be taken literally as describing the way in which this discourse of darkness identifies its own heart as an abyss, as a token of endless reflexivity at the focus of its blazon.[4]

Marlow describes his approach to the river in a revealing way, recalling some of the names of the trading posts the ship passes, 'names that seemed to belong to some sordid farce acted in front of a sinister back-cloth', and the preliminary distortions and alienation of meaning suffered by the traveller. The remark has a sharp reflexive force, too, identifying the teller's awareness of the performative act's theatricality, as the enjoyment of performance shades into a hysteria. As against this he places the 'natural' sounds of the sea and the physical vitality of the people who live by it – observed in such a way as to mark the irrelevance and sterility of the European enterprise and its alien view:

> The idleness of a passenger, my isolation amongst all these men with
> whom I had no point of contact . . . seemed to keep me away from the

truth of things, within the toil of a mournful and senseless delusion. The voice of the surf heard now and then was a positive pleasure, like the speech of a brother. It was something natural, that had its reason, that had a meaning. Now and then a boat from the shore gave one a momentary contact with reality. It was paddled by black fellows. You could see from afar the white of their eyeballs glistening. They shouted, sang; their bodies streamed with perspiration; they had faces like grotesque masks – these chaps; but they had bone, muscle, a wild vitality, an intense energy of movement, that was as natural and true as the surf along their coast. They wanted no excuse for being there. (*HD* 61)

This account has in it more than a vestige of the stereotypical prejudiced view of the European in Africa. The appeal to a natural, physical fineness in the alien race has a very long history in European thinking, stretching back to Montaigne's cannibals by way of Rousseau's noble savage. Conrad's own romantic temperament was just such as to be caught briefly by the glamour of the idea before probing beneath it. But the language he makes Marlow use contains its element of caricature, slipping into turn-of-the-century gests[5] of masculine conversation, 'these chaps', to remind us of the dramatic frame of the assembled company on the *Nellie* and the conventions of discourse which belong to it. Indeed the way in which Marlow's discourse slips in and out of different levels and conventions is one of the most striking ways in which Conrad hints at the level of experience which lies outside any easy exposition.

F. R. Leavis criticizes the excess of language:

The same vocabulary, the same adjectival insistence upon inexpressible and incomprehensible mystery, is applied to the evocation of human profundities and spiritual horrors, to magnifying a thrilled sense of the unspeakable potentialities of the human soul. The actual effect is not to magnify but rather to muffle.[6]

But Leavis doesn't take account of the theatrical nature of the performance. It's melodrama, surely, this thrashing about after effect, but it's not, in the structure of the narrative, a melodrama of the author. It's a convention suiting this man, this fictive audience, which, somnolent as they are, need hardly pay any attention. It signals a failure to find signs sufficient for the impression the speaker wishes to leave with his auditors.

A Rousseauesque romantic sentiment is active behind Marlow's description of Kurtz's abandoned black mistress, in the view of one perceptive critic, Ian Watt, 'the most affirmative image in the narrative, the embodiment of the confident natural energy of the African wilderness'.[7] Here Watt, too, is working within a European conceptual and emotional structure by adopting without question Marlow's words 'wilderness' and 'natural'. If the Africa which the woman inhabits is a wilderness, that is the result of the exploitative industry of European exploiters, and the way it has become a wilderness is through their subversion of an accustomed civil order which is no more 'natural' or 'unnatural' than any other. If it is not a wilderness, neither Conrad nor the *Société Anonyme Belge pour le Commerce du Haut Congo* would be able to see that. Nor would his fiction, 'Marlow'. The vitality of the woman is a kind of cipher to suggest what is only half seen or understood – a vitality and energy which remains despite the corruption and the confusion. It retains the weakness of a cipher, for all the high colour that Marlow gives her. This 'wild and gorgeous apparition of a woman' is the product of a European imagination rioting in the ignorance of its African experience:

> She was savage and superb, wild-eyed and magnificent; there was something ominous and stately in her deliberate progress. And in the hush that had fallen suddenly upon the whole sorrowful land, the immense wilderness, the colossal body of the fecund and mysterious life seemed to look at her, pensive, as though it had been looking at the image of its own tenebrous and passionate soul. (*HD* 135-6)

Inside all this hokum, almost Haggard-like in its fantasy of Africa, there are hints both of a sense of inadequacy and of a glimpse of reality in the observer. But it isn't an observation of Africa. It may be the beginnings of a realization of self, catalysed by Africa.

Elsewhere the hokum takes the form of threatening fantasies in which fear dehumanizes the real human presence:

> they faced the river, stamped their feet, nodded their horned heads, swayed their scarlet bodies; they shook towards the fierce river-demon a bunch of black feathers, a mangy skin with a pendent tail – something that looked like a dried gourd; they shouted periodically together strings of amazing words that resembled no sounds of human language; and the deep murmurs of the crowd, interrupted suddenly, were like the responses of some satanic litany. (*HD* 145-6)

When Marlow asks Kurtz 'Do you understand this?' the manner of Kurtz's answer is interesting:

> I saw a smile, a smile of indefinable meaning, appear on his colourless lips that a moment after twitched convulsively. 'Do I not?' he said slowly, gasping, as if the words had been torn out of him by a supernatural power. (*HD* 146)

What is described here is not *what* is known, but *how* it seems to be known; the 'indefinable meaning' is in the smiling, not the knowing; whatever illumination lies inside the obscenity is as white as the exterior of a whited sepulchre, a vision catalysed by the ignorance which invaders bring with them.

Marlow embodies a potential locked within a limitation and/or a reversal of that, a limitation locked within a potential. However, both potential and limitation include the turning away from the assumed common role and common understanding of Europeans in Africa to hearing 'the voice of the surf' 'like the speech of a brother', and perceiving the Africans to be 'as natural and true as the surf' (*HD* 61). That is a sea-change worthy of notice, in which Marlow suggests the possibility of a turn from this alien-ness, this European-ness, to recognition of common humanity. But the whole fiction, plotting as it does a difficult and dangerous journey into a sense of the ultimate failure of European culture, forbids the potential to transcend the limitation completely. The two are locked into each other.

What Conrad can and does do is to explore the myth of Africa in such a way as to reveal the contradictions, the vulnerability, the ignorance and treachery implicit in the European's concepts of self and of civilization. Just beneath the surface of European civilization there is always 'the Eldorado Exploring Expedition':

> Their talk . . . was the talk of sordid buccaneers: it was reckless without hardihood, greedy without audacity, and cruel without courage; there was not an atom of foresight or of serious intention in the whole batch of them. (*HD* 87)

Conrad's vision is, resolutely, a moral one, and that, perhaps, is its partial failure. Conrad is very effective, satirically, in suggesting the feebleness of the culture and the ideals the colonists bring to Africa with them. The Company's chief accountant is eloquent of this, with his meticulous turn-out: 'That's backbone. His starched collars and got-up shirt-fronts were achievements of character.' He is also very effective in the ironic contrasts he draws between the pride of European culture in its *efficiency* and the muddle on the ground in Africa, where a full-time brickmaker makes no bricks for lack of essential materials, where the boat remains inoperative for weeks because a few rivets are not in the right place, where the manager of the inner station is allowed to drift into madness, out of control of the central organization. Conrad conveys powerfully the sense of this mess as moral and psychological failure.

Worse than the barbarism they construct in imagination, though uncomfortably like it, the invaders may meet isolation within a world perceived as having immense but formidably hostile power, organized according to some kind of ordering principle inaccessible to European minds, but nevertheless projected by their European-ness.[8] The ideal of intellectual clarity embedded in European pragmatism and its universal explanations covers imperfectly a profound fear of something unexplained at work in every mind. The terror is released by the unfamiliar world of Africa, converted by the fearful confusions of the observer. It was as if they were 'travelling back to the earliest beginnings of the world, when vegetation rioted on the earth and the big trees were kings' (*HD* 92-3), like visitors to a prehistoric world or an unknown planet. 'We could have fancied ourselves the first of men taking possession of an accursed inheritance, to be subdued at the cost of profound anguish and of excessive toil' (*HD* 95).

The sense of dislocation goes together with the comedy of impotence. Marlow describes an episode in one of the dirty little 'civilizing' wars Europe was conducting, with all solemnity, at the time:

> In the empty immensity of earth, sky, and water, there she was, incomprehensible, firing into a continent. Pop, would go one of the six-inch guns; a small flame would dart and vanish, a little white smoke would disappear, a tiny projectile would give a feeble screech – and nothing happened. Nothing could happen. There was a touch of insanity in the proceeding, a sense of lugubrious drollery in the sight; and it was not dissipated by somebody on board assuring me earnestly there was a camp of natives – he called them enemies! – hidden out of sight somewhere. (*HD* 61-2)

Marlow's first words: 'And this also . . . has been one of the dark places of the earth', direct us with some irony to three things. First, by implication, to the European myth of Africa, 'the dark continent' (though Marlow never mentions Africa by name). Second, to a view of history and civilization in which Europe plays the bringer of light. Third, to the fragility of the culture which Europe wills upon Africa. Later he speaks of a change, not in the place, but in the idea of the place, from a glorious empty mystery to 'a place of darkness', and the river sinisterly

> resembling an immense snake uncoiled, with its head in the sea, its body at rest curving afar over a vast country, and its tail lost in the depths of the land. And as I looked at the map of it in a shop-window, it fascinated me as a snake would a bird – a silly little bird. (*HD* 52)

In the arrogance and insecurity of the European consciousness Africa appears again and again as a place to find one's self. Sometimes as a test of daring, sometimes in a grand theoretical and poetic way, as Jung sought to find evidences of the collective unconscious in Africa. It is much more rarely that Europeans hope to find individual consciousness there, recognizing other people in their other-ness. Ideas of mystery, ideas of darkness, ideas of godlike grandeur lurk here, such as those hinted at in Kurtz's report to the International Society for the Suppression of Savage Customs, projecting the imperial sway as 'an exotic Immensity ruled by an august Benevolence. It made me tingle with enthusiasm. This was the unbounded power of eloquence – of words – of burning noble words.' Under the luminescence there is the real dark continent of 'Exterminate all the brutes!' (*HD* 118), as Marlow finds in the margin of Kurtz's text. Yet further beneath that margin is that heart of the title, nothing to do with geographical centres, much more to do with a perceived failure of European civilization glimpsed through a continent of darkness in the mind.

The brief comedy of Marlow's examination by a doctor in the city of the whited sepulchre has more point than it appears to claim. The doctor makes enquiries about madness in Marlow's family, observes with scant tact that it would be "'interesting for science to watch the mental changes of individuals, on the spot, but . . . '" "Are you an alienist?" I interrupted' (*HD* 58). It is no simple coincidence that Freud's enquiries into psychoanalysis began in Vienna, that city of imposing surfaces, in the midst of the decadence of a European empire, whilst at the same time Europe launched into its headlong rush to create great external empires in the continent which Europe called dark. Freud's Vienna, Leopold's Brussels, Marlow's city of the whited sepulchre, Edwardian London too, were becoming disturbingly aware of the gulf which existed between the plausible work and hidden forces the word cannot suppress. Journeys into the interior were full of reverberations; if the travelling was physical it trailed along the rags of the mind; if psychological, it carried kit for a tropical jungle.

In Britain this was the age of *Dr Jekyll and Mr Hyde* (1886), the trial and imprisonment of Oscar Wilde (1895), *The Time Machine* (1895), *The Turn of the Screw* and 'The Jolly Corner' (1898 and 1909), and *Sons and Lovers* (1913). In Europe it was time for Symbolism, and latterly, Proust and Dada. European artists in a multiplicity of ways were celebrating or suffering the power of the suppressed to compromise or destroy. An intelligent contemporary like Edward Garnett was able to recognize immediately this element of the tale in a review dated 1902:

> the art of 'Heart of Darkness' – as in every psychological masterpiece – lies in the relation of the things of the spirit to the things of the flesh, of the invisible life to the visible, of the sub-conscious life within us, our obscure motives and instincts, to our conscious actions, feelings and outlook.[9]

It is one of the distinctions of *Heart of Darkness* that it enables us to perceive a continuity between the paradoxes of the psyche in individual man and the unconscious history of Europe as it entered into a dangerous episode. It was, as it were, the beginnings of a self-analysis for Europe in which relays of authors sat discreetly behind the couch taking notes which are still not complete, and in which the message is still garbled by inconsistencies of code, and by the insecurities of the scribes. We might, then, expect from the fictions, the travel literature, the autobiographical writings of colonists, explorers, visitors, if not light on the Africa which Stanley called 'the dark continent', then at least illumination of the secretive interior life in European men and women. In Europe it was a time when that internal life clamoured particularly loudly for recognition and appeasement in a form of discourse appropriate to its urgent force. In the context of this secret agenda there was no way in which Europe could pretend to discover Africa in any sense beyond the drawing of maps and the exploitation of human, agricultural, or mineral resources. There was deep psychological uncertainty, the beginnings of an attempt at reappraisal of Europe's role in the world, but that did not in any way weaken the political, economic, and military drive for grandeur simply in possession of vulnerable lands and peoples.

The magic of possession was the key, as Conrad himself saw, and transferred from Europe as a whole to Kurtz:

> You should have heard him say, 'My ivory.' Oh yes, I heard him. 'My Intended, my ivory, my station, my river, my – ' everything belonged to him. It made me hold my breath in expectation of hearing the wilderness burst into a prodigious peal of laughter that would shake the fixed stars in their places. Everything belonged to him – but that was a trifle. The thing was to know what he belonged to, how many powers of darkness claimed him for their own. (*HD* 116)

Kurtz is a scapegoat, in the accurate, ancient sense of the word. There is a kind of expiatory magic in the tale which consigns, or tries to consign, the sins of Europe, to abbreviate them into 'Kurtz' and drive him into the arms of those 'powers of darkness'.

The scramble for Africa was in some ways a more cruel experience for the continent than slavery. The slavers murdered millions, condemned millions to chattel slavery thousands of miles from their homes. The new colonialism destroyed whole societies, impoverished and weakened ancient cultures, and, almost incidentally, killed and enslaved millions more. It reduced many of the rest to wage slavery and set about destroying their government, ways of worship, and patterns of social relationship. Once again Edward Garnett was quick to see the link, remarking that Conrad's art 'implies the catching of infinite shades of the white man's uneasy, disconcerted, and fantastic relations with the exploited barbarism of Africa'. Even if Garnett, characteristically for his time, assumes that Africa must be barbarous, he hints at the other barbarism, the madness of the exploiter too. Unadmitted amongst all the mixed motives which drove the colonizers on was a fascination for what they saw as 'dark', for a world in which social and moral restraints might be ignored, and fantasies of power played out without the accustomed sanctions. It goes without saying that there was no notion of the kind of civil, legal, and political order of the communities they invaded and frequently brought close to destruction.

The two women in *Heart of Darkness* shadow each other in a way which is deliberately indeterminate but hints strongly at the perversions of consciousness which the exploiter brings with him to Africa. The Intended

> put out her arms as if after a retreating figure, stretching them black and with clasped pale hands across the fading and narrow sheen of the window. Never see him! I saw him clearly enough then. I shall see this eloquent phantom as long as I live, and I shall see her, too, a tragic and familiar Shade, resembling in this gesture another one, tragic also, and bedecked with powerless charms, stretching bare brown arms over the glitter of the infernal stream, the stream of darkness. She said suddenly very low, 'He died as he lived.' (*HD* 160-1)

The allusive frame of a descent into and return from hell, recalled from ancient myth, is at its clearest here – 'a tragic and familiar Shade', 'the infernal stream, the stream of darkness'. What is not clear at all is that the infernal stream acts, as it does in Greek mythology, as a boundary between regions which are distinct – the world of light and the world of dark. It isn't even clear that the conventional European moral meanings of 'dark' or 'black' are meant to be secure. Kurtz's African lady, described here as 'brown', not black, is given tragic status, without losing any of the warmth she is credited with elsewhere. And though the 'Intended' has fair hair and pale hands, she is said to stretch her arms 'black' across the river. The colour of mourning, or a constructive confusion of the symbolism of black and white? She inhabits, after all, a 'whited sepulchre'.

In calling her a 'tragic and familiar Shade' Conrad, through Marlow, sets yet more associations to work – 'shade' takes on a dual meaning, at once spirit or ghost and, in association with 'tragic', actress. By contrast, the deserted mistress takes on a different quality of tragedy: if the epic analogy is what is in our minds (and it is there, somewhere, for many readers), the memory of Dido deserted by another cruel traveller might shadow the text for a moment, while the Intended becomes, ironically, the apparition of a failed Penelope. Or it may be that the reader of Conrad would recall, almost as a gloss upon the nature of Kurtz's treason, this passage from the close of *Lord Jim*:

> But we can see him, an obscure conqueror of fame, tearing himself out of the arms of a jealous love at the sign, at the call of his exalted egoism. He goes away from a living woman to celebrate his pitiless wedding with a shadowy ideal of conduct. Is he satisfied – quite, now, I wonder? We ought to know. He is one of us – and have I not stood up once, like an evoked ghost, to answer for his eternal constancy?[10]

Marlow's ambiguous experiences, Marlow's misgivings, are present in our minds as contextualities webbed with tragic and epic reminiscences as we read what the Intended says. Her rhetoric does have a theatrical aspect – it is grief for the edification of an audience, a public, not a private faith and knowledge which she declaims. 'Familiar', too, has the simple enough meaning of well known, but in this ambiguous context the word evokes the notion of the 'familiar' who intervenes between the spirit world and the world of the living – a sense which might very readily occur to the contemporary reader in a turn-of-the-century Europe, much preoccupied as it was with psychical research and communication with 'the beyond'. Conrad himself had a sceptical attitude towards such shenanigans with spirits, as is suggested by his 'Author's Note' to *Youth* (the volume which first contained *Heart of Darkness*), where he is lightly dismissive about the various ways in which critics have interpreted Marlow: 'he was supposed to be all sorts of things: a clever screen, a mere device, a "personator", a familiar spirit, a whispering "daemon".'[11] But there's no doubt that the quality of communicated experience in *Heart of Darkness* carries with it possibilities of modes of suggestiveness which go far beyond anything placed concretely before the reader in the text, and which may add legitimacy to half-fulfilled suggestions of things beyond, or buried deep in our experience. Following Garnett, who was better placed to know the complexities of Conrad's mind, we might say that he explored a subconscious experience, though the further we go into a neo-Freudian and post-Freudian world the less we can be sure about what this means.

The 'Author's Note' marks Conrad's half-surprised realization of the oblique powers he has discovered:

> It was like another art altogether. That sombre theme had to be given a sinister resonance, a tonality of its own, a continued vibration that, I hoped, would hang in the air and dwell on the ear after the last note had been struck.[12]

It is, indeed, one of those works which prompts one to speak of an 'overdetermined' quality, the melting of the various complex elements one can isolate into a whole which creates its own mode and standard, a work in which the whole personality, known and unknown, is fused in a passionate heuristic.

In a letter to William Blackwood dated 1902, Conrad indicates how central he thought the interview between Marlow and the Intended should be in the whole design of the work:

> the interview of the man and the girl locks in – as it were – the whole 30000 words of narrative description into one suggestive view of a whole phase of life, and makes of that story something on quite another plane than an anecdote of a man who went mad in the Centre of Africa.[13]

So when the Intended asks for Kurtz's last words, it is no more than might be expected that the exchange takes on a quality of awe befitting a message from the underworld, or, what might be the same thing, a report from the dark side of the mind, illuminated at last:

> I was on the point of crying at her, 'Don't you hear them?' The dusk was repeating them in a persistent whisper all around us, in a whisper that seemed to swell menacingly like the first whisper of a rising wind. 'The horror! the horror!'
> 'His last word – to live with,' she insisted. 'Don't you understand I loved him – I loved him – I loved him!'
> I pulled myself together and spoke slowly.
> 'The last word he pronounced was – your name.' (*HD* 161)

The question usually asked about this passage is 'why did Marlow lie?' Perhaps the more pertinent question is whether he *was* lying, or admitting a complex and elusive truth sheathed in the form of a lie. There's no doubt that

Marlow displays feelings of guilt at telling the Intended what she wanted to know, and, what is more important, failing to do Kurtz justice by so speaking:

> She knew. She was sure. I heard her weeping; she had hidden her face in her hands. It seemed to me that the house would collapse before I could escape, that the heavens would fall upon my head. But nothing happened. The heavens do not fall for such a trifle. Would they have fallen, I wonder, if I had rendered Kurtz that justice which was his due? Hadn't he said he wanted only justice? But I couldn't. I could not tell her. It would have been too dark – too dark altogether. (*HD* 162)

There is not a word here about lying, though to be sure it is natural enough to infer that lying is what Marlow is worrying about, with the melodrama of the whispered sound 'The horror! the horror!' still reverberating in our minds.

However, it is possible to interpret Marlow's conscious failure as one of equivocation, as allowing the Intended to continue to believe in the noble, ideal Kurtz, the Kurtz of words, to allow her to 'know', to be 'sure'. 'The horror!' is more than an abrupt negation of these faulty ideals and noble words. It is, as Marlow remarks elsewhere, 'as though a veil had been rent' – the phrase recalls the moment of Christ's crucifixion and the rending of the veil which conceals the inner sanctum of the temple (Matt. 27:51). It is thus the revelation of a negation or absence,[14] or else that what has been expected in an outer space is only to be looked for within. And, directly after the passage quoted, Marlow is described as 'indistinct and silent, in the pose of a meditating Buddha' (*HD* 162), an image which points further into negation. 'The horror!' is thus, by association, given an air of greatness, a prophetic force commensurate with revelations of a momentous absence. It may be too petty to interpret Marlow's words to the Intended simply as consolation – even though Marlow defensively calls it a 'trifle'. Ian Watt is one of those who find in the 'lie' 'a humane recognition of the practical aspects of the problem: we must deal gently with human fictions, as we quietly curse their folly under our breath'.[15] It may be that and something else as well.

What form does the 'lie' take? Marlow tells the Intended that Kurtz said her name. Name? In the text she is 'the Intended', just that, we are given no other name. To be sure we can treat the 'name' as an absence, an item locked in the fictive memory of a fictive narrator, but 'the Intended' has become so integral a part of Marlow's enactment, so much a part of 'Kurtz and his litany of possessions', that it is the only available 'name' in a fiction which centres around a naming, around what a naming does, performatively, and on what happens when a name is substituted for a compendious vision.

This Intended is said to have the beauty of a 'great and saving illusion that shone with an unearthly glow in the darkness, in the triumphant darkness from which I could not have defended her – from which I could not even defend myself' (*HD* 159), the beauty of a noble falsehood at the centre of darkness. She is the Intended, not just in the commonplace sense of the betrothed, but in the sense that she embodies all that which Kurtz intends, the illusion which sustains the citizens of a 'whited sepulchre' in their sense of imperial destiny. That 'unearthly glow in the darkness' is something she carries with her, both glowing illusion and circumambient darkness, as Kurtz once did. If 'the horror' within the abyss is, indeed, what Kurtz possesses in 'his' Intended, then the intention of the discourse is centred, or decentred, in that abyss; 'The center is at the center of the totality, and yet, since the center does not belong to the totality (is not part of the totality), the totality *has its center elsewhere.*'[16]

Earlier in the text there is a brief anticipation of the 'lie' scene; an ambiguous passage:

> 'I laid the ghost of his gifts at last with a lie,' he began, suddenly. 'Girl! What? Did I mention a girl? Oh, she is out of it – completely. They – the women I mean – are out of it – should be out of it. We must help them to stay in that beautiful world of their own, lest ours gets worse. . . . You should have heard the disinterred body of Mr Kurtz saying, "My Intended." You would have perceived directly then how completely she was out of it.' (*HD* 115)

There's a certain gallant sexism in this exclusion, but it's more than a clumsy, conventionally male compliment. It has the effect of separating 'the girl' from 'my Intended' – the reality from the ideal, but, at the same time, wrapping the girl – all 'the women' – in a protected illusion. Kurtz was a possessor: '"My Intended, my ivory, my station, my – " everything belonged to him.' But Kurtz's real gifts are nothing to do with this lust to possess, or to protect 'the women' with an endearing illusion; they are the skills of Teiresias, Oedipus, or Gloucester, skills which enable him to see, *in extremis*, what we fear to be truth, the deep falsity of all our dedications. 'I laid the ghost of his gifts with a lie', therefore, can be seen as prevarication, permitting the lie which is there already to exorcize the ghost of prophecy.

The primary narrator gives fair warning to the reader in the first few pages of *Heart of Darkness*, in a passage which directly comments on Marlow's first spoken words – '"And this also," said Marlow suddenly, "has been one of the dark places of the earth"' (*HD* 48). He tells us too that Marlow's tales are not like those of other seamen, like the cracking of a nut:

> to him the meaning of an episode was not inside like a kernel but outside, enveloping the tale which brought it out only as a glow brings out a haze, in the likeness of one of these misty halos that sometimes are made visible by the spectral illumination of moonshine. (*HD* 48).

I take this to be one of the purposes of the frame of the novella, the trapping of the story-teller and his audience in a tidal suspension of movement, and in a darkness in which Marlow is 'indistinct'. The 'resonance', the 'tonality', the 'continued vibration' which are, for Conrad, 'another art altogether', lie in an indeterminacy which acts as a caution to the reader who is caught by the need to discover meaning, though, as J. Hillis Miller remarks, the 'halo' of meaning itself 'depends for its existence on the reader's involvement in the play of light and dark which generates it'.[17]

However, we need to hazard at least one certainty. *Heart of Darkness* is in no central way about Africa – not Conrad's revelation of the secret of a whole continent after a day's stroll. It is a re-invention of Europe in terms of representative consciousness and proving experience. This re-invention, as I have called it, takes place through complex relationships between the persons of the tale, arranged around the figure and voice of Marlow.

Conrad's use of Marlow is a way of presenting the tale inside a fiction of telling. It's an old device – older than Chaucer or Boccaccio. Its age is of a kind peculiarly appropriate to a tale which uses Africa, and it is one of the ways in which the tale claims an obscure but real relationship to the actual place, in that Africa is still a continent of tales, of tellers and listeners. Marlow recounts the way he discovers a printed book, *An Inquiry into some Points of Seamanship*, 'in a delicious sensation of having come upon something unmistakably real' (*HD* 99), only to find what seem to be notes in cipher (it turns out to be Cyrillic script) in the margin – 'an extravagant mystery'. The security of the literate in the written word is mocked, but so too is the apparent simplicity of the spoken word, mocked by the extravagance of Marlow's language.

The device of the spoken tale within the printed book brings us closer to the root of narrative. Whilst the reader remains a solitary with his page of signs in front of him, he is offered, as part of the propositions of the fiction, the imaginary role of auditor, the fundamentally social role of participant in a tale-telling. Marlow, the teller, also becomes a participant in a common act, but in a profoundly ambiguous way. His experience of the tale which he tells becomes a withdrawal too – a withdrawal into a meditative private world from which others are excluded. The auditor is alienated from the teller, or the teller from the auditor, with images borrowed from oriental meditation: 'Marlow sat cross-legged right aft, leaning against the mizzen-mast. He had sunken cheeks, a yellow complexion, a straight back, an ascetic aspect, and, with his arms dropped, the palms of hands outwards, resembled an idol' (*HD* 46), 'lifting one arm from the elbow, the palm of the hand outwards, so that, with his legs folded before him, he had the pose of a Buddha preaching in European clothes and without a lotus-flower' (*HD* 50), and 'Marlow ceased, and sat apart, indistinct and silent, in the pose of a meditating Buddha' (*HD* 162). The reader is in an ambivalent position, as solitary reader and, imaginatively, participant in a social act. His ambivalence echoes the ambivalence of the teller: Marlow the teller of tales, one of us; and Marlow the alienated, the withdrawn, who seems almost to occupy a space and time of his own, as if from a distant culture, intervening in the insecurity of Europe, helpless in the swing of the tide.

Marlow's telling of the tale, then, is as much the object of attention as he is the channel of our perceptions, and this uncertainty generates much of the power of the novella; as Marlow himself says, 'sombre enough, too – and pitiful – not extraordinary in any way – not very clear either. No, not very clear. And yet it seemed to throw a light.' His relationship with Kurtz compounds the ambiguity. Marlow and Kurtz are twinned by the fiction. We are only able to see Kurtz through Marlow, and the thrust of the fiction is towards a point where Marlow, it is hinted, cannot see himself or the world around him except in ways which are altered crucially by the psychic and emotional experience of his encounter with Kurtz.

The Kurtz we perceive is Marlow's perception, and the special intimacy in that linkage caused by the frame of tale-telling through the darkness to a close-knit group never completely erases our knowledge that the oral tale is inside a written discourse. Conrad invents Marlow to invent Kurtz: this might, as some critics say, 'distance' author from object, but it also implies the need for distance, the sense that this one must be held at arm's length, since it is dangerous. Dangerous not least in the fact that the homozygotic relationship abolishes any inner boundary between the glow of light and its darkness, though it retains and offers a sort of external division.

There's another effect of the twinning. Kurtz is a man of words, and it is through words that he exerts power in the world of Europe. The brickmaker of the Central Station (who seems never to make bricks) praises him for the rhetoric of his ideals:

> 'He is a prodigy. . . . He is an emissary of pity, and science, and devil knows what else. We want,' he began to declaim suddenly, 'for the guidance of the cause intrusted to us by Europe, so to speak, higher intelligence, wide sympathies, a singleness of purpose.' (*HD* 79)

This side of Kurtz inspires fascination, admiration, dedication, declamation, since it so persuasively embodies all that Europe 'stands for' in Africa; it is doubtless connected too with what, for the Africans, makes him a false god. And yet, Marlow tells us, 'The wastes of his weary brain were haunted by shadowy images now – images of wealth and fame revolving obsequiously round his unextinguishable gift of noble and lofty expression' (*HD* 147) – 'obsequiously' is marvellously eloquent of the coercive power which that voice possessed. Again, under this, 'there was something wanting in him – some small matter which, when the pressing need arose, could not be found under his magnificent eloquence.' The 'wilderness' – the word is used by Marlow – has whispered to him

> things about himself which he did not know, things of which he had no conception till he took counsel with this great solitude – and the whisper had proved irresistibly fascinating. It echoed loudly within him because he was hollow at the core. (*HD* 131)

Marlow, like Kurtz (like Conrad), is an artist with words. Marlow too is compared with an idol. And it is he who brings back this story from an encounter with 'the heart of darkness'. It is only he who is equipped to share the ultimate horror with Kurtz and relate it to the collection of auditors on the *Nellie* – and to us. If Marlow's 'lie' – 'the last word he pronounced was – your name' – implicates the Intended (though only ambiguously the girl herself) in the horror, everything Marlow does, and the way he is described by the primary narrator, implicates him. If Marlow is presented as communicating some kind of wisdom, that wisdom is in the knowledge of emptiness – a continent of emptiness, but not Africa. In a shadowy (or luminous) way, what Marlow learns is what all Europe knows, a darkness somewhere in its own interior.

What Kurtz knows lies in a space created between two women, one of whom is all that he whitely intends. The other, who is not named either, matches her with a dark inexplicable warmth. Their duality adds to a sense which is present throughout the *novella*, that the whole episode acts covertly through a sexual metaphor. Marlow penetrates the unknown continent, travelling along a river which is coiled like a serpent, thrusting towards a final experience which is entirely different from what he expected – not the enlightenment of the idealistic Kurtz, but his horror. In the process the women are as marginalized as the blacks; they become semantic markers only. If we can describe Marlow's journey as invagination, a probing into an interior which, when it is discovered, becomes equally the outer surface, the *novella* turns out to need both Africa and women to complete its strategies. They are needed, but strictly in that metaphorical role: they retain intrinsic meaning only vestigially. Africa becomes the vast reservoir of man's subconsciousness and limitless vitality, a world of origination and ambivalence, cruelty and shame, but in doing so stops being Africa. Women become majestic ways of defining men, revealing their power and charm, their inadequacies and lies, metaphorically, indeed, becoming men's virtues and vices, no longer women. *Heart of Darkness* is concentrated and potent; it is also incorrigibly the work of a white and a male. Europe's rage to possess Africa, without knowledge of what the possession would yield, has attracted the metaphor of rape many times. It is a metaphor deeply and ambivalently at the heart of Conrad's darkness.

3

Olive Schreiner: *The Story of an African Farm*

Olive Schreiner is an almost exact contemporary of Joseph Conrad, born just two years before him in 1855, though her first fiction, *The Story of an African Farm,* was published in 1883, a dozen years before *Almayer's Folly.* They have in common a peripheral relationship to the English-speaking world, the strong awareness of something destructive and constricting at its heart, and a conscious alienation from its materialist drive. Conrad's Africa, like his other geographies, is the product of an encyclopedic vision: it is not quite real, except as far as it exists in Conrad's perception. It is this that makes the detective work of Norman Sherry[1] so fascinating. It enables us to follow the history of the real Joseph Conrad, but does little to enlighten the process by which actual events were turned into fiction.

Conrad's fiction absorbs the person, the pain, the reality and the unreality. Schreiner's fiction is the direct expression of the person, and though the events and persons described in the fiction are altered from actual histories, the voice proclaims their closeness to present feeling. Showalter remarks, 'That voice, soft, heavy, continuous, is a genuine accent of womanhood, one of the chorus of secret voices speaking out of our bones, dreadful and irritating but instantly recognizable.'[2] But it is Schreiner and the women she influenced, Dorothy Richardson, Woolf, and Lessing, who found the language, taught us to hear what had never before been given appropriate form.

The Story of an African Farm, like *From Man to Man* (1927), is transparently based upon Schreiner's own life, particularly on her memories of childhood. That childhood is bound in so closely with African landscape and African society that Africa becomes a necessary condition for it, whereas Conrad's experience of Africa is entirely contingent. The opening words of *African Farm* are a description of the semi-arid land of the Karoo which is deeply estranging:

> The full African moon poured down its light from the blue sky into the wide, lonely plain. The dry, sandy earth, with its coating of stunted 'karroo' bushes a few inches high, the low hills that skirted the plain, the milk-bushes with their long, finger-like leaves, all were touched by a weird and an almost oppressive beauty as they lay in the white light.

In one spot only was the solemn monotony of the plain broken. Near the centre a small, solitary 'kopje' rose. Alone it lay there, a heap of round iron-stones piled on one another, as over some giant's grave. Here and there a few tufts of grass or small succulent plants had sprung up among its stones, and on the very summit a clump of prickly-pears lifted their thorny arms, and reflected, as from mirrors, the moonlight on their broad, fleshy leaves. (*AF* 35)[3]

This has some of the disconcerting effect of a picture by le Douanier Rousseau. The image of a bright moon in a blue sky creates a paradox of time and of light, arresting time, light, and the landscape revealed. The whole effect is one of conspiracy to alienate. It has something to do with the enumeration of objects, the sense given that each object is placed under the light of the moon to complement, or, as the prickly pear does, to reflect it, as from mirrors. The enumeration continues with the enumeration of sleepers under the moon's light. The milk-bushes have been given 'long, finger-like leaves', the iron-stones made into part of a giant's burial ritual, humanized just enough to consort on equal terms with the peculiarly still homestead and the sleeping humans. By now the dream is outside them, encompassing the sleeper rather than inhabiting his or her consciousness. Clingman remarks that Schreiner's work sets out 'a "colonial" problematic; it is settled and alien at the same time'.[4] The passage accomplishes the paradox obliquely, by means of visual metaphor.

The passage is characteristic of Schreiner in its estranging effect; it is also characteristic in its occasional sentimentality, describing Em's 'innocent face of a child in its first sweet sleep', Lyndall's 'quite elfin-like beauty', and Waldo's 'great head of silky black curls'. The estrangement and the sentiment belong together: Schreiner's adult view of childhood is habitually coloured by a dream-like sense of loss – and loss is involved with recollections of the metaphysical anxieties of childhood. Waldo lies there in the moonlight counting the clock and the death of men; Schreiner, with her worried *fin de siècle* atheism, vicariously indulges his childlike grief.

The sentimentality is characteristic in another way too. In any society there is a tension between a collective ethic and consciousness on the one hand, and individualism on the other. In such a deeply fractured society as Schreiner describes, identification with the collective values of a society presents peculiar problems. Individualism becomes the means of flight. And individualism has its own forms of sentimentality. The consciousness of a society as the enemy of talent, the gaoler of imagination, tempts the writer to create heroes of the imagination who are destined to experience a tragic fall. Hardy's Jude avoids the sentimental trap by complex means; George Eliot's Dorothea doesn't. Olive Schreiner never quite loses the desire to make us fall in love with her characters, particularly her children, by making them perfect and hard done by.

The moon-world has its counterpart sun-world, red as the moon-world was white, full of heat, aridity and movement as the other was still and coolly dream-like:

> The plain was a weary flat of loose red sand sparsely covered by dry karroo bushes, that cracked beneath the tread like tinder, and showed the red earth everywhere. Here and there a milk-bush lifted its pale-coloured rods, and in every direction the ants and beetles ran about in the blazing sand. . . . The two sunflowers that stood before the door, out-stared by the sun, drooped their brazen faces to the sand; and the little cicada-like insects cried aloud among the stones of the 'kopje'. (*AF* 38)

The plants preside stilly over the moonscape; in the red sunscape it is the insects who dominate, and the plants are defeated by the light. The dream-like eschatological anxiety of the night world gives way in Waldo to exploratory ritual; the slate, the pencil, the rituals of self-education mutate into the building of an altar. The 'heap of round iron-stones piled one upon another, as over some giant's grave' which had presided over the moonscape are echoed, but with absorbed, intent, ant-like activity, in the sunscape:

> Looking carefully, he found twelve small stones of somewhat the same size; kneeling down, he arranged them carefully on the cleared space in a square pile in shape like an altar. Then he walked to the bag where his dinner was kept; in it was a mutton chop and a large slice of brown bread. The boy took them out and turned the bread over in his hand, deeply considering it. Finally he threw it away and walked to the altar with the meat, and laid it down on the stones. (*AF* 39-40)

Such games, rituals, childhood explorations of meaning, attempts to construct models of elusive purpose in the universe, are peculiarly important in Schreiner. The motif reappears with extraordinary effect in the first chapter of *From Man to Man*, 'The child's day'. They are described with all the care and attentiveness to detail with which, for instance, Defoe describes his castaway making a spade, or the inhabitants of his plague city disinfecting a purse full of coins. They have, in part, a similar effect – man is shown to be *homo faber*, the maker, artificer. But, whereas Defoe, eighteenth-century Englishman, concerns himself with the imperative of surviving isolation, inventing surrogates for a lost society, Schreiner, nineteenth-century colonist and woman, lovingly and painfully describes the powerless artifice with which a growing understanding attempts to compel meaning in a hostile land. *Homo faber* in Defoe cannot be contracted simply to *homo oeconomicus*, as Ian Watt would argue,[5] but that will do for a start. In Schreiner the foundations are more complex – man the maker has its origins equally in *homo ludens, homo philosophicus*, and *homo somnians*: the substructures of the practical world are in play, speculative thought, and dream, and each of these merges into the others.

Later, Waldo laboriously constructs the working model of his invention, a machine for shearing sheep, only to have it destroyed by the hypocrite Bonaparte Blenkins. Waldo's ingenuity is certainly compatible with the progressive, materialist ideal of the nineteenth century, but it is something more. The machine is built out of the same impulse as the stone altar: they are both attempts to connect the active, restless intelligence with a meaning obstinately absent from the world. His name, Waldo, and that of Em, Lyndall's sister, and Ralph Iron (Schreiner's pen-name for this work), together form a homage to Ralph Waldo Emerson, but one which is compromised by irony in a world ill-prepared for Emerson's idealism.[6]

Reading Olive Schreiner in the last decades of the twentieth century is disconcerting in this respect: that the issue we expect to be central appears to be peripheral. By the 1880s white colonists had appropriated most of the best land in South Africa, destroying or exploiting other racial groups on the way. Reading Schreiner we have to put up with Nguni and Sotho being called kaffirs or niggers, Khoisan called hottentots and bushmen, though the most obvious racial or cultural prejudice is, perhaps, reserved for the Afrikaners, who are represented by the gross, lazy, spiteful, self-indulgent Tant' Sannie and her equally unpleasant niece Trana. The Irish fare nearly as badly in the farcical figure of Blenkins.

But Schreiner's South Africa was very different from the South Africa of today. Almost all blacks – most whites too – lived a rural life. The Rand goldfields were not discovered until 1886. Diamonds had been discovered in 1867-71, which led to the British annexing the semi-autonomous state of Griqualand West, ostensibly to protect the Griquas from exploitation by the Afrikaner republics. It was a profitable piece of feigned morality but it didn't protect the Griquas or any other blacks. By June 1871 the population of the territory had grown to 37,000, perhaps only a third of them white. The episode pointed directions for the future in racial labour relations. There was no legal regulation of wages or working conditions, and there were no safety measures or compensation for injury or death. Labourers were paid a weekly wage of 7s. 6d. or 10s., supplemented by rations. Water cost 2s. 6d. a bucket, but brandy was cheaper. There was no way in which black workers could organize to defend themselves, or even have any sense of a common identity, until the process of urbanization and industrialization had gone much further.

Expropriation, exploitation, massacre, and inter-tribal warfare had destroyed or weakened traditional communities. In many cases independence, authority, and a collective identity were maintained with dignity and courage, as in the case of Moshoeshoe, ruling his refugee kingdom from Thaba Bosiu. But there was as yet no concept of an African identity beyond tribe or community to meet the changes which history, diamonds, and the white expropriator were forcing upon Southern Africa. Similarly there seemed to be no way in which even the most well-meaning white could face the problems posed by the disruption except by sympathy and haphazard charity.

Ruth First and Ann Scott argue that *African Farm* is effectively 'a statement about the violence of colonialism'. The blacks, they say, are made peripheral:

> But that was the point about the colonial condition: Africans were kept so far outside white society that that in itself was a statement about it; hence the violence of Bonaparte and Tant' Sannie's behaviour. . . . Olive was writing, in fact, about what colonialism did to whites, and in her novel the children are both symbol and expression of that system and its consequences.[7]

Their argument has a certain evasiveness. Olive Schreiner transcended her own society and culture, becoming one of the first great feminists, a distinguished socialist in an era of remarkable socialist intellectuals, and, flawed as her discussion of race in 1908[8] may have been, it shows she had ideas which were progressive for her time. But her sense of community with women, with the working class, or with people of other races, proceeded, paradoxically, from rebellion against community. Showalter gives us a portrait of the writer as neurotic isolate, her writing 'saturated with ardent emotion, adolescent to the point of solipsism in its privacy. The labors of construction and plotting were beyond her; her greatest joy came in the recording of an intuitive flash, or a political harangue.'[9]

But that was the only way: only a hermetic script could serve for escape (partial though that may be) from the ideological pressures of colonial life, womanhood, class-consciousness and racism in rural South Africa at the time of the Kimberley diamond rush.

It is no surprise that her attitudes to the complexities of her own society were muddled – particularly in an early work like *African Farm*. When Tant' Sannie expels the black herdsman's wife and her child from the farm, we are made to admire the Good Samaritan in Otto, the old German, whose charitable sense of duty makes no distinction between black and white. But we are not given any sense that the black woman might respond to disinterested love, deserve it, or even understand it. She is described in the way that whites in racist societies are taught to see blacks:

> She had a baby tied on her back by a dirty strip of red blanket; another strip hardly larger was twisted round her waist, for the rest of her black body was naked. She was a sullen, ill-looking woman, with lips hideously protruding.
>
> The German questioned her as to how she came there. She muttered in broken Dutch that she had been turned away. Had she done evil? She shook her head sullenly. Had she had food given her? She grunted a negative, and fanned the flies from her baby. (*AF* 87)

'Sullen' is used again and again. Why shouldn't she be sullen? She is separated from the ways of life which once gave dignity and purpose in her own community. She has been obliged to work for another's profit, that living has now been taken from her, and a white man gives her a little food and the loan of a coat. Perhaps inadvertently, Schreiner has given a sharp account of the impotence of individual charity.

It doesn't help that elsewhere in the book there is a portrait of a 'Kaffir' which contains something rather like Rider Haggard's facile romantic view. Umbopa in *King Solomon's Mines* (1885) was 'a magnificent man; I never saw a finer native. Standing about six foot three, he was broad in proportion, and very shapely. In the light, too, his skin looked scarcely more than dark except here and there where deep black scars marked old assegai wounds.' Laurens van der Post testifies to the effect of Haggard on a sensitive white child in South Africa in the first years of the twentieth century, encouraging progressive feelings about the relations between the races.[10] But it's difficult to sympathize when Lyndall uses something very like this patronizing admiration (intermixed with bitter ironies) as a way of criticizing the feebleness of a white, Gregory Rose.

> There at the foot of the 'kopje' goes a Kaffir; he has nothing on but a blanket; he is a splendid fellow – six feet high, with a magnificent pair of legs. In his leather bag he is going to fetch his rations, and I suppose to kick his wife with his beautiful legs when he gets home. . . . There is something of the master about him in spite of his blackness and wool. . . . He is the most interesting and intelligent thing I can see just now, except, perhaps, Doss. He is profoundly suggestive. Will his race melt away in the heat of a collision with a higher? Are the men of the future to see his bones only in museums – a vestige of one link that spanned between the dog and the white man? He wakes thoughts that run far out into the future and back into the past. (*AF* 227-8)

In all the complications of Olive Schreiner's feminism, too, there is a profound ambiguity which is perhaps expressed in Lyndall's attitude to Gregory's effeminacy. This insecurity is not resolved by the strange heroism of his feminine services to Lyndall at the end of her life. But amongst the crush of competing possible interpretations of Lyndall's mockery of Gregory there is one that is interesting in its irony. For all her feminist rhetoric, perhaps, Lyndall is confused about the stereotypes of gender and morality; she shows herself uncertain as to what to admire and what not to admire in a man. She cannot help but be so confused – there is no available language in her society to aid her to point the full potential of man or woman.

Neither can Gregory Rose understand, but both he and Lyndall *act* the denial of those stereotypes in their living, she to her destruction, he to his extraordinary (and extremely unlikely) credit. The fact that Lyndall chooses to mock Gregory's personality with the example of a stereotypically masculine black is Schreiner's way of casting ironic doubt upon the passive view of race which Lyndall and Gregory share, as well as the prevalent view of gender roles.

> Gregory was not quite sure how to take these remarks. Being about a Kaffir, they appeared to be of the nature of a joke; but, being seriously spoken, they appeared earnest: so he half laughed and half not, to be on the safe side. (*AF* 228)

The puzzle Schreiner puts to us through Gregory's uncertainty is not just Gregory's. It contains a whole series of questions about the assumptions which Schreiner, with no other audience to address than a white, male-dominated society in the imperialist 1880s, *knew* were inscribed in the language, the morality, the religion, in all the institutions of her day. They were the assumptions of power, and they could not be assaulted, except, perhaps, through irony and through a sentiment which aspires to tragedy. Lyndall, eventually, suffers the sentimental tragedy. The passage quoted above is one enfolded expression of the irony.

Schreiner is trapped in her own historical *locus*, tainted by the ignorance of the invading barbarian tribe. But at the same time she records the deadliness of the tribe, the suffocation and destruction of the trap. Tant' Sannie and Bonaparte Blenkins are not simply conventional grotesques, though the savage humour which defines their spitefulness, hypocrisy, and ignorant self-satisfaction might well be seen to draw intelligently on the still lively tradition of the picaresque. They are portraits of power, and of that kind of power which is generated by a culture of exploitation. Those – especially those children – who have a capacity to imagine other kinds of world have to perceive it through a crazed distorting glass of adult ideology.

In the very chapter when Bonaparte arrives, off-stage, at the farm, Waldo and Lyndall become the channels through which we perceive something of this. First, Lyndall's romanticized history of the real Bonaparte ironically places the awful Blenkins. But it also expresses Lyndall's own sense of deathlike confinement and confused fascination with power; she imagines Bonaparte's last days on St Helena: 'when he walked near the shore it seemed to him that the sea all around him was a cold chain about his body, pressing him to death'. Then Waldo hesitantly offers another version of history in place of Em's conventional acceptance of Christian dogmatism, a history which admits of other kinds of human achievement than that of Bonapartes, either the Corsican or the Irish variety. The vision of history which Waldo glimpses is one that is vast in extent, though its vocabulary is still touched by racial distortion in speaking of 'the time when the little Bushmen lived here, so small and so ugly, and used to sleep in wild dog holes, and eat snakes, and shot the bucks with their poisoned arrows'. But Waldo goes on to speak of this old artificer with respect and excitement – this *homo faber* whose paintings, though quite recent in time, witness a common culture which is our best contact with a continued and shared humanity:

> 'He used to kneel here naked, painting, painting, painting; and he wondered at the things he made himself,' said the boy, rising and moving his hand in deep excitement. 'Now the Boers have shot them all, so that we never see a yellow face peeping out among the stones.' He paused, a dreamy look coming over his face. 'And the wild bucks have gone, and those days, and we are here. But we will be gone soon, and only the stones will lie on here, looking at everything like they look now. I know it is I who am thinking,' the fellow added slowly, 'but it seems as though it were they who were talking.' (*AF* 49-50)

Curious the sentiment which the destroyer discovers once he has completed a genocide. One is reminded of the mysticism of van der Post, his conviction that the San possessed insights into life which we have lost. I wonder whom we will destroy next to discover such another truth.

Waldo's dream nostalgia for a lost culture does not seem so remarkable now. It was in nineteenth-century rural South Africa. It is also remarkable in the way it summarizes the need to destroy which characterizes the culture which enfolds and rules them – Lyndall, Em, and Waldo – and which gives passion to its ignorant desires. Tant' Sannie and Bonaparte Blenkins become a devastating tragi-comic account of the power which the white culture wields to destroy, not only the black and the brown, but also its own 'free' children, leaching their humanity and intelligence to preserve its claim to possession. It is as if the colonist is driven to make room for his 'civilization' by the thing he does best – destruction. And the design of destruction shapes the imaginative life to the extent that, after they have done their worst with other racial groups, the exploiters turn restlessly to initiative in their own tribe as a present danger to be settled as soon as possible.

I have dubbed both Waldo and his shadowy twin the San painter, '*homo faber*'. I did this before I remembered that Waldo's full name is Waldo Farber. The name is from a German root meaning 'colour' or 'dye', and seems to be a subtle means of linking Waldo more firmly to his Daedalian 'Bushman' counterpart, the rock-painter. The link is further strengthened elsewhere. Waldo is writing to Lyndall, telling her of his work and his travels, as he becomes more and more alienated from white society. The brutalizing effect of the constant, wearying work as a waggon driver changes him: 'My body was strong and well to work, but my brain was dead', 'You may work a man till he is a devil. I know it, because I have felt it.' At last he passes out, unconscious from over-indulgence in brandy, and he is saved, possibly from death, by a San.

> The Bushman boy was grilling ribs at the fire. He looked at me, and grinned from ear to ear. 'Master was a little nice,' he said, 'and lay down in the road. Something might ride over master, so I carried him there.' He

grinned at me again. It was as though he said, 'You and I are comrades. I have lain in a road too. I know all about it.' (*AF* 257)

Waldo has gone through something like the regression into barbarism of Kurtz – not a whit less important because it is described without the melodrama of *Heart of Darkness* – to discover something important about himself, which is connected with the 'Bushman'. Already, in the episode of the painting, the felt connection between the two has become an image of the creativeness and the community of the human race. Waldo discovers his own humanity and that of the 'Bushman' by a kind of *via negativa*, almost out of our vision, like Bruegel's Icarus. The courtesy, charm, and humour of the San suggests delicately that such community is anything but barbaric, particularly when it is set against Waldo's experience of the barbarity of the 'European' community.

In *From Man to Man*, too, Schreiner employs the figure of the San to convey an independence of mind and judgement which belies the slave status. Griet, a child bought from her 'Bushman' mother 'for a pair of old shoes and a bottle of wine' (*FMM* 104),[11] shows her perspicuity for the first time in her judgement of Veronica Grey. Griet is mischievous in the tricks she plays to express her dislike, but Schreiner conveys the fullness of her personality in a way which she seems unable to do with 'Kaffirs'. There are indications that, if she had finished *From Man to Man*, Griet might have played a larger part, representing a sensed continuity with past millennia of human understanding:

> She bent her head a little on one side to listen, as for all the long generations of the past her foremothers had listened on the great pathless plains for the coming step of the antelope that meant food, or of the enemy that meant war – death. (*FMM* 342)

Elsewhere in *From Man to Man*, we can observe Schreiner struggling towards a more adequate understanding of race, and 'civilization'. For instance, in 'Fireflies in the dark' Rebekah tackles the prejudices of her sons and their embarrassment at sharing their home with Sartje, Frank's illegitimate black daughter. She tells them to imagine the invasion of earth by 'terrible white-faced strangers' (*FMM* 418), whose technology is so advanced that it challenges the pride which we earthmen have in our 'little cities and little inventions, our ships and our books and our telescopes and our laws and our manners' (*FMM* 418). They called us 'The Inferior Races' and destroyed our culture:

> there was no place for us unless we could serve and be of use to them. They broke down our little countries and our little governments and our little laws; they took all the earth. They said, 'Work for us; that is all you are good for; we will let you go on living if you are of use to us.' (*FMM* 421)

This is of its time in building fables out of the excitement of Percival Lowell's 'discovery' of canals and a superior civilization on Mars, but beyond its time in its critique of European colonial authority. It even goes some way to anticipating the philosophy of black consciousness: 'Because they despised *us*, we began to despise *ourselves!*' What it does *not* do is to grasp and convey the idea that the *soi-disant* superior race might have anything to learn from people they conquer. The fantasy imagines a total passivity in the conquered race: 'when they did nothing to teach us their wisdom and make us grasp their freedom – then we despised ourselves; and so we died' (*FMM* 423). As a fable for racists it has its virtues, and it would have been difficult for someone like Schreiner to imagine the possibility of a true, invigorating reciprocity between white and black.

Like *Heart of Darkness*, *African Farm* contains an account of its own aesthetic, and, again, the aesthetic is a matter of indirectness, multiplicity, multivalence, indistinctness of meaning. But, whereas *Heart of Darkness* declares a paradoxical silence at the heart of understanding, the aesthetic of the stranger in *African Farm* is one which permits the triumph of *interpretation* in a multitude of intelligibilities:

> the attribute of all true art, the highest and the lowest, is this – that it says more than it says, and takes you away from itself. . . . If we pick up the finger and nail of a real man, we can decipher a whole story – could almost reconstruct the creature again, from head to foot. But half the body of a Mumboo-jumbow idol leaves us utterly in the dark as to what the rest was like. We see what we see, but nothing more. There is nothing so universally intelligible as truth. (*AF* 169)

We note the cultural arrogance, and are unable to excuse it by observing that the speech is put into the mouth of a fictional character. Transparently Olive Schreiner is responsible for what is said; she accepts the racist language and thought implicit in making the image of falsity in art 'a Mumboo-jumbow idol'. It's as easy as it is necessary to condemn this, though such grossly insulting terms could be used at that time with no consciousness of their hurtfulness. What is more interesting is the easy optimism, the facile assumption of the triumph of clarity – even if clarity is many-faceted – in 'There is nothing so universally intelligible as truth.'

But there is much to redeem the passage. In a faulted way it suggests the limitations of language in capturing and fixing meaning. It endows the reader with a certain independence. It recognizes that the reader may stand obliquely to the author's construct, while discovering tectonics of meaning, emotion, and consciousness which may have been only partly, or indirectly, or not at all, available to the author.

African Farm is a strange example of a real intelligence prematurely engaging with the destructiveness of its own society, observing with a critical eye the mechanisms of power, both sexual and racial, achieving a real, though partial, independence from its materialist, exploitative ideology. Schreiner was on her own, and bound to make mistakes. It is part of her strength that she concedes the insecurity of her argument.

Perhaps the greatest of these mistakes is in the chapter 'Gregory's womanhood'. Reaching out as it does, to an experiment in the fictional reversal of male-female stereotypes, the episode succeeds in achieving a fine dottiness. This isn't in Gregory's care for Lyndall, his delicacy of temperament, or his wearing of women's clothing. It is not even in the sentimental death of Lyndall – like that of Clarissa Harlowe a way of challenging, fictionally, the passive values of a social conspiracy. It is rather in the silence of Gregory. Gregory reverses the male-female conventional roles, to be sure, but ends up imitating a female stereotype. Gregory is a marvellous nurse, but, as Florence Nightingale had proved in reality (though not in the myth) the best nurse is not necessarily the quiet, amenable, silent, 'feminine' servant some men dream about.

Schreiner was an extraordinary woman, and perhaps the most extraordinary thing about her was the way in which she brought the contradictions that were implicit in her life to the surface, against the *decorum* of her age. And yet, though they are brought to the surface, they are never resolved; it is in their lack of resolution that the energy and the suffering, the sharpness and the lack of definition, the poignancy and the occasional absurdity of her work lies. 'The worst of this book of mine is that it's so womanly,' she wrote of *From Man to Man*. 'I think it's the most womanly book that ever was written, and God knows that I've willed it otherwise!'[12] Elaine Showalter identifies part of the problem: 'men are redeemed by female suffering, while women perish in teaching the lesson. . . . The heroines are granted only the narrowest of possibilities.'[13] Maybe the problem for a twentieth-century reader is that the book isn't 'womanly' enough. And yet Schreiner's fiction is one of the foundations upon which are based our changed ideas of woman as self-reliant, creative, and strong.

4

William Plomer: *Turbott Wolfe*

Gandhi founded the Natal Indian Congress in 1894, the year after he arrived in South Africa, and the techniques of Satyagraha were developed in that country over the next twenty years.[1] But Gandhi and his followers regarded the African in much the same way as European colonists might – as a savage innocent liable to be corrupted by European ways of life. It was only eighteen years later, in January 1912, that the cause of the majority began to find a vehicle for expression of its political will in the newly launched African National Congress. At first this was a deferential and cautious organization. Eight ruling African monarchs were given the position of Honorary President; its other leaders were Christian, liberal, and middle-class in outlook. It promoted a morality bland enough to appeal to as many white sympathizers as possible, and was wedded to gradualism, evolution, and compromise. There was no question of using economic weapons like the withdrawal of labour. Nevertheless it was the first organization of Africans, as opposed to members of tribal groups, the first to see Africans as one nation.[2]

At the same time the labour movement was growing in the white community. In the Cape, where racial attitudes were relatively tolerant, there were those in the movement who opposed any kind of colour bar out of socialist principle. Even here, many workers, among them stonemasons, plasterers, and bricklayers, operated a colour bar; and on the Rand, trade unions justified similar measures by speaking of the class struggle and the protection of white interests in the same breath.[3]

The large employers aimed to keep labour cheap and amenable by deploying selectively the threat of undercutting whites with cheap non-white labour. After the Boer War the mine owners tried to maximize their profits by paying black workers even less than they had in the days of the Afrikaner Republics, with the result that the number of black workers fell and so did production. The employers responded by importing indentured Chinese labourers to work at a rate *below* the African wage. The issue of the protection of white labour against non-white competition became the prime one for the South African Labour Party.

There was a more radical element which worked against the racism of white workers. This minority was at first divided into splinter groups, but a series of incidents pushed its members into recognizing common cause. First there was the Russian revolution, with all that followed in other countries. Then, in May 1921, there was the Bulhoek massacre. A messianic sect known as the Israelites gathered every year in Bulhoek location in the eastern Cape, on land belonging to their prophet Enoch Mgijima. While they were waiting for the Messiah to arrive they would not work for a wage, and this alarmed white farmers. The police sent nearly 1,000 men to Queenstown and on Empire Day, 24 May 1921, attacked them with support from machine-guns and artillery. In ten minutes the killing was over, and 190 men died. Jan Smuts defended the action in parliament.[4]

The episode helped to precipitate the setting up of a South African Communist Party, in July 1921. It looked to Soviet Russia for its inspiration, but it was essentially a movement which grew out of the social, political, and racial situation in South Africa. The most novel aspect of its programme was its determination to break through the racial barrier, its conviction that this was the only way in which there could be justice for all groups in society, black or white, rich or poor. It was the first, and for a long time the only, group in South Africa in which whites worked for an anti-racialist programme, and it led to a South African phenomenon which is little understood outside that country; the identification of whites who oppose racism root-and-branch as Communists. In July 1921 a spectre began to haunt South Africa, and its name was democracy.[5]

The great majority of the members of the miners' union in the Transvaal insisted on a strict colour bar. The mine owners, on the other hand, argued for the relaxation of the colour bar on moral and economic grounds. The economic grounds were pressing: since 1913 African wages had risen by only 9 per cent for an underground shift of twelve hours, while white miners' pay had gone up 50 per cent. The owners therefore proposed certain changes in the contract system, a complex matter, but one which the white miners believed eroded their rights and privileges.

A strike for the maintenance of white privilege began in the coal mines. The Communists, under S. P. Bunting, attempted to redirect the strike: 'What to fight for? . . . Wages, then, not colour, is the point to strike about and so far as this is a strike to maintain wages, it deserves the support of all Labour, including the coloured and native workers themselves', but such arguments had little effect. The African miners continued to work as well as ever without their highly paid white overseers, and in some pits record production was achieved. At times Communist opposition to colour prejudice was eroded; a famous red banner carried at Fordsburg carried the slogan 'Workers of the World, Fight and Unite for a White South Africa'. Commandos were raised by striking miners, there were attacks on black workers as well as white, and, amidst confusion as to aims and tactics, a general strike was called. At no time was the Communist Party able to control events, but exaggerated publicity was given to its activities.

Smuts declared martial law. Police and troops, with air support, bombs, artillery, machine-guns and tanks, forced the surrender of the commandos, and about 250 people were killed in what came to be known as the Rand revolt. Forty-six people were charged with murder, eighteen were sentenced to death and four actually hung, sixty-seven were convicted of treason or sedition. Out of about 5,000 people who were arrested nearly 1,000 appeared in court.[6]

It is, then, disingenuous of van der Post to write, in his 1965 'Introduction' to *Turbott Wolfe*:

> the Communist agent, he is called 'Bolshevik' by Plomer, and the immense potential of Russian influence in Africa, are important elements in the story. Considering that when *Turbott Wolfe* was written the Revolution in Russia was barely seven years old, the country ruined by civil war, disease and famine and its power in the world negligible, I find this an impressive example of visionary writing. (*TW* 49)[7]

The USSR was weakened by the White Terror, by western intervention and internal economic problems. But the ideas which it represented were potent. Van der Post, who began his career as a journalist on the *Natal Advertiser*, knew well enough the way in which Government and Press had exploited 'the Bolshevik menace'. Elsewhere in his 'Introduction' van der Post, to emphasize Plomer's originality, implies that there was no opposition to racism in the white South African community (*TW* 41). It is a difficult thing to exaggerate the depth of racism in the white community but it is not true that Plomer was alone in connecting the possibility of a non-racist future with the ideas of the Communists.

David Rabkin[8] is surely right in linking Plomer's novel with Sarah Gertrude Millin's *God's Stepchildren* (1924) as very different responses to the same question – that of miscegenation. Hitler's favourite South African novel (ironically Millin was a Jew) attacks the 'soft' British view of race, following the fortunes of the Reverend Andrew Flood, a liberal who elects to marry a 'Hottentot', and his descendants, through four generations. The novel is hardly original in expressing the irrational terror of the settlers. It may be that its conventional attitudes were given a sharper edge by the fact that there now existed, in South Africa, a group of people who argued for the abandonment of racialism, and that they were supported by a much feared international movement.

Miscegenation was never a part of Communist policy, but racialist domino theory has always had clear lines of argument: 'Once you get . . . the next thing will be . . . and that will be the end of civilization as we know it.' *Turbott Wolfe* is original in that it *recommends* miscegenation. If that were all, it would be a curiosity, but it's more than that. It is very much a young man's novel, at times brilliant in its savage satire on European mores, the hypocrisy, viciousness, and self-satisfaction as well as the failure of the well-meaning. But it is also somewhat unstable in tone, with an insecurity which seems deliberately to be reflected, even satirized, by Plomer's narrative technique. Later, Plomer himself was to reflect that he was 'attempting to reach by a short cut what can only become visible by taking an arduous road', adding that the result is 'crude and immature, and disfigured by an unpleasant superficial smartness or vulgar cleverness'.[9] Though Plomer uses the word pejoratively, 'disfiguring' might be taken as the point of the whole discourse, the use of a calculated indecorum to subvert the *figures*, the distinctive forms or shapes through which a society projects its sense of the proprieties. In this sense what Plomer later perceives as its crudeness is its principal virtue – short cuts were the only paths available, even if they involved hazards.

Turbott Wolfe was published in 1926 by the Woolfs at the Hogarth Press, which had published *The Waste Land* only four years before, in 1922, and there are ways in which it seems to echo the tonalities of that work, not least in the way that it appears to allude to *Heart of Darkness*. The poem which concludes the narrative reveals a Conradian subtext by the prominence it gives to the word 'horror'. It is supposed to have been found among the papers left by Friston, after his death travelling towards an appointment with the mysterious 'Bolshevik'. It is not a very good poem, but it does express a complex idea, a paradoxical relationship between freedom and action which might derive from a reading of existentialists. The last two stanzas of 'Manifesto, By a Man in a Trap' read:

I yawn, when I was used to wince,
At such clandestine vileness done –
Fear has withered swiftly since
HORROR was written on the sun.

Doors, mouths, and periods open, shut:
Time will not give what time has lacked.
I am constrained to play a part –
An actor, only free to act.   (*TW* 215)

The career of Friston, the supposed poet, expresses that aspect of the novel in which it is a journey into the heart of the matter, discovering in the dreary inadequacies of European society in Southern Africa a horror which can only be exorcised by dramatic (even melodramatic) action. And yet it also, with schizoid caution characteristic of a liberal conscience, views such action as a trap, or as a role in which the individual loses his identity. In Appendix I, in another of Friston's papers entitled 'The Politico Aesthete', we have another self-deprecating expression of the problem:

He staggers, poor man, under the weight of the past; and he struggles, poor man, under the load of the future. He has not got over the French Revolution when he is faced with the Russian. . . . He would like to focus his attention on the point where the rational in his character coincides with the concupiscible; but is it really his character, he wonders – ?(*TW* 212)

One of the ways in which Plomer seems indebted to Conrad in this novel is in the use he makes of a primary and secondary narrator. In Plomer this device expresses the divided nature of a consciousness in an even more radical way than Conrad. It is Turbott Wolfe who is the secondary narrator, recounting the story as he lies dying in E—, a seaside town in England. But, whereas in Conrad (or in James's *The Turn of the Screw*) the primary narrator remains unnamed, in *Turbott Wolfe* the primary narrator is given a name – William Plomer. This has a disturbing effect, since the name is used strategically, only at points where the emotional contradictions implicit in the narrative become particularly demanding. The shadowy primary narrator – little more than a self-effacing device – is suddenly wrenched into the foreground as a person with a reality outside the fiction, independent of the text, intrusive, anomalous, destructive of the claims of fiction. In that a persona with the same name as the author is inserted into it, the text tends to re-form as a dialogue between selves, with a multiplicity of ironic relations between versions of self. We might once more recall *The Waste Land*, with its allusion to Baudelaire:

'You! hypocrite lecteur! – mon semblable, – mon frère!'

Wolfe is recollecting falling in love with a black girl, Nhliziyombi, but failing, for reasons that he cannot understand, to do anything about his feelings. He remains, as he is nicknamed by the blacks, Chastity Wolfe. He confesses to having been in love against conscience, against reason, and 'against *myself*'. And he explains his failure to fulfil the love as a matter of vanity:

I saw that I should be sacrificing *my own opinion of myself.*
    I suppose you think I mean that I was white and the girl was black. My good William Plomer, pray accept my assurance that that had nothing whatever to do with it. I am too much the humanitarian to be colour-blind. . . . but there appeared to be a great forbidding law, like all great forbidding laws, subcutaneous. Conscience, did I say? What had conscience to do with it? There may have been a mystery. There may have been an illusion. (*TW* 92-3)

The sentence which strikes me most forcibly in this is 'I am too much the humanitarian to be colour-blind.' The first reaction, perhaps, is to read it as an error – to import a negative, or to alter colour-blind to 'colour-prejudiced'. Then, perhaps, there is an attempted reversal – the real humanitarian is *not* colour-blind, he rejoices in the diversity of humanity, black and white and brown. But if we take this road we are soon brought face to face with its inconsistency with the text around it. There is a real confusion here. It is, after all, 'Turbott Wolfe' speaking, and there are other ways in which 'Turbott Wolfe' is aware that something might be wrong, with his memory, with his understanding, with his sense of reality: 'There may have been a mystery. There may have been an illusion.' We are given a double reason to walk round what 'Turbott Wolfe' says, to reconsider it: the author, by suddenly appearing in his own person and name, has separated 'William Plomer' from what 'Wolfe' says, and 'Wolfe' himself has cast doubt on it by saying 'There may have been an illusion.' He repeats it:

I can almost believe that there was an illusion.–

. . . The window-curtains in that room were strewn with patterned faded poppies that moved, nodding maliciously, as the curtains moved; promising an anodyne; waiting, heavy-budded, for a time when the room should be empty and obscure; waiting for a time when Turbott Wolfe, nicknamed Chastity, should be no longer there; succeeded, perhaps, by nothing but the ghost of his ecstatic voice. (*TW* 93)

This is eloquent in an obscure way, and the obscurity is part of the eloquence; it is an eloquence that leaves almost everything in doubt. It may be that the ending distantly alludes once more to *Heart of Darkness*, promising nothing left of Wolfe, as there was nothing left of Kurtz, but 'the ghost of his ecstatic voice', nothing but impotence and contradiction, nothing but irrelevance and illusion to define the abyss of 'mystery'. And in this respect, perhaps, it becomes an effective portrait of a tender conscience in its failure to act, its obscene humanitarian chastity, like the poppies anodyne yet obscurely malicious.

Another aspect of this complex vision of failure is given in the figure of the missionary, Nordalsgaard. He is about to retire to Europe after forty years and is suddenly aware that he has accomplished nothing:

he had gone out with gifts and weapons, this man. His blood had been tradition; his brain, knowledge; his body purpose. He had gone out . . . to conquer the world, to conquer time. It was not a wreck: you could not call it a failure, this. It was defeat. . . . What had he done? What had he done? He had wounded history. (*TW* 128-9)

Nordalsgaard's defeat becomes the summary of a greater matter, the arrogance and incompetence of European missionary idealism in the face of history. Shortly after this passage the assembled company sing hymns: 'But above the droning could be heard, with a distinct and awful and unceasing significance, the loud roar of chaos'. The work abounds with resonances, and I suppose this might well remind one of Forster's *A Passage to India* – it's not unlikely that Plomer had that work fresh in his mind, since it was published in 1924. As in that work the sound of the Marabar cave defies final interpretation, Plomer's sense of the chaos remains ambiguous, but there is one clue to suggest what it is *not*. Plomer slips in a reference to Couperus in Java, and what he calls 'the hidden force', and this in its turn might alert one to the epigraph from Couperus: 'As for the native, he reads his overlord with a single penetrating glance: he sees in him the illusion of civilization and humanity and he knows they are non-existent.' The chaos is not in the black world, the 'native world'. It is in the illusive world of Nordalsgaard, and of

Wolfe, who fails to come to terms with it, who remains 'chaste', who is not constrained, as Friston is, with the paradoxical freedom of the actor, to act.

The girl Nhliziyombi expresses part of this. She is never seen with the kind of discrimination which suggests an understanding of her inner life, the richness of her individuality. Of course not, she is always seem with the eyes of Turbott Wolfe, for whom she is simply a kind of illusion. But even through his account we can perceive her knowledge of him and his kind, her gentle scorn for *his* illusion. He gives her a gold pin:

> 'Are you giving it?' she asked incredulously.
> 'It is yours.'
> She was alarmed at being favoured by a man she had come to know as Chastity, and exclaimed softly:
> 'O, white men!'
> Then she ran down the path, checkered with shadows. Nor did she look back. (*TW* 94-5)

The novel is about choices and failures to choose, about the conflict between duties and aesthetic satisfactions. And, to a great extent, it is about the way in which such dilemmas are peripheral to history. In one way the most potent image of this is a character who only exists on the margins of the novel. Tyler-Harries, a rich aesthete, maker of editions-de-luxe and founder of the Pomegranate Press, sails into South Africa to make a beautiful book, sails out again on a rotten cargo boat by the eastern route, only to drown with all his manuscripts and photographs. It's uncomfortable self-satire, a comment on the effrontery of attempting to summarize Africa in a book written from the very edge of its manifold experience.

5

Laurens van der Post: *In a Province*

The failure of the Labour Party to represent anything but the short-term interests of the white working class led to an electoral pact between the Labour Party and the Nationalists in the aftermath of the Rand revolt. It also led eventually to a closer alignment of interests between the Communist Party (CP) and the African National Congress (ANC). In 1927 Gumede, representing the ANC at the Congress against Colonial Oppression and Imperialism in Brussels, declared: 'I am happy to say that there are Communists also in South Africa. I myself am not one, but it is my experience that the Communist Party is the only party that stands behind us and from whom we can expect something.'[1]

At about this time began an alliance of interests between Communists and African Nationalists which grew, not entirely smoothly, but strongly, for many decades. One non-Communist Afrikaner, André Brink, has written of another Afrikaner, Bram Fischer, that, at a very much later time:

> he discovered that the only people prepared to suffer for convictions similar to his – people who could have all the luxury they wanted if they chose, but who identified themselves to such an extent with the deprived majority that they were prepared to forgo all that and risk imprisonment, banishment, or even death – were members of the Communist Party.[2]

The emphasis of the party's policy moved towards advocacy of a black republic, and its influence grew. E. J. Khaile, a member of the CP's executive, became the ANC's general secretary. On the other hand the Industrial and Commercial Union, the black trade union, elected to expel its Communist members, including Khaile and two other members of its growing council, La Guma and Gomas.[3]

In the parliamentary election of 1929 two CP candidates – both of them white, as was required under the constitution – stood for two of the Cape Province seats then elected by black voters. Bunting stood for Tembuland and Wolton for Cape Flats. Their manifesto offered citizenship rights for everybody, the removal of colour bars from the constitution and the repeal of discriminatory laws, a fair redistribution of land, equal wages for equal work, the recognition of African trade unions, free primary education, and freedom of speech and assembly. This was to be within the framework of a workers' and peasants' republic 'wholly independent of the British or any other empire' in which the African would have the fundamental right of self-determination.

It was the most enlightened electoral programme ever offered to a South African electorate, but Wolton and Bunting lacked a grass roots organization, the government-supported African organizations worked against the CP, and there was widespread intimidation of voters by white hooligans. Bunting's campaign in Tembuland, which was centred around Umtata (the site of the main police barracks, the principal employer in Umtata), provides much of the material for the central episode in *In a Province* (1934).[4] Bunting is the basis of Burgess in the novel, and Tembuland is disguised as Bambuland, Umtata as Paulstad. In the historical episode there were acts of police intimidation, arrests and prosecutions, and ugly incidents involving white racists, some but not all of which are reflected in the novel. Bunting did better than Wolton with 289 votes, but neither came close to winning. After the election Bunting, his wife Rebecca, and his agent Gana Makabeni were convicted on a charge of promoting inter-racial hostility. The Supreme Court upheld their appeal against the conviction.

But there was a white reaction. The Nationalist government which took office in June 1929 as a result of this general election went on the offensive against the radicals. The great depression was beginning, the fascists were in power in Italy, and the Nazis were on the brink of achieving power in Germany. Racism, forcible management of labour, and state violence were becoming the resort of populist politicians throughout the world. Some members of the new South African government, like Oswald Pirow, the Minister of Justice, were strong Nazi sympathizers. Pirow's under-secretary, van Rensburg, was later to be *kommandant-general* of the Ossewabrandwag, the spearhead of fascism in South Africa during the 1930s and through its *Stormjaers* responsible for acts of sabotage during the 1939-45 war. Pirow himself founded the New Order, which agitated for a fascist system of government. And the Greyshirts (National Socialist Party) were active throughout the 1930s.

Another event in the background of *In a Province* was the campaign organized by the newly formed League of African Rights, which included a great petition for civil rights and anti-pass demonstrations on Dingaan's Day, 16 December 1929. This is a day of great divisive national significance both for the Zulus and for the Afrikaners, since it commemorates the defeat of Dingaan's Zulu impis by the Afrikaners in 1838. Dingaan's Day is disguised in *In a Province* as the anniversary of the defeat of the Bambuxosa nation, the day on which the revolutionary Burgess holds his meeting in Paulstad. It may be that Pirow deliberately provoked violent incidents to justify measures to strengthen the state's powers, particularly over the dissident individual. Certainly it helped him to gain support for a bill to amend the Riotous Assemblies Act. This had the practical effect of making any action, whether it was likely to be riotous or not, difficult in the extreme for any group of which Pirow and his friends disapproved. The bill was supported, not only by relatively moderate Nationalists like Hertzog, but also by Smuts, who called for measures to suppress 'communist propaganda'. Pirow's hand was strengthened by the Supreme Court's judgement on the successful appeal of the Buntings and Makabeni against their sentences. The bill, and the deliberate provocation which may have been used to justify it, is referred to with little disguise in van der Post's novel (*IP* 240-1).[5]

In a Province owes something to *Turbott Wolfe* in the way in which it is plotted. This is not so much in the use of multiple narrators, though van der Post, rather awkwardly, and in a very significant way, does allow the omniscient author to foreground himself, briefly, in the last two paragraphs. The indebtedness is rather in the way in which the central character, van Bredepoel, is seen at the beginning as somebody who is suffering from a deep sickness. *Turbott Wolfe* is dominated tonally and atmospherically throughout by the eponymous character's sickness unto death, as seen by 'William Plomer' his visitor. Van Bredepoel is visited by Simmering, an 'absurdly sensitive' character who quickly disappears from the narrative after doing nothing but suggest that van Bredepoel go to Paulstad to convalesce. This episode is followed by an account of the stages by which van Bredepoel fell into sickness. As in *Turbott Wolfe* it is a sickness generated by problems of inter-racial relationship, so acute that they become internalized in illness.

In *Turbott Wolfe* the relationship with Nhliziyombi is not described with any attempt at insight into the mind of the girl. The relationships between the members and sympathizers of the rather dotty political organization, Young Africa, are in a satirical, caricaturing vein. The moments of insight are in those places where Wolfe is seen as the prime object of the novel's attention rather than as its trustworthy narrator. Van der Post's novel is very different.

The place occupied in *Turbott Wolfe* by Nhliziyombi is taken by Kenon Badiakgotla. Van Bredepoel recalls the time he first came from Vergelegen (the name means 'far away' in Afrikaans), a remote farm in an Afrikaans-speaking community, to Port Benjamin. In his boarding house he meets Kenon, a young man of his age who also comes from 'far away', from the land of the Bambuxosa. He likes Kenon, and spends a great deal of time in his company, listening to his stories of the Bambuxosa, of the Tokoloshe (a mischievous priapic character who is the subject of many African stories) and of Masakama, the heroic founder of the Bambuxosa tribe.

Van der Post catches very well the kind of excitement which members of a highly literate culture feel when they discover the richness and energy of a culture which is primarily oral. Johan finds in Kenon a reminder of the way in which voice and gesture may be the subtle medium of a complete and coherent understanding of the world. Europeans tend sentimentally to associate these skills with the past, with the Greeks, their myths and epics, with bards and scops, with Hebrew prophets and the sagas. In van Bredepoel the fascination is dual. It draws him in, makes him wish to share in the power of that knowledge, and it makes him aware of his own exclusion:

> His imagination was deeply stirred and van Bredepoel, listening, sometimes imagined himself back in a lost world of epic poetry, back in that old, old Africa, which lay there beyond the mountains, its stony face turned to the sun. (*IP* 63)

It is one of the more deadly and subtle strategies of assumed cultural superiority to romanticize the products of another culture, to make a world which is patently *there* into 'a lost world', something which, however 'old', is also new, into part of a past – as epic is for Europe – part of 'that old, old Africa', and self-indulgently to dramatize our own feelings of exclusion from a 'lost' culture – 'its stony face turned to the sun'. Of course it never was 'lost' any more than the Victoria Falls were when Livingstone discovered them. This is once again the European's assumption of centrality, but, paradoxically and simultaneously, the experience of marginality, the sense of a European culture and people clinging on to the edges of Africa. To van Bredepoel or to van der Post, with their family allegiance both to an Afrikaner way of life and to a *Hollands* past, the experience is complicated – the Afrikaner believes that if he does not belong he does not exist. But for van Bredepoel, and for van der Post, the double sense of being part, yet being other, is a problem which becomes a quasi-mystical summary of human-ness. Van Bredepoel looks at the mountains, serene and remote, as if

> they pointed an inarticulate moral at the frantic town below him. And he was reminded that Port Benjamin was only a small European pendant to a long necklace of African land; that behind that barrier of mountains lay the Africa from which he came and to which he might one day have to return. (*IP* 13)

The relationship between Johan and Kenon is a kind of love affair. It has no superficially sexual element, though some of the whites in the boarding house use innuendo to imply misbehaviour. But in a very South African way Johan's affection is as condescending as it is tender. White South Africans, especially if they have been brought up on a farm, are apt to assert that they *understand* the rural African – they played with them as children and so on. They will often add that they do not understand the urban blacks, the educated blacks, the radicals. The doctrine of white supremacy has its basis in this assumption that whites can understand the needs of the rural poor and the strengths of the tribal tradition better than the blacks do themselves, and the rejection of the black urban viewpoint as impertinent. Van der Post is not entirely imprisoned in the white laager of prejudice. Neither is his character Johan, in that he is drawn deeper and deeper into his relationship with Kenon Badiakgotla, and discovers respect as he learns more. But the career of Kenon is one which fits in very well indeed with paternalistic white assumptions about blacks, and van Bredepoel's love for him remains within that mode. Johan can withstand the crude insults, 'nigger-kisser' and the rest, thrown about by the members of the Paulstad club, because his unconventional friendship nevertheless remains within what are, for him, tolerable limits. He can be kind to Kenon, do things for him, and Kenon, in return, can entertain him from the deep storehouse of his own culture.

But, for that relationship to continue, Kenon must remain an innocent, and for this to be secure his identity must be presented as a tribal identity. It would be difficult to imagine van Bredepoel adjusting to the kind of relationship Burgess has with Daniel (one of the residual racialist habits in this novel is that blacks are usually referred to by their first names – Kenon, Daniel – and whites by their surnames – van Bredepoel, Burgess). Van Bredepoel observes with puzzlement the easy working relationship between the two men:

> For the first time he was coming into contact with a native who had succeeded in winning through difficulties under which thousands of his people succumbed, succeeded so well that he was preparing to lead others after him. Now Burgess had the utmost confidence in Daniel, but van Bredepoel could never get inside his mind. (*IP* 141)

Van Bredepoel, and apparently van der Post with him, expects that kind of instant access to another man's mind – at least a 'native's' mind – that he *claims* in understanding rural Africans. And he is deeply suspicious when he isn't allowed the illusion of understanding. In a self-protective manoeuvre, he soothes the wound of insecurity by finding limitations in Daniel. His mind is

> strictly limited, but amazingly clear and accurate. The black man's vision was focused on only one aspect of life and never left it for a moment. He had before him always, as under a microscope, the point where white and black people came into contact. (*IP* 142)

Van Bredepoel finds a way to admire the man while hinting that his political and social intelligence stunts him.

So when Kenon comes to town you may be sure there is danger threatening his charming innocence. He becomes corrupted by Port Benjamin and its mores. He takes up with a syphilitic coloured girl. He goes with friends to a whorehouse, gets involved in a brawl with white sailors, is imprisoned and comes out with a changed personality. Later on he has the effrontery to come to the *front door* of Mrs Harris's boarding house, in a taxi, wearing clothes which are different from those which the innocent tribal boy had worn on coming to Port Benjamin. Now he is dressed

> in a new double-breasted suit of a rich purple material. The coat was cut very short and well tucked in at the waist so that the trousers, which were exceptionally wide, filled out like a skirt behind. On his feet were a pair of white and brown suede shoes, narrowly pointed and very high-heeled. (*IP* 103)

The stereotype comfortably ratifies a white South African's sense of what is right and wrong. The clothes (which, it may be, Kenon wears well and which please both him and his friends) break rules, and, as we know, rules are made by rulers.

The crisis which causes van Bredepoel's sickness is a consequence of his growing friendship with Burgess, the Communist, who raises in its most acute form the question of responsibility. The question isn't an abstract one for Johan; it is repeatedly seen by him in terms of his friendship with Kenon. The matter is sharpened by an incident in which a black orator is shot by a hooligan who is part of a white mob. The incident seems partly to have been modelled on a race riot at Durban on 17 June 1929, in which shots were fired from the crowd, eight people killed and over 100 injured.[6] The investigating commissioner, Justice de Waal, blamed white hooligans. There was another relevant incident in a township outside Potchefstroom in December of the same year. In this second incident about 100 whites invaded the township, two black Communists, Marks and Mofutsanyana, were shot at, and Hermanus Lethebe, a local party official, was killed. The murderer was subsequently acquitted by the white jury.[7]

Van Bredepoel's reaction to the killing worries Burgess, and he quickly diagnoses the problem:

> it's possible to reconcile the flesh and the spirit. I confess that if I had to live in the duality you are in, I wouldn't be able to work. It's your duty to yourself to work for something you respect. If there's nothing in this life you love, there must be something it lacks that you love, and you must work to give it one day the thing you love. (*IP* 160)

Johan can find no answer to Burgess's reproaches. Johan has a delirious dream which orchestrates the internal debate. He imagines he sees Kenon dragged along by a dog-chain held by the cartoon-like plutocrat of Burgess's posters. He resists the impulse to save Kenon because 'It isn't my affair', and then hears Burgess's voice saying

> 'You allow yourself to feel sorry only because otherwise your essential indifference would be intolerable to you. No pity is worth the name of pity unless it has the courage of the actions that pity demands.' 'It isn't my business,' he murmured back, and then, getting angry, shouted: 'And neither is it yours.' (*IP* 162)

Turbott Wolfe runs away from his conflicts to die in England, but van Bredepoel recovers from his sickness to attempt to face up to the problem. He goes to Paulstad to recover, realizes that Burgess is about to wage a political campaign there, and stumbles across a plot in which the police arm three blacks with old weapons in order to provoke repressive action and justify white violence. One of these blacks turns out to be Kenon, who has followed the conventional progress of the corrupted innocent by becoming addicted to *insangu* (cannabis). In the ensuing fracas Kenon is killed, and van Bredepoel is shocked deeply by his latest experience of racial violence.

This is where van der Post poses the problem of choice in its most acute form. Before the critical meeting Burgess makes his interpretation of the position clear. 'All your life you've been sitting on your little liberal fence, with your fears on either side', he says to Johan, ' . . . You must come down on one side for your happiness' (*IP* 223-4). The appeal has a dimension beyond South Africa. The effects of Italian colonial administration were to be seen in Cyrenaica, where Graziani had reduced the population from 225,000 in the 1920s to 142,000 in 1931. Ethiopia was to be invaded in 1935. Marcello Caetano, Salazar's successor, was later to make the Portuguese position on African labour abundantly clear: 'The blacks are to be organized and enclosed as productive elements in an economy directed by whites.'[8] The racism and the cult of violence in the new Germany had already become clear. Pirow and his like had accelerated the rate at which South Africa was travelling in that direction as a means of preserving and extending the power of the white community. At the same time, under the leadership of Stalin, the USSR was entering its most repressive phase. Burgess says:

> We must all decide now, once for all, to commit ourselves either to the past or to the future. No one shall have rest, no artist, no writer, no worker, no politician, no one, until he has taken this decision, for the individual is subordinate to society, and when the structure of society is breaking down the peace of the individual goes with it. (*IP* 224)

Van Bredepoel's reservations revolve around Burgess's 'the individual is subordinate to society' and the low priority Burgess assigns to 'the peace of the individual'. The conflict now becomes a debate between individualism and collectivism. Angrily, Johan rejects Burgess: 'I refuse to help you, even as a spectator; I won't add one more cell to that mass-mind' (*IP* 224).

After the meeting van Bredepoel moves further in expressing his philosophy of individualism. It is a view which has respectable antecedents – the Dostoevsky of *Notes from Under the Floorboards* for instance. The debates between behaviourist and mentalist in psychology, stimulated by Pavlov's animal experiments, had effects outside psychological circles, and Pavlov's behaviourism appealed to the materialism of the Soviets.

> Man, they tell you, is only a machine; put him in a certain environment and he must react in a definite and calculable way. He cannot help himself, only his conditioned reflexes can. And what conditions these reflexes? Environment. (*IP* 242)

In retrospect Johan's final attitude seems indefensibly feeble, far away from the anger, the despair, the hope of Dostoevsky, more a matter of *il faut cultiver notre jardin*. He decides he is going to buy a farm and grow potatoes:

> Each one must take heed by himself, and the system will in the end take heed of itself. If the system perpetuates a colour-prejudice, we can

counteract it by refusing to admit a colour-prejudice in our own lives, we can live as if no colour-prejudice existed. (*IP* 246)

Can you? After Sharpeville and Soweto, the juggernaut years of the 1980s grind on, destroying everything except the hypocritical stubbornness of the white leaders and the courage, determination, and passion of the majority. Van Bredepoel's rhetorical condemnation of Burgess seems much less relevant than it might once have seemed:

Life is bent low with hate. But take heart. For here, where your footsteps disappear, so near that if you stretched out your hands you could almost feel them, come the feet of the generations that trample the dim future, and there may be love at their side. (*IP* 254)

6

Karen Blixen ('Isak Dinesen'): *Out of Africa*

The Baroness Blixen knew how to tell a story, and that, for her, meant first of all speaking, not writing. You cannot learn how to tell a story without listeners, and this is the best gift Africa gave her – it was a continent as full of listeners as Europe is full of readers.

> the art of listening to a narrative has been lost in Europe. The Natives of Africa, who cannot read, have still got it. . . . But white people, even if they feel that they ought to, cannot listen to a recital. . . . They have been accustomed to take in their impressions by the eye. (*OA* 194)[1]

Behind Karen Blixen's narratives we can distinguish the rhythms of speech, the brief anecdotal flights, of a teller of tales who wants above all to hold the listener's attention. Such skills are often possessed by writers using their second or third language (Conrad and Nabokov as well as many African writers), perhaps because one listens so much more in conversation if it is in a language one has had to learn after childhood. 'Writing', Derrida remarks, 'can never be totally inhabited by the voice';[2] the illusion of speech is a comfortable conspiracy, but it permits one occulted effect which makes Blixen's discourse very different from that of the African story-teller working in the presence of an audience. Her art is totally self-centred.

Out of Africa (1937) is a hymn of nostalgia for lost possession. It begins: 'I had a farm in Africa, at the foot of the Ngong Hills.' It ends with the loss of that farm. But it is not only the farm she possesses or loses. She strives to make everything and everyone her own, to arrange them around her like a bower-bird, subordinating everything to her personality. Finch-Hatton, Berkeley Cole, the Ngong Hills, Lulu, Kamante, Farah, all are there to extend the self.

In a habit of phrasing which will strike the ear of many Europeans differently from the way it might be heard by a Kikuyu or a Sikh, she speaks again and again of 'my natives', 'my coloured people', as when she tells how Finch-Hatton will not let her give a ring to Pooran Singh, 'for he used to complain that whenever he gave me anything I would at once give it away to my coloured people' (*OA* 312). For her the pleasure of having is made more acute when ownership is insecure, where possession has to be won repeatedly.

Her relationship with Denys Finch-Hatton is of this kind; it becomes settled only when, with a final romantic gesture, she chooses him a grave in the Ngong Hills. It is only to be expected, so deeply self-indulgent is the symbolism of her sentiment, that she should later discover that lions frequent his grave.

She speaks of the creatures she domesticates, or tries to, as 'wild' – Finch-Hatton himself, and Kamante: 'Rarely, rarely, have I met such a wild creature, a human being who was so utterly isolated from the world, and, by a sort of firm, deadly resignation, completely closed to all surrounding life' (*OA* 32). Kamanate was not wild; he was starving, sick, not far from dying. Before she could help to save his life (as, to her credit, she did) Blixen had to accommodate him to her world by beginning to tell a story about him: he was a wild creature. It's a compliment, much as Montaigne turned round the word *sauvage* into a compliment. But it is a compliment which places him in a separate compartment of the mind, fine, but not as 'we' are, not hobbled by something we call civilization.

This condescension is surrounded again and again by animal imagery:

> The discovery of the dark races was to me a magnificant enlargement of all my world. If a person with an inborn sympathy for animals had grown up in a milieu where there were no animals, and had come into contact with animals late in life . . . [her case] might have been similar to mine. (*OA* 25)

Lulu the fawn, on the other hand, is fancifully granted a fairy-book humanity. She is saved from the stew-pot to be the heroine of the anthropomorphic romance, with the satisfactorily fairy-book conclusion that the belonging was never complete, a matter of extraordinary grace and favour, so that she can go back at last to live with her *bwana* in the bush: 'Lulu of the woods was a superior, independent being, a change of heart had come upon her, she was in possession.' Lulu changes from 'a young princess in exile' (*OA* 72) to a queen, and the glamour Blixen projects on to her is something of her own desire, a matter of serene *possession*.

Such pretty stories again and again strive to force reality to submit itself to the will of Karen Blixen, masking the human pain and sorrow which was Africa – pain and sorrow not least because the Blixens, the Coles, and the rest 'had a farm', had brought their way of possession and their own kind of self-centredness to Africa. Ngũgĩ wa Thiong'o makes a telling point in relation to this. He cites Blixen's story of Kitosch, who disobeyed a white settler's instructions by riding a mare instead of leading it, and was flogged so severely that he eventually died. In the subsequent trial the defence revolved around a question of intention, not whether the settler intended to kill, but whether the cause of death was the flogging or Kitosch's own determination to die:

Kitosch said to him that he wanted to die. At four, the child said, he again said that he wanted to die. A little while after, he rocked himself from side to side, cried: 'I am dead!' and died. (*OA* 241)

Medical witnesses were called to testify that if an African decides to die he can do so at will. 'On this point, the first doctor stated, he could speak with authority, for he had been in the country twenty-five years, and knew the Native mind.' Another doctor agreed, but the 'district surgeon, who had done the post mortem examination, pronounced death to be due to the injuries and wounds that he had found upon the body.' In the end the jury (white) accepted the 'wish to die' theory. They 'knew the Native mind'. The settler, found guilty of 'grievous hurt', got two years, as Ngũgĩ remarks 'probably on his own farm'.

Ngũgĩ's comment is: 'The irony is not Blixen's. She accepts the theory. What, of course, Kitosch said was, 'Nataka kufa' which means: 'I am about to die, or I am dying.'[3] He is right, of course. She accepts the theory (though she detests the verdict) and accepts the translation that goes with it:

his firm will to die, although now removed from us by many years, stands out with a beauty of its own. In it is embodied the fugitiveness of the wild things who are, in the hour of need, conscious of a refuge somewhere in existence; who go when they like; of whom we can never get hold. (*OA* 243)

The strange thing is that twice, in *Out of Africa*, she shows herself aware of the real meaning of the phrase. 'At the time when Waweru Wamai, of Nyeri, was about to die – *na-taka kufa*, wished to die, they have it in Swaheli – he had two wives' (*OA* 108). Later one of Chief Kinanjui's sons asks her to come to his father's village, 'for he was dying: *Na-taka kufa* – he wants to die – the Natives have it' (*OA* 286). It is not easy to decide why she suppresses this vital evidence of a miscarriage of justice. One can only conclude that she elects to *pretend* to believe the false interpretation. As Ngũgĩ says, it's not irony. The clue is in Blixen's resort once more to admiring talk of the fugitiveness of wild things, the beauty we cannot hold or possess. The disgraceful injustice has to be forgotten for some will-o'-the-wisp romantic beauty which makes 'the native' into an animal too proud to be captured by a 'civilized' society.

'I had a farm in Africa' covers a good deal of history, and no literature is innocent of history. The prize for the British in East Africa was the highlands where the Kikuyu lived, but it was not only the Kikuyu who suffered. The foundations of British rule in Kikuyuland were made by the trader John Boyes, who manipulated a people weakened by famine and smallpox until he was in a position of considerable power. He was ultimately arrested by the British authorities for 'dacoity' – armed robbery. But the authorities who replaced him were not remarkably more responsible. Between 1902 and 1906 the Iraini and Embu Kikuyu were violently suppressed. In the February 1904 expedition against the Iraini:

The official report put the number killed at 400, but Meinertzhagen, who was personally involved, considered 1,500 to be a modest estimate. This figure, however, was cut out from Meinertzhagen's report on Eliot's instructions, as Eliot feared that Hinde would get into trouble if such a large casualty list reached England.[4]

The Sotik were attacked in June 1905 (92 killed; 2,000 cattle, 3,000 sheep and goats looted); 400 Gusu tribesmen were killed a few months later. In Kisumu province there was even fiercer resistance. In 1905-6 the British, with Masai and Somali mercenaries, attacked the Nandi for the sixth time. This time 1,117 died, nobody knows how many were wounded, and 16,000 cattle and 36,000 sheep were slaughtered. Then the civilizers moved back to the Embu to kill 406 of them. The northern Bugusu, who had trekked north to avoid the British, were attacked twice in 1908, with more than 200 deaths. In London these incidents were defended specifically as part of 'our civilizing mission'. Basil Davidson reports the warning sent by an under-secretary at the Colonial Office, saying that surely it was not necessary to go on

'killing these defenceless people on such an enormous scale.' His name was Winston Spencer Churchill. 'One might almost say,' concluded another official comment of 1906, 'that there is no atrocity in the [Leopoldian] Congo – except mutilation – which cannot be matched in our [East African] Protectorate.'[5]

The main continuing military effort was against northern nomadic tribes, Turkana, Somali, and others. Among some of the tribes of East Africa economic warfare, in the form of cattle-raiding, was a way of life. But when the raid was over the victors would return to their own territory, leaving the vanquished to build up their stock again. The British stayed and took the land and the people as well as the cattle for themselves. The water-cooled Maxim gun, which was capable of firing 600 rounds a minute, had proved itself to be a very useful aid to colonial settlement.

Less brutal kinds of coercion supported the bloodshed, and were approved by Westminster in its ancient role of 'whited sepulchre'. Kinanjui, who has already been mentioned, was first employed by the British as a caravan headman. He proved so amenable in this role that the colonial governor nominated him as chief of the Kikuyu in the area around Nairobi. The post of chief had never been part of Kikuyu practice or custom, and replaced an ancient and subtle traditional Kikuyu system of elders, a system more difficult to manipulate and less easy to understand for the civilizing governors of the East African Provinces. The solution of the difficult problem of the Masai proved more difficult. Lenana (his authority as *laibon* was spiritual rather than chiefly) died at Ngong in March 1911, expressing a wish that the two branches of the Masai should be reunited in the South. The British so manipulated this request that the northern Masai area was made available for Europeans by eviction and forcible resettlement.

By such means the farm at the foot of the Ngong Hills was secured for the Baron Blixen and his bride. The Africans who lived on the land, by right of tribal custom, changed their status. They became what Karen Blixen calls them throughout; they became *squatters*. The right of the settlers to 'have a farm' was secured by murder and sustained by extortion. People who had never lived in a cash economy were forced into it by hut taxes and poll taxes, devices to make the 'native' *work*, for total strangers, on land which had been his, to produce a crop he could not consume. The instrument of this form of progress was a system which in some ways closely resembled the feudal pattern which had been abandoned in western Europe centuries ago:

> The squatters knew that in order to stay on the land they had got to work for me one hundred and eighty days out of each year, for which they were paid twelve shillings for every thirty days. . . . they must pay the hut-tax to the government, of twelve shillings to a hut. (*OA* 317-18)

This time the Baroness is not telling tales – she has had a disturbing glimpse of the reality behind her life for the last eighteen years – the things which made the coffee bushes flower, what kept Finch-Hatton's plane aloft and gave her time to write her stories. But there is some comfort, for she still 'knows the mind of the Native'. She tells us about their ignorance of 'an underlying universal principle', which they ignore at their peril, the right of the new owners of the farm to evict them: 'In some respects, although not in all, the white men fill in the mind of the Natives the place that is, in the mind of the white men, filled by the idea of a God' (*OA* 318).

Now the 'Natives' discover that if the godlike Baroness sells the farm they are not even squatters. They become homeless. They depend upon the energy and persistence of a very persuasive woman to find 'my squatters' anywhere at all to live in this colony, with its civilizing mission. The new owners had given the 'squatters' six months' notice:

> This to the squatters was an unforeseen and bewildering determination, for they had lived in the illusion that the land was theirs. Many of them had been born on the farm, and others had come there as small children with their fathers. (*OA* 317)

7

Evelyn Waugh: *Scoop* and Joyce Cary: *Mister Johnson*

Karen Blixen was much less prejudiced than many of her white contemporaries. She observes skills, dignity, and wisdom among her black acquaintances, even if the observation is marred. Indeed, it is her very self-centredness which enables her to see much that others were not able to see. Kamante, Farah, and others were useful to her personally: they contributed considerably to her sense of her self, so she could not help but glimpse something of their reality as humans.

But she wrote *Out of Africa* in the 1930s. It would not be true to say that race prejudice was deeper in that decade than it had been before, despite the rise of Hitler and the operations of the Ku Klux Klan. In earlier ages it had been so easy and customary a part of the white consciousness that the massacre, torture, or mutilation of black, brown, or oriental peoples had been justified as part of Europe's civilizing mission. Mussolini's mayhem in Ethiopia was not unusual – it happened later than most colonial adventures, that's all.

Simultaneously film entertainment was drawing upon the deep well of prejudice and misinformation acquired long before moving pictures had been invented, now given even greater immediacy and penetration by the power of visual images. Audiences which had grown up playing with golliwogs and reading Little Black Sambo books were now given animated stereotypes in cartoons, with exaggeratedly large lips and grotesque hair styles. The first silent films usually portrayed blacks as slaves – there were six versions of *Uncle Tom's Cabin* between 1903 and 1927. Griffith's *The Birth of a Nation* (1914) was explicitly racist, but in later films racism was more dangerously implicit, and blacks appeared only as comic railway porters or shoeshine boys with rolling eyes and gravel voices, honest old retainers, off-screen choirs singing spirituals, or as porters carrying loads for white explorers in improbable jungles. The convention of the terrified black man-servant also began with Griffith in *One Exciting Night* (1922). Generations grew up imagining an Africa centred around Johnny Weissmuller's Tarzan, studio jungle, tigers and all. Even Paul Robeson, with his grave and powerful personality, could do little to redress the balance since many of the films he appeared in, like *Sanders of the River* (1935), were set in *Boy's Own* versions of a cardboard Africa.

In this climate works were written in the 1930s which were treated very seriously by European critics despite the fact that their view of blacks was far closer to the Hollywood fantasy than to the reality. A case in point is Evelyn Waugh's *Scoop* (1938). *Scoop* is a by-product of Waugh's experience as a war correspondent in Abyssinia (Ethiopia), during the Italian attack on that country in 1935. *Scoop* disguises Ethiopia as Ishmaelia, and ignores the terror and the pain of that military rehearsal for the world war by concentrating on the comic aspects of journalism. It replaces the real thing by a comedy civil war off-stage, led by comic black communists and comic black fascists who are both bought by external powers anxious to control mineral interests.

The plot involves inventing a form of government more amenable to comedy than the Emperor Haile Selassie. Waugh replaces the Emperor and his government by a comically corrupt Afro-American family, the Jacksons, and this gives Waugh the chance to use all the available templates of cartoon, film, and *Boys' Own* fiction caricature, stretching from the founder of the dynasty, 'a pious old darky named Mr Samuel Smiles Jackson from Alabama' (*S* 75),[1] to the present of the fiction. An interview with one of the ruling family presents a version of the comic female Negro servant so familiar in American films of the 1930s and 1940s transported into a position of national power and influence:

> Mrs Earl Russell Jackson was in the lounge. 'Good morning, madam,' said Corker, 'and how are you today?'
>
> 'I aches,' said Mrs Jackson with simple dignity. 'I aches terrible all round the sit-upon. It's the damp.'
>
> 'The Press are anxious for your opinion upon a certain question, Mrs Jackson.'
>
> 'Aw, go ask somebody else. They be coming to mend that roof as quick as they can, and they can't come no quicker than that not for the Press, nor nobody.' (*S* 93)

A bitter satire might have been written which was based on the experiences of war correspondents in Ethiopia, and it might have castigated powerful figures connected with the Ethiopian government. But Waugh evades that possibility, because it would have involved some responsibility to a world which was incredibly distant from his own interest. It does perform one satirical task well. It gives an account which is wildly exaggerated, but satirically pointed, of the comic indiscretions, the gullibility and false invention of journalists looking for newsworthy stories in a world they neither understand nor care about. It also attacks the mechanisms by which the newspaper magnates demand these lies. *Scoop* is essentially satire as relief of tension in the manner of a curse: to excommunicate the enemy from the city, the tribe, the church, or the golf club, in this case to excoriate the editors and journalists who had intruded into Waugh's life, indeed the whole of the newspaper industry. But if the scapegoat[2] is to be driven out into the wilderness, or if the Goddess Dullness, surrounded by her attendant hacks, is to uncreate the Universe, returning all to original Chaos, then there must be a wilderness or a Chaos in the fiction. That's where Africa comes in.

Joyce Cary's *Mister Johnson* (1939) is the last of his novels set in Nigeria. Cary served in Nigeria as magistrate, administrator, and soldier for seven years between 1913 and 1920, and there is no doubt that he attempts to convey a sense of his affection for the African in *Mister Johnson* – in his preface to the novel he speaks of his wish to convey

> the warm-heartedness of the African; his readiness for friendship on the smallest encouragement. . . . I can't forget their grins (and laughter – an African will laugh loudly with pleasure at any surprise.) . . . It is not true that Africans are eager but fickle. They remember friendship quite as long as they strongly feel it. (*MJ* 8-9)[3]

M. M. Mahood contends that, 'like almost every masterpiece', the novel 'has been misunderstood from the day of its publication'. She adds that 'I have heard sensitive English readers protest that *Mister Johnson* is a "patronising" book.'[4] It's difficult not to recognize the tone of the white 'expert' on Africans in a passage like the one quoted above – it's not far from that of Blixen's witness who 'knows the native mind'. Malcolm Forster summarizes much of the case for Cary's benign intentions:

> Cary was in favor of imperialism insofar as it offered opportunities to expand the lives of the colonialized peoples but not when it became an alternative oppression to the one they already suffered. Obviously Johnson's life *has* been enriched. Of course, it might have lasted much longer had he been left to live out his days in a primitive village. But it would never have been so rich.[5]

Other readers must now read Cary in the light of black writers like Chinua Achebe, who evokes the richness of so-called primitive villages in *Arrow of God*, or Elechi Amadi, who creates a resonant mythology of African life before white control.[6]

Mahood argues that the record of the evolution of the book in Cary's notebooks refutes the idea that Cary is patronizing. Johnson, she argues, is shown to be an artist, with the resilience, gusto, and generosity of the free imagination. But, for all the affection Cary shows, 'Mister Johnson' must be incompetent, improvident, capable only of living in the present; indeed Cary explains his controversial use of the present tense throughout the novel by saying that 'it was chosen because Johnson lives in the present, from hour to hour' (*MJ* 9). Cary does not generalize this by actually *saying* that this is how all Africans live – indeed 'Mister Johnson' is, in this respect and others, contrasted to the postal clerk, Benjamin. But the ineradicable impression left by the book is that this is what Africans *are* like. It is the black man as friendly, cheerful fool. Celia Rudbeck's pet name for Johnson is 'Wog', and

Mahood concedes that in some of his moods Rudbeck treats him as 'the real quaint, a sort of attendant nigger minstrel'.[7]

The climax of the novel is when Rudbeck, who has not the heart to allow the condemned 'Wog' to be executed in the normal way, responds to Mister Johnson's dog-like devotion by putting him out of his misery, as you *would* do with a favourite animal. Seeing Rudbeck with the gun, Johnson

> triumphs in the greatness, the goodness, and the daring inventiveness of Rudbeck. All the force of his spirit is concentrated in gratitude and triumphant devotion; he is calling at the world to admit that there is no god like his god. He bursts out aloud 'Oh Lawd, I tank you for my frien' Mister Rudbeck – de bigges' heart in de worl'.'
>
> Rudbeck leans through the door, aims the carbine at the back of the boy's head, and blows his brains out. Then he turns and hands it back to the sentry. 'Don't forget to pull it through.' (*MJ* 248-9)

Mahood speaks of the 'imaginative liberation' of Rudbeck, 'the realization that Johnson is not absurd, or dangerous, or pathetic', but 'gifted with the mastery to shape his own life and even to shape its close'.[8] I have tried to concede as much as I can to this reading, but find it impossible to miss an element of obscene comedy. I have also tried to modify this by a search for a bitter and laconic irony. This, after all, must be one of the places where the greatness of Johnson's heart has to be shown. But the cringing hyperbole of Johnson worship of Rudbeck and the comedy dialect representation of Johnson's last speech are intolerable. Diagnostic in a terrible and shameful way is the word 'boy' in 'aims the carbine at the boy's head'. It is not a tender reflection on Mister Johnson's youth. It is a failure to concede the adulthood of a man. It is once again the damaging illusion which we met in *Out of Africa* that, for the African, the white man is a kind of God – the same illusion which turned Kurtz mad before he died – which suffuses affection with a deadly contempt for the worshipper. But, as Conrad knew, such contempt destroys the man who seems to be worshipped more completely than the one who seems to worship.

8

Elspeth Huxley: *The Flame Trees of Thika*

Elspeth Huxley arrived in Kenya in the same year as the Baroness Blixen. She did not publish her account of her experience, *The Flame Trees of Thika*, until 1959. Like *Out of Africa* it touches upon what, for many European readers, is a profound vein of nostalgia: for most readers today a nostalgia for an experience they have never had, and which now has the glamour of the impossible dream.

The Baroness Blixen gives us a late opportunity to discover the illusive freedom of the aristocrat in feudal possession, release from the constraints which have usually bound a woman in European society. She can take a lover or two, bind herself to them in mutual fantasy, and her game of courtly love will be nourished by the 180 days a year her 'squatters' are bound to work to support her.

Elspeth Huxley's account of Kenya in 1913 and 1914 is very different, partly because it is an account of childhood, partly because it was written in the 1950s. By 1959 Jomo Kenyatta had been back in Kenya for thirteen years. The 'Mau Mau' war, which lasted from October 1952 until the capture of Dedan Kimathi in October 1956, had effectively put an end to the prospect of permanent domination by colonial settlers, and Kenya was given political, if not economic, independence in 1963. Elspeth Huxley knew that her childhood was an episode in the history of a world that had disappeared. It wasn't possible for Huxley to write, or her readers to read, without at least some knowledge of what had happened in the concentration camps at Athi River, Iruhuru, Simba, and at the most notorious of all, Hola. The interrogation and 're-education' of freedom fighters there often meant systematic torture and sometimes meant death. At the time of Mau Mau ninety-five Europeans died, and so did about 2,000 of their African supporters, but the number of Mau Mau supporters who died will never be known. Certainly it was more than 11,000.

Her readers would know, too, what the British government and the western press were anxious that the world should know, that Mau Mau was violent. It was likely to be when the revolutionaries had only *pangas* and spears, whereas the government forces and the settlers were well armed. Gross acts of violence committed by men in uniform are frequently tolerated by groups who see their privileges endangered, while similar acts, committed by those who seek to dismantle their privileges, are condemned by 'decent people'. Elspeth Huxley was not equipped to understand revolutionary activity like that of Mau Mau, but it had to change the way she thought about her own past.

In *Flame Trees* the old attitudes of the settler are there, of course. The colonialist claim to 'understand the native mind' is somewhat muted, but it is implicit everywhere. In the later autobiographical volume *The Mottled Lizard* (1962) it surfaces with a new shine given by the quasi-scientific observations of European anthropology. For instance, she reports the findings of a Swedish anthropologist on the Wakamba ritual of the third circumcision, and comments in the kind of way which might be thought appropriate for a professional expert on the native mind, a member of the Monckton Advisory Commission on Central Africa (as Huxley was). She defends such rituals against the charge of barbarism, saying that they foster 'fortitude and self-discipline'. She denies the usual colonial assumption that Africans are simple, spontaneous children of nature, telling us that if you look beneath the surface, you can see that Africans

> lived like so many Gullivers, bound by innumerable threads of custom, and allowed so little room for manoeuvre that the individual personality was cabined and confined. Their behaviour . . . recalled the complexity of some highly sophisticated, mannered society such as the court of Versailles in the eighteenth century. While people drank from calabashes, dressed in skins or blankets, relieved themselves in the bush and had created scarcely any art . . . ritual purification had to follow a hundred small, daily actions and a complex system of fines and penalties existed to cover every small or great transgression.[1]

The trappings of understanding are there, but the cultural perspective is so fixed that an unprejudiced reader must gasp in astonishment. One set of prejudices is replaced by another set which are thought to be more complimentary. The fault is not entirely Huxley's – she is herself 'cabined and confined' by the conventional assumptions which are built into our social, political, educational, intellectual, and verbal behaviour.

Even anthropologists who are trained to be objective are not free from the disease. Colin Turnbull, the author of popular anthropological accounts like *The Forest People* and *The Mountain People*, is a case in point. Turnbull disliked the Ik of northern Uganda, about whom he wrote in *The Mountain People* (1973). The Ik had been prevented from following their ancient pattern of life by resettlement to make way for a game reserve. This, and climatic changes, had led to starvation, and a way of life which, in Professor Turnbull's account, sacrificed social morality for individual survival. There's no objection to his disliking the Ik, any more than there might be to the Ik's disliking him. But Professor Turnbull was asked by the Ugandan authorities to advise on what course of action should be taken with the Ik. His recommendations amounted to a complete and systematic destruction of the Ik culture by forcible dispersion, separate into random groups of no more than ten, regardless of family and kinship. There is no attempt to find ways in which the tribe could be rehabilitated, helped to resume a life of dignity and coherence, or even left alone. When the Ugandan government sensibly rejects his plan, the anthropologist is reduced to hoping

> that their isolation will remain as complete as in the past, until they die out completely. I am only sorry that so many individuals will have to die, slowly and painfully, until the end comes to them all. . . . hatred must be reserved for the so-called society they live in, the machine they have constructed to enable them to survive.[2]

Flame Trees is less occupied with this kind of judgement. It is, on the other hand, enlightening about the settler society which imposed itself upon Kenya in the years before the First World War. Its subtitle is *Memories of an African Childhood*, and, though we must not trust it as a direct account of what a child saw, heard, and thought, the adult romance of a childish past has its real interest in the way in which it provides a view from beneath the adult world for which Blixen had such sentimental affection. Whatever virtue the work has is in its perspective of exclusion. The child is partly admitted to, partly excluded from, an adult world, observing but only partly under-standing where she cannot fully participate. So the dashing, sensitive, hand-some Ian Crawfurd, who lives his romantic, erratic life travelling in the bush with his Somali servant, plays a role somewhat like that of Denys Finch-Hatton. We understand both of these men in terms of their relationship to an idea of masculine beauty or charm or joy which is very European, very British, a nostalgic echo of nineteenth-century romanticism which persists into the early twentieth century. Lawrence of Arabia represents one potent version of this pseudo-myth.

The kind of glamour which accretes around the images of such men is a product of a settled, urban, literary culture which craves to fill an absence in itself. The absence, perhaps, is all that an oral, or a rural, or a nomad culture *seems* to possess: the capacity to live without fear of death, and for the moment only, the idea which lies behind the lost vitality of epic or romance. It's part of a wider, insidious complex of pseudo-myths, which all praise the adventurer who elects to live outside the conventions of society, and by boldness to conquer – land, money, power, the bush, the sea, space, himself – and it's given a spurious historical depth by, for instance, the romantic version of the buccaneer, by Drake and Raleigh. It is a part of the British dream of Empire, and goes together with the assumption that in places like Africa the career of the adventurer may validly be judged without any concern for the effect it has on the people. The pseudo-myth gives a context for the adulation of Cecil Rhodes as well as T. E. Lawrence.

A more subtle, but cognate, idea of masculine achievement was explored by Ernest Hemingway. Tales like 'The Short Happy Life of Francis Macomber' and 'The Snows of Kilimanjaro' were written after brief and superficial experience of Kenya on safari. As so often in Hemingway the action is simple, brutal, self-consciously primitive, however subtle the inner implications which are glimpsed through the story might be. Killing and dying, sex, drink, the challenge to the self-consciously masculine sensibility of confrontation with wild animals, or confrontation with one's own fears (which may amount to the same thing) – these are the boundary posts, and yet at the same time the starting-points, of Hemingway's fiction. And paradoxically the outcome is an acute consciousness of the vulnerability of man, the power of self-doubt, and the seductiveness of death.

These African tales of Hemingway's are wonderful in their way, but curiously close to Blixen's in their sensuous self-centredness, and the way in which their elaboration of the self employs the heroic idea of the adventurer. There in Kenya, the adventure can be bought; the chance to confront one's destiny becomes an odd kind of ritual which involves the purchase of a white hunter as guide, and black bearers to carry the tents and tables and cot-beds and chairs and the whisky, so the experience of a natural environment can be buffered against too bleak an alienation. So if, in 'Francis Macomber' or in 'Kilimanjaro', the escapee from Oak Park, Chicago, or the Kansas City *Star* gives an account of the primal experiences of initiation and of death, it is in an environment where the hunter must pay to have around him reminders of a more conventional life. This conventional white life has its own irksome ritual structures. Macomber brings his wife and her adultery, the nameless writer in 'Kilimanjaro' brings whisky-soda and his unwritten stories. Around him, unnoticed, the Masai and the Wakamba, the Kikuyu and the Nandi are undergoing different kinds of ritual initiation and similar kinds of death. But in their case initiation, ritual, and death are a necessary structure, a part of the requisite stock of knowledge which shapes a life, and a community's life. The structure which Hemingway offers is compensatory and arbitrary, an instrument of flight which is interpreted as knowledge only in terms of the fiction.

In Blixen and Huxley the pseudo-myth of the dashing adventurer is sustained by another – that of the woman who stays at home tragically awaiting the return of the wanderer. Like the Baroness Blixen, Lettice Palmer in *Flame Trees* is beautiful, cultured, made interesting by a somewhat irregular sexual past. Instead of the syphilitic Baron there is Hereward, that stereotypically military English figure of the officer and gentleman with stiffly conservative opinions – one of the stereotypes which really walks and breathes, because the Herewards of the world actively choose the stereotype as a way of life.

Seen retrospectively, by the adult rebuilding in the imagination a world of childhood which has disappeared, this trio, and, in a different way, the girl's parents Tilly and Robin and neighbours like Alec Wilson and Mrs Nimmo, become paradigmatic of that world. The effect is not simply romantic, or tragic, or nostalgic, or affectionate. As with Chekhov's *The Cherry Orchard* and its inhabitants, the fate of the inhabitants is fundamentally comic, essentially absurd. Comic because it is doomed to end, absurd because it does not believe that it ever can.

The pity is that Huxley is elsewhere so gripped by the doomed opinions and the arrogant manners of her society that one is unsure whether she is aware of anything but the nostalgia and affection. Whatever she meant, Huxley has illuminating moments. Again and again they are to do with the vulnerability, the marginality of the colonist's world; I would add the irrelevance, if colonization had not so decisively changed the life of Africa. Whatever way you read this, for instance, it speaks volumes about the European presence in Kenya:

> Indeed respect was the only protection available to Europeans. . . . The least rent or puncture might, if not immediately checked and repaired, split the whole garment and expose its wearer in all his human vulnerability. Kept intact, it was a thousand times stronger than all the guns and locks and metal in the world; challenged, it could be brushed aside like a spider's web. (*FTT* 16)[3]

The problem of interpretation is all the more acute and interesting in that Huxley frequently dwells upon the ways in which the settlers become aware of disrespect; tokens of the independence of mind of the Africans filtering through to them, as in the names given to white men, or the tricks which they used to get their own way. Perhaps the respect was not so magical after all, but a recognition that, if they went too far with these 'ghosts' who lived on their land, what happened to the Nandi could happen to them.

9

Graham Greene: *The Heart of the Matter* and *A Burnt-Out Case*

The rhetoric of these two works concerns the dilemma of Man suspended between human affection and moral imperatives. It projects a sustained sense of the ironies surrounding a striving towards self-understanding, and, through these, a search for rediscovery of the modality of tragedy. In the end, though, tragedy is the wrong word, despite Greene's will to see everything in terms of human failure to meet a more human truth, and Greene's insistent concern with metaphysical suffering.

In that sense the location is not essentially important. David Lodge, remarking on the indebtedness of Greene to the French Catholic literary tradition and its 'decadent origins in its fascination with evil', notes that one can lose much by concentrating too much on this aspect of Greene's work. Lodge then adjusts the balance by praising *The Heart of the Matter* (1948) for 'the superb realization of time and place, of the petty, exhausting tensions in a colonial society, of racial conflicts and contrasts, of the work men do'.[1] Allott and Farris remark, 'At the sensuous evocation of place Greene is deficient . . . but in *The Heart of the Matter* this weakness is made to contribute to a planned spareness of dramatic incident.'[2] On the other hand M. M. Mahood remarks that

> the colony in which Scobie serves is in the novel for the most part a backdrop, at best an atmosphere, but never a society. Here surely in the social life of Sierra Leone was the chance for an objectivity that would have resisted our sentimental empathy with Scobie's projection of his emotional needs on the world around him.[3]

I agree with Mahood. However much each detail may represent something actually to be found in the Sierra Leone of the war years the totality is a deliberate metaphor. Its 'weakness' of 'sensuous evocation' is paradoxical. An insistent and narrow focus on signals of *anomie*, hi-jacking a time and place to express a state of mind, is, indeed, an evocation of a sensuous state. It can be said to be both weak and strong in the way in which a child's repeated cry of pain might be.

I don't wish facilely to complain that Greene's fiction is morbid. Allott and Farris quote T. S. Eliot on Baudelaire:

[His] morbidity of temperament cannot, of course, be ignored. . . . We should be misguided if we treated it as an unfortunate ailment or attempted to detach the sound from the unsound in his work. Without the morbidity none of his work would be possible or significant.[4]

Eliot also remarks that

there is something artificial and even priggish about Goethe's healthiness, as there is about Baudelaire's unhealthiness; we have passed beyond both fashions, of health and malady, and they are both merely men with restless, critical, curious minds and the 'sense of the age'.[5]

The problem with Greene's morbidity and its relation to a 'sense of the age' is a certain lack of that curiosity and criticism, a triumph of the artifice of discomfort over understanding.

This is not just a matter of those characteristic details – the cockroaches and mosquitoes, the steamy heat and sudden squalls of rain, the sweat and the sleepless nights. The parody of Descartes which the cabin-passenger writes at the beginning of *A Burnt-Out Case* (1960), 'I feel discomfort, therefore I am alive', might usefully stand as an epigraph to all of Greene's serious work, and this exploration of disease is given narrative force by evocation of the expatriate's disturbing experience of dislocation. But this re-creation is a *literary* one; its coherence is a sparse imaginative coherence, in which it is difficult to draw boundaries between the accurate (or inaccurate) reporting of the atmosphere and the element of mindscape. The traveller's notebook is raided to provide crisp hard detail to give credibility to the fable. But vultures, tsetse flies, corrugated iron, gin at midday, become inscaping properties of a paper hell, admonitory foretastes of the fate which the melancholy Scobie chooses for himself in his suicide. The trouble is that such countries of the mind may become hypostatized, that they might mythologize rather than 'realize' (to use Lodge's word) a time and a place. Greene's West Africa is thus a cultural artefact of a dangerous kind.

It is no surprise to find that there are strong hints of a relationship between Greene's fictions and Conrad's *Heart of Darkness*. The title of *The Heart of the Matter* hints as much; Querry's river-boat journey to the final station in *A Burnt-Out Case* has deliberate parallels with Conrad's fiction; *The Human Factor* has an epigraph from Conrad which summarizes succinctly a theme which grows from melancholy meditative traditions in the Catholic Church: 'I only know that he who forms a tie is lost. The germ of corruption has entered into his soul.'

Like Conrad, and unlike, for instance, Joyce Cary in *Mister Johnson*, Greene eschews any claim to psychological insights into black African characters. Blacks appear in marginal roles, as servants, brothel-keepers, wharf-rats. In *Heart of Darkness*, however peripheral and however marginalized blacks are, we are given some sense of their inhabiting a living world outside Marlow's field of vision. In *The Heart of the Matter* they do little more than the vultures. The greatest area of danger for Greene, though, is in the relationship between Scobie and Yusef, the Syrian trader.

We might attempt to neutralize the inter-racial problems of that relationship by treating it as an account of the moral and spiritual dangers involved in personal or financial relationships between public servants and businessmen. But Greene's narrative is not quite so innocent as this. Scobie and Yusef are seen to have different sets of values, and these are linked to cultural, if not racial, differences. It isn't at all easy to say how much of Scobie's behaviour is owing to his flawed sense of integrity as an official, how much to his imperfect Catholicism, how much to his Britishness. In the same way it's difficult to say how much Yusef's actions, and his capacity to act as catalyst to Scobie's decline, are supposed to be put down to his acquisitive business instincts, how much to the fact that he is not, as Conrad's Marlow might have put it, 'one of us'.

His relationship with Yusef is more difficult than his adultery with Mrs Rolt. Painful and destructive though the latter is, it follows a pattern which is comprehensible. We are aware of what adultery may mean in a Catholic context of confession and repentance, death and damnation; we are aware, too, that in this context pity may have a damning as well as a saving power.

As far as we are told, and as far as we are given the ability to understand, Yusef is about as innocent, and about as guilty, as Mrs Rolt. His using Scobie to frame Tallit, or lending him money and expecting favours in return, or blackmailing him to help in the smuggling of gemstones, is made to be part of a shabby code of practice which is second nature to him. But there is a difference. Mrs Rolt's acquiescence in her affair with Scobie can't easily be interpreted as a criticism of non-Catholics. Yusef's actions carry with them an implication which is difficult to erase that to get mixed up with Syrian businessmen is to play with fire; one item in a litany of prejudices which the officials of the West African colony might chant over their pink gins at sundown as a reassertion of tribal identity.

Greene is very good at identifying and placing such prejudice, and has an excellent ear for the ugly, repetitive patterns of words in which they are expressed. Listen to Harris:

> 'I hate the place. I hate the people. I hate the bloody niggers. Mustn't call 'em that you know.'
> 'My boy seems all right.'
> 'A man's boy's always all right. He's a real nigger – but these, look at 'em, look at that one with a feather boa down there. They aren't even real niggers. Just West Indians and they rule the coast.' (*HM* 13)[6]

In Sierra Leone the descendants of the freed West Indian slaves were and are a powerful group. Unlike Waugh, Harris isn't inventing complete nonsense. But the half truth makes the racism even more ugly. And the way in which Greene reports it leaves no doubt that it is an ugliness he recognizes, closely associated as it is with those images of ever-present death which are so much a thumb-print of Greene's style. The passage continues:

> A vulture flapped and shifted on the iron roof. . . . this was one of those occasions a man never forgets: a small cicatrice had been made on the memory, a wound that would ache whenever certain things combined – the taste of gin at midday, the smell of flowers under a balcony, the clang of corrugated iron, an ugly bird flopping from perch to perch.
> 'He loves 'em so much,' Harris said, 'he sleeps with 'em.' (*HM* 13)

Harris's words are heraldry, the emblems of solidarity in a community's self-protective systems. Wilson, the newcomer, is being taught the code. But Scobie, who is placed by such racialist taunts outside the bounds of a decent colonialist virtue, is subsequently seen to be operating within a much more demanding concept of propriety, one in which he is required to see himself, not simply as representing a colonial government, or an imperial, ruling society, or even the white man, but Man – humanity subject to an eternal system of duty and morality.

It is a matter of fictional propriety, then, that the world which surrounds Scobie should echo the dangers within the mind. The world of sin in which an imperfect man endeavours to understand motives, limit his self-mutilating mistakes, is, in a conveniently available trope, echoed by the treachery and violence of an external setting. But such tropes may seep beyond the boundaries of the fiction and become persuasive as assessments of a real world. Greene is none too careful about the relation between the ethical figure and the racial overtones it might be seen as carrying:

> Somewhere in the darkness two rats scuffled. . . . the natives called them pigs and ate them roasted: the name helped to distinguish them from the wharf rats, who were a human breed. (*HM* 36)

The strategies of language and imagery are such that sin and anarchy are regularly expressed in terms of animals and blacks, responsibility and order in terms of the lonely white man struggling with a world which threatens him. It's a more insidious form of the Victorian commonplaces: 'the dark continent' and 'the white man's burden', all the more powerful because of Greene's skills in language and his high moral tone. For instance the sense of smell, as has often been observed, seems to have reserved for it a privileged pathway into otherwise inaccessible regions of the mind. Scobie finds a bottle in the corner of a warehouse which one of the black policemen tells him is 'native medicine'. Its stench nauseates, Scobie feels polluted and throws the bottle into the water: 'the contents were scattered on the air, and the whole windless place smelt sour and ammoniac' (*HM* 37).

There is a constant pressure urging us to see Scobie as an alien in a dangerous world of evil, a world in which his own culture, his own sense of values, his own notion of responsibility, disable him from understanding what he is doing. The wharf becomes part of a purgatorial or infernal world, with nameless metaphysical horrors waiting everywhere to be released:

> He should have left the bottle where it stood: it had been placed there for one purpose, directed at one person, but now that its contents had been released, it was as if the evil thought were left to wander blindly through the air, to settle maybe on the innocent. (*HM* 37)

But if Scobie, like Pandora or Adam, releases an evil, it is not entirely race-innocent. The evil he senses surrounding him is not given a name, isn't placed in the ideal regions of ethics or eschatology; it's simply given a smell, and the smell encompasses the anxiety of place: it becomes African. The guilt by association extends to the police station in a passage which, perhaps unconsciously, reproduces the worst of racialist habits of language: 'Outside the brothel on the left-hand side the girls were sitting along the pavement taking a bit of air. Within the police station behind the black-out blinds the scent of a monkey house thickened for the night' (*HM* 37). There's a melancholy syntax of self-wounding in which moral imperatives are transubstantiated into sensuous distaste, a shuddering pleasure which obscures the world perceived as thoroughly as it reveals the horror of perceiving.

European attitudes towards Africans change slowly. In the Belgian Congo changes were slower than in most colonial territories. A very few white-owned enterprises controlled most of the workforce – Davidson gives the figures for the middle 1950s as 3.17 per cent of employers controlling 51.15 per cent of the wage-earning workforce, and therefore an exceptionally high proportion of the cash economy.[7] Catholic missionary schools monopolized education. The Belgian authorities had introduced a system somewhat similar to the Portuguese *assimilado* system, in which those blacks who showed sufficient accommodation to Belgian values and standards were given 'civic merit cards' and certain privileges. In 1957 Patrice Lumumba wrote that only 884 such cards had been issued.[8]

When political independence came, it was sudden. The policies of the colonizing power, the commercial and industrial monopolies, and the paternalistic attitudes of the church, had ensured that there were very few blacks with experience of power. On the day of independence only three black civil servants were above grade four of the service, the *Force Publique* had no blacks above the level of NCO, blacks were largely confined to menial tasks in agriculture and industry. The Belgian authorities had been consistent in treating their black subjects as children, and now contemptuously granted nominal independence, perhaps in the hope that their charges would beg them to return. The secession of Katanga under Moise Tshombe, supported and encouraged by the mining companies, was the boldest device attempted by the exploiters to retain control over what they regarded as rightly theirs.

The sequence of declarations of independence in Africa, and in particular the events of 1960, were part of the education of Europe, or at least some Europeans, in the meaning of democratic government. It helped to advance a process which had been stimulated by the Second World War – a slow, difficult and painful reconsideration of the racialism which had been an integral part of European culture for centuries. *A Burnt-Out Case* was written as the process took place.

The narrative follows a pattern sufficiently similar to that of Conrad's *Heart of Darkness* for the two works to invite comparison. In both a journey into the interior of Africa by river-boat ends in the final station, the *terminus* of the ordinary alien traveller. But both books deal with journeys which go beyond the ordinary, in which the alien travellers become figures for a momentous reassessment.

There is something slightly diagrammatic in *A Burnt-Out Case*, an avoidance of the dark energy of *The Heart of the Matter* or *Heart of Darkness*. Unlike Scobie, unlike Marlow, Querry does not, and is not meant to, force himself upon us as a version of our deepest selves, a vehicle for profound doubt in our own integrity and motivation. I think this is reflected in his name – Querry is somewhere between Query and Quarry – the name sets up rather obvious multiple ironies, but encourages us, perhaps, to see him from outside, as a problem somewhat different from our own.

Querry has entered into a mutilated state of emptiness, drained of creativity, imagination, sexuality, hope, belief: above all drained of the capacity for love. As a character he makes no claim to the reader's belief other than as the embodiment of this negative idea. If he's an Orestes, the quarry of Furies, then the Furies are created or attracted by the follies of his self-destruction and cynicism, and take human forms. As Mahood remarks, 'the hunters – the Ryckers, Father Thomas, and Parkinson – are not merely the recipients but the *personifications* of the resentment and hatred, pride and false pity that Querry thought he had left behind him.'[9] If he is, despite his disbelief, a quester, Deo Gratias with his Pendélé is a grail of shabby manufacture, and Africa, 'the region of uncertainty, of not knowing the way about', becomes, as Mahood says, 'a blank space through which to travel in search of a character'.[10] Querry writes to Dr Colin, explaining why he does not wish to work for the community as an architect: 'A vocation is an act of love: it is not a professional career. When desire is dead one cannot continue to make love. I've come to the end of desire and to the end of a vocation' (*BOC* 52).[11]

We know only the church name given to Deo Gratias, not the African name he undoubtedly has. Only a perfunctory attempt is made to present him as having an African identity. There is an ambiguity about the nature of his God – it is not precisely the God the missionaries have brought with them, but in part the God of his ancestors too. For a man of that name, and for a novel of this nature, this might be the important fact, but there's little else we know about Deo Gratias.

In an episode which is central to the book Deo Gratias wanders into the forest, beyond the leprosarium, beyond the river-boat's terminus. His staff, a leper's staff, but perhaps, ambiguously, the staff of a pilgrim too, has been found in the forest. As nightfall approaches and Deo Gratias has not returned, Querry sets out to find him, absurd as this is for a stranger to the forest.

There's a spiritual allegory here. But there is a dimension to it which is explicable only in terms of Africa and European man's changing experience of it. The leper who has found Deo Gratias's staff refuses to accompany Querry into the forest, and at first Querry's reaction is what one might expect from the average colonial who thinks of Africans as 'these people':

> He could not blame these people for their fears: a man had to believe in nothing if he was not to be afraid of the big bush at night. There was little in the forest to appeal to the romantic. It was completely empty. It had never been humanized, like the woods of Europe, with witches and charcoal-burners and cottages of marzipan; no one had ever walked under these trees lamenting lost love, nor had anyone listened to the silence and communed like a Lake poet with his heart. (*BOC* 56)

How can Querry *know?* Greene himself must have known that some African forests were not empty of the accumulated emotion of fable and fantasy, if only through Amos Tutuola, whose work had received such acclaim in European literary circles during the 1950s and after.[12] Tutuola was a revelation for European readers; he enabled them to rediscover the danger and the fun of a world of belief in transition from an orate to a literate culture. There was a patronizing side to their admiration, but a genuine excitement as well.

But Querry's essential arrogance is more intimate than a simple culture blindness: intimate in the sense that it is a central vice in the structure of Greene's moral universe: it is Querry's belief that he believes in nothing. The 'emptiness' of the forest is a metaphoric extension of the deliberate emptiness of imagination in Querry: 'But if, like these Africans, one believed in some kind of divine being, wasn't it just as possible for a god to exist in this empty region as in the empty spaces of the sky where men had once located him?' (*BOC* 57). The walk in the forest becomes a way of recognizing that such emptinesses might be filled by something: 'he had lived with inertia so long that he examined his "interest" with clinical detachment' (*BOC* 58). He speaks with Dr Colin about that night, of the strangeness he felt in being needed by Deo Gratias, and his puzzlement with the word 'Pendélé', saying that he had 'never properly listened to an African talking before. You know how one listens with half an ear, as one does to children' (*BOC* 60).

In this Greene recognizes a persistent culture of arrogance, to which Europeans are peculiarly vulnerable in the presence of Africans. Querry finds, to his own surprise, that he can learn something from somebody else, and the person from whom he can learn is the very one he has never learned how to listen to.

And yet Greene has made the choice, in the structuring of his fiction, of making that connection of understanding through a pair of victims. Or rather, he chooses to make a highly self-conscious, a self-proclaimed victim, discover unwonted pity and concern for someone who has never chosen to be a leper or a victim. Querry may never have listened to an African before, in the arrogance of his culture, but it is significant that the first and only voice he is able to hear is that of a victim. Europeans are rather good, given the right occasion, at pitying victims. Many of them will be honest and full-hearted in their charity, and cherish the illusion that they understand. What remains infinitely more difficult to cope with is the recognition of the independence of the victim, his ability to decide for himself.

Colin hazards a guess as to the meaning of the mysterious word 'Pendélé': 'I've an idea that it means something the same as *bunkasi* – and that meant pride, arrogance, perhaps a kind of dignity and independence' (*BOC* 60). Querry casts doubt upon Colin's interpretation: 'I am certain he meant a place. . . . Perhaps there is more than one "Pendélé" in the world' (*BOC* 60-1). The implication is that there are multiple suggestions in the word, and to be sure the art of fiction thrives upon a multiplicity of meanings dissolved in an uncertain text. But there is supposed to be some special character in the ambiguity, something given it by the brief tenderness of an unexpected communication. It is as if Greene has chosen to make Querry a desperate version of Marlow in *Heart of Darkness*, a man who is infinitely weary in the ways of the world. Greene makes his Querry return to gather another, quite different word, one which he cannot completely understand, but this time spoken by an African. And this time, as nation after nation in Africa becomes independent, among them Leopold's old fiefdom in the Congo, amongst the many suggested meanings or near meanings of this new word, independence is one – not simply political, but spiritual, cultural independence.

The indeterminacy of meaning in 'The horror! the horror!' is not lexical, not specific to a culture, nor to interference in meaning between languages and cultures. The lucidity of the world yields to a doubt about its meaning, especially in the context of the equivocal 'The last word he pronounced was – your name' (*HD* 161). 'The horror! the horror!' expands the discourse beyond its centre, reverberating beyond the tale. 'Pendélé' has a different quality of ambivalence, abandoning the discourse to a perplexity.

The word occupies a variable space in which psychological, cultural, political, religious, even mystical interpretations of independence, dignity, pride, may be entertained. The puzzle, frankly, is much less interesting than it should be. It has something to do with the constricting relationship between Deo Gratias and the world of *dependence* which the well-meaning missionary Fathers have set up in the interior of Africa. 'He had felt strangled his last day in the leproserie; of course he didn't use the word "strangled", he told me there wasn't enough air, he wanted to dance and shout and run and sing. . . . So he set out to find this place beside the water' (*BOC* 60). As Dr Colin succinctly puts it: 'These people here are all dying – oh, I don't mean of leprosy, I mean of us' (*BOC* 61).

The weariness of Querry is enfolded in the weariness of Europe. Such a weariness is the foundation of much of Greene's rhetoric throughout his fiction, but, perhaps, here, it comes near to straying out of the intense and serious self-centredness with which Greene endows so much of what he writes. He is aware, as some Europeans are, of the multiplicity of victims, 'the wretched of the earth', and of the victimizing role of Europe throughout the centuries. That register of concern is won. What is more difficult is the recognition of immense creative energy in Africa, and perhaps what Greene does in *A Burnt-Out Case* is to stop just short of pointing to that, to make it recognizable in its absence from his discourse.

10

Alan Paton: *Cry, the Beloved Country*

Whatever critical judgement one makes about *Cry, the Beloved Country* (1948), it has to be admitted that it is a landmark in the history of European perceptions of the African condition in South Africa, Ngũgĩ is scathingly critical of the 'good Christian souls in Alan Paton's *Cry, the Beloved Country*, who suffer without bitterness, and move through an oppressive régime without even being stirred to anger'. He compares the novel with *Uncle Tom's Cabin* and identifies Paton's imaginative failure as an inability to see the African 'in an active causal-effect relationship with a significant past. Kumalo has no god; he can only look to the merciful white man's god for deliverance.'[1]

All that has happened between the 1940s and the 1980s ensures that a book should never again be *praised* for being like *Uncle Tom's Cabin*, as *Cry* was by the old *Daily Herald* when it was first published:

> Mr Paton's book should do for the native African what *Uncle Tom's Cabin* did for negro slaves in America. And I think it is a better book than *Uncle Tom's Cabin*. It is written in a beautiful biblical style of English, and not biased in favour of one side or another. It is a calm and clear statement, in human terms, of South Africa.[2]

Harriet Beecher Stowe's work has become such a byword for white condescension and black complicity in the process of subjugation that it is not easy to recall the kind of significance it had when it was first published, in serial form, in 1851. Precisely because it was never a 'calm' statement, though it was a very clear one, it became a rallying point for the people of the northern states of the USA in their rejection of slavery, and had no small part in the wave of feeling which led to the American Civil War and the freeing of slaves. In an impressive argument, written from a feminist point of view, Jane P. Tompkins urges that the kind of sentimental power it represents has been undervalued by critics writing in a male-dominated tradition.[3] Tompkins argues that such a fiction as Harriet Beecher Stowe's is not to be considered as realism, but as typological narrative, that its characters are not defined psychologically but soteriologically, that is according to their state of grace, whether saved or damned.

Stowe had her effect in a world in which black freedom depended more than anything else upon a radical change in white sentiment: if the change in sentiment produced changes in political and military action, that might be to the good, but such changes had to be sustained and realized by a change in ideology which was at least as sentimental as it was conceptual:

There is one thing that every individual can do – they can see to it that *they feel right*. An atmosphere of sympathetic influence encircles every human being; and the man or woman who *feels* strongly, healthily and justly, on the great interests of humanity, is a constant benefactor to the human race. See, then, to your sympathies in this matter! Are they in harmony with the sympathies of Christ? or are they swayed and perverted by the sophistries of worldly policy?[4]

Much less was achieved by *Cry*. In the late 1940s it was beginning to be apparent that, though changes in European sympathies were important, they were less important in the end than awareness among black Africans of their identity, their collective power, and their inevitable destiny. Paton's novel has its strongly soteriological dimension: it works on the Christian conscience and the Christian sense of a common humanity. But that growing sense of strength – Black Power, Black Consciousness as it came to be known much later in different manifestations – was growing in South Africa in a way which did not suit Paton's perceptions of salvation. Paton is alarmed by the politics of collective action amongst urban workers, and the damned become those who seek such action.

Cry helped, in its time, to give focus to sentiments which were growing in importance amongst a small group of whites in South Africa. In the latter years of the Second World War political attitudes in South Africa were in a malleable state. After the battles of Britain, Alamein, and Stalingrad fascist organizations like Ossewabrandwag became less popular in appeal, and lost more ground still with the defeat of the Axis powers. Simultaneously, white South African soldiers fighting abroad found themselves working with people of other races, and through organizations like the Springbok Legion and, after the war, the Torch Commando, showed courage in working for change. Women of all races were very active too, particularly in the Black Sash. *Fighting Talk*, one of the best journals opposing racial discrimination, had its origin at this time in the South African armed forces.

There was an opportunity for a change in sentiment among the whites. It didn't last long, and nothing much was achieved in political terms: the Nationalists were victorious at the polls in 1948 and strengthened their hold over the white population in successive years. But, partly through the influence of *Cry* (published, as it was, in the year of the Nationalist victory at the polls), a small non-Communist white opposition was organized, seeking to use peaceful conventional parliamentary means to persuade the white electorate to extend some kind of justice to the majority of the population. Five years after *Cry*, in 1953, the Liberal Party of South Africa was founded.

It was allowed to continue in existence for a few years, and Alan Paton served as its president.

Much more important was the beginning of a new stage in the development of the ANC. In 1943 the African Youth League was formed. Four of its founders have since become well known, almost synonymous with the liberation movement in South Africa: Nelson Mandela, Oliver Tambo, Govan Mbeki, and Walter Sisulu. They saw the role of the ANC as a positive adaptation to the urbanization and industrialization of Africans, and actions such as boycotts and withdrawal of labour as appropriate to these changing circumstances. But they worked closely too with non-blacks, whether Christian or Communist, who showed commitment to a common cause, like Ruth First and the Reverend Michael Scott. This situation is reflected in *Cry*. Many of the whites who were broadly sympathetic to the cause of the subject peoples of South Africa were incapable of imagining anything of value in the society of the urban African which was developing, haphazardly, painfully, but with enormous energy, all around them. A white urban society was comprehensible: it was possible to be proud of its achievements and aware of its deficiencies (how one identified the achievements and the deficiencies was another matter). But a black urban culture – that was terrifying.

Even the conventions of racial dominance permitted certain kinds of highly coded, carefully structured admiration for black tribal society. These are reflected in white South African popular literature, from Rider Haggard to Wilbur Smith. There is the proud Zulu aristocrat like Umbopa, the manly equal, but nevertheless the servant, of Sir Henry Curtis in *King Solomon's Mines*. The pattern seems to sell well still. In the *Courteney Trilogy* of Wilbur Smith the broad-shouldered, sexually active, rough, tough fighting hero Sean Courteney is accompanied by Mbejane, a kind of squire to his master's picaresque errantry, black, but of course not very black. Mbejane is Umbopa rehashed for the second half of the twentieth century, with the same kind of carefully veiled homoeroticism giving spice to the relationship:

> The whites of the eyes had no yellow in them and the nose was more Arabic than negroid. His colour was dark amber and his skin shone with oil. . . . 'How are you called?' Sean asked, noticing the breadth of the man's chest and the way his belly muscles stood out like the static ripples on a windswept beach.[5]

Of course, Mbejane turns out to be the rightful heir to the Zulu throne which Cetewayo has usurped.

The second pattern is related to the first, though it is addressed to a less callow audience. It has a slightly more developed view of the values and structures of an African tribal society, but an equally arrogant confidence in the comprehensiveness of its knowledge of Africans. This attitude views with alarm the catastrophes that lie in wait for the innocent black tribesman, or the virtuous black Christian traditionalist, when he first attempts to cope with urban life.

In *Cry*, as in *In a Province*, the possibility that there is sufficient strength, flexibility, and coherence in the personality of the rural immigrant to adapt, to find new modes of life suitable to a new society, is simply not entertained. One of the dangers which alarm both writers is the radical politician who exploits the credulity and innocence of his black audience and makes their situation worse. In both books there is also the wiser figure of the white man who has the black's interest at heart, and knows better than the black man how to achieve it. In real life there *are* honest and innocent people (some of them black ministers of religion) who are confused by city life, just as there are exploitative politicians, and field charity workers of great integrity. But both fictions work by enlisting the sympathy of a white readership whilst leaving it with some of its most dangerous prejudices. The rhetorical thrust of the fiction moulds attitudes and gratifies prejudices which are stronger because they are allowed to remain unconscious. Mphahlele remarks of Paton's characters: 'We can almost hear them groan under the load of the author's monumental sermon.'[6] You can also almost hear the vigorous nods of assent from white readers who sympathize, but don't want that sympathy to interfere too much with their view of the world.

One of the effective means is the chosen style. In Wilbur Smith belly muscles which stand out like ripples on a windswept beach (though a bit peculiar when you begin to think about it) have the right kind of triggering effect upon a certain simple kind of sensuous imagination. Paton's choice of style is in a different convention, in what the *Daily Herald* described as 'a beautiful biblical style of English'.

If you look closely, it is nothing of the sort, if by 'biblical' you mean like the Authorized Version of 1611. In *Cry* Paton employs deliberately simple, declarative sentence structures which are decorated by self-consciously lyrical archaisms, *some* of which may be drawn ultimately from the Authorised Version:

> There is a lovely road that runs from Ixopo into the hills. These hills are grass-covered and rolling, and they are lovely beyond any singing of it. . . . It is well tended, and not too many cattle feed upon it; not too many fires burn it, laying bare the soil. Stand unshod upon it, for the ground is holy, being even as it came from the Creator. (*CBC* 7)[7]

'Lovely beyond any singing of it' is nowhere near AV, or any other version of the Bible. At a guess I would place its provenance in nineteenth-century stage-Irish, or else in Victorian ballads. 'Even as it came from the Creator' has a churchy ring about it, which might ultimately derive from the Bible, but the sentence as a whole is contrived in its reverential solemnity. Paton attempts a style consistent with all that is most attractive to him (and the implied reader) in African society. This requires the kind of simplicity which city-dwellers imagine they are nostalgic for, which (they imagine) is to be found in rural life.

Stephen Kumalo and his wife have some education; enough at least to be able to read and write in English, but their Zulu society is largely a pre-literate one, and this is important in the construction of the fictional pattern, particularly in the management of the relationship between the assumed reader and the text. When Kumalo's wife reads the very important letter from the Reverend Theophilus Msimangu, 'She read it aloud, reading as a Zulu who reads English' (*CBC* 10). The sentence might seem without any critical loading at first glance, but its function is to place Kumalo's wife as someone who is ill at ease in the sophisticated world of literacy. In its context it is a signal, a largely affectionate one, addressed to the white city-dweller, that these rural folk are not threatening 'our way of life', and that they possess simple integrity, of a kind that 'you and I' are daily in danger of losing. If they are to preserve that integrity they must be protected (perhaps – the implication is buried rather deep – from too fluent a literacy).

The dialogue between Kumalo and members of his family has a simplicity of syntax and of vocabulary which would be eminently suitable for the nursery. It has the occasional syntactical structure – 'go well' and 'stay well' as formulaic words at parting for instance – to remind one that it is Zulu translated. Zulu is as rapid, complex, and capable of subtlety as any other language, as Paton, who spoke Zulu, knew. The great majority of whites could choose to think otherwise, comfortable in the assumption that 'kitchen kaffir' or 'fanagalo' represents all that there is in the language and culture of the servant race. They would, perhaps, feel challenged by a representation of conversation which indicated anything more difficult. But an inarticulate dignity which moves with painful slowness and never aims above its proper station in life presents no such challenge:

> – This letter, Stephen. You have heard it now.
> – Yes, I have heard it. It is not an easy letter.
> – It is not an easy letter. What will you do?
> – Has the child eaten?
> She went to the kitchen and came back with the child.
> – Have you eaten, my child?
> – Yes, umfundisi.
> – Then go well, my child. (*CBC* 10)

At no point is Stephen Kumalo, or any 'good' black character, allowed to speak in a way which is either much more complex or much more rapid than that. White characters, speaking in English, can gabble away sixteen to the dozen without losing 'goodness'. But Stephen's brother John, the dangerous politician, is different. When Stephen asks how life is different in Johannesburg, John answers 'Well, that is difficult. Do you mind if I speak in English? I can explain these things better in English' (*CBC* 33). This is the first sign of his corruption, that he cannot explains things in the simple and slow language spoken by Stephen. He uses the insidious skills of English to criticize the forces which bind together Stephen Kumalo's life – the tribe, the chief, the church – and to argue that these forces are no longer important in the city, no longer the forces that are going to shape the future of the black South African.

Either by accident or design these are the arguments the ANC youth, among them Mandela and Tambo, were making. Those forces which are seen to be receding in importance – the tribe, the chief, the church – were the most powerful conservative forces in black society, the greatest natural allies of those whites who wished merely to temper the injustices of a divided society with charity and good will, or, more sinisterly, to use the traditional patterns of order to hide those injustices from the outside world. The theory of *apartheid* which was developed in the 1950s depends a great deal on the maintenance and development of tribalism and an obsolete system of chiefly government. John Kumalo speaks:

> at least I am free of the chief. . . . He is a trick, a trick to hold together something that the white man desires to hold together.
>
> He smiled his cunning and knowing smile, and for a moment addressed himself to his visitors.
>
> – But it is not being held together, he said. It is breaking apart, your tribal society. It is here in Johannesburg that the new society is being built. Something is happening here, my brother. (*CBC* 34)

And the cunning politician says much the same of the church. When the *Daily Herald* reviewer wrote that the book is 'not biased in favour of one side or another', he may not have fully understood the changing situation in South Africa, or what the 'sides' really were. Forty years later it does not look so cunning and corrupting to deny that a man must be meek and obey the laws of man.

The Reverend Msimangu is implicitly contrasted with John Kumalo – both of them speakers of restraint, but different kinds of restraint; both speakers who could justify the fears which possessed the whole of a white society and begin a revolution. But Msimangu holds back out of Christian principle, John Kumalo out of corrupt self-interest:

> There are some men who long for martyrdom, there are those who know that to go to prison would bring greatness to them, there are those who would go to prison not caring if it brought greatness or not. But John Kumalo is not one of them. There is no applause in prison. (*CBC* 160)

The implication of this is deeply offensive to the new black culture, and the careers of Mandela and many others have abundantly proved its falsity. There is a proper anger, a decent discontent abroad; it is the blessed who are marching on Pretoria: the mutilated children of Soweto, the disinherited of Crossroads, those who survive their 'independence' in arid homelands, the workers who bear down every day upon every white city from egg-box townships to do the white man's work for him. The churchmen who serve them are now Tutus and Naudés and Boesaks, the heirs of Luthuli not of Msimangu.

The title, *Cry, the Beloved Country*, demands a passionate concern, and, to be fair to Paton, the concern is there; it is powerful, it thrusts through the book from beginning to end. But it is an odd kind of passion, which holds within itself a fear of passion, a concern with correct limits rather than with desperate needs. I spoke of the culture of white South Africa as *permitting* certain kinds of admiration of the black. In the same way, behind *Cry* there is a hidden ethic of permission, both for black and for white, a grotesque parody of the negative structure of the Old Testament Commandments, with no 'Thou Shalt' shining through. It is, perhaps, at its most poignant here, where Stephen Kumalo tells his son's woman what Absalom has done:

> – Have you heard of your husband? he asked. Only the word does not quite mean husband.
>
> . . . . . .
>
> – He is in prison, for the most terrible deed that a man can do.
> But the girl did not understand him. She waited patiently for him to continue. She was surely but a child.
> – He has killed a white man. (*CBC* 99)

There is no irony. The most terrible deed a man can do is to kill a *white* man, and the girl was a child for not knowing that. There is sadly a sense in which, in South Africa, that is true. In that world race has its terrible imperatives. I don't think that Paton was aware of what he meant when he wrote that sentence, but he meant it, all the same. And it fits, in a precise way, with the coy diffidence of 'the word does not quite mean husband'. Paton is acutely sensitive, as every white South African is, to *decorum*. Morality habitually takes the form 'thou shalt not kill a white man', 'thou shalt not fornicate'; it is not *permitted*, it is not the *law*.

Paton is following an instinct which is absolutely sure when he makes Jarvis's intellectual and moral testament, a document which is intended to make a white reader search for the truth hidden in his contradictory instincts, a matter of discrimination between what is *permitted* and what is not. The first part of the document which we are given begins in the middle of the sentence:

> was permissible. What we did when we came to South Africa was permissible. It was permissible to develop our great resources with the aid of what labour we could find. It was permissible to use unskilled men for unskilled work. But it is not permissible to keep men unskilled for the sake of unskilled work. (*CBC* 126)

This part of the document, about a page long, uses the word 'permissible' twenty-five times. It is deeply wrong, I believe. Wrong because it seeks for a universal authority in terms only of limits to proper action, and not in terms of rightness of purpose or response. It argues in terms of the bounden duty of the white, and not in terms of recognizing what power is and what it does. And, in the end, it is hopelessly one-eyed in its condescending Europo-centricity:

> Our natives today produce criminals and prostitutes and drunkards, not because it is their nature to do so, but because their simple system of order and tradition and convention has been destroyed. It was destroyed by the impact of our own civilization. Our civilization has therefore an inesca-pable duty to set up another system of order and tradition and convention. (*CBC* 127)

And yet, Jarvis's document *is* about contradictions, about deep fissures in understanding which hinder the most intelligent and sensitive as well as the most stupid of whites. It is the strange, partial success of *Cry* that, like Jarvis's posthumous manuscript, it identifies the contradictions which mar it – not in such a way as to justify the book as a whole, but at least in such a way as to recognize with partial success its own problematic. The last words which Jarvis writes are of the confused and inconsistent God the whites have created in South Africa:

> The truth is that our civilization is not Christian; it is a tragic compound of great ideal and fearful practice, of high assurance and desperate anxiety, of loving charity and fearful clutching of possessions. Allow me a minute . . . (*CBC* 134)

The pathos of those last words of a well-meaning man read by his sorrowing father should not blind us to the contradictions: he wasn't allowed a minute to do all the things that were needed, but no end of minutes would not have been enough unless the problem was understood and the right means chosen. Paton reveals his own position very clearly in the book when he writes about the miners' strike.

The historical strike referred to happened in August 1946. The mine owners had used the war to increase their profits, and this involved maintain-ing very low levels of pay for black workers who were doing work previously done by whites for high wages. As Jack and Ray Simons remark: 'The mines were being subsidized by peasant families throughout the sub-continent, who produced from forty-five to sixty per cent of their household income and depended for the rest on money earned by the working miner.'[8] The Cham-ber of Mines refused to negotiate with the African Mine Workers' Union, and embarked on a campaign of victimization and espionage. The Lans-downe Commission, chaired by one of South Africa's most distinguished judges, reflected the confused attitudes of many white liberals by showing itself in favour of the development of African trade unions but discovering malevolent Communist influences, and deeming that the miners 'had not yet reached the stage of development which would enable them safely and usefully to employ trade unionism'. Paton echoes these attitudes towards 'simple people, illiterate, tribal people':

when they strike they go mad; they imprison mine officials in their offices, and throw bottles and stones, and set places on fire . . . they can do great damage, and endanger human life, and bring the great industry of South Africa to a standstill. (*CBC* 162)

Seventy-six thousand men struck for a wage of 10 shillings a day. They were forced back into the mines with clubs and bullets. Nine Africans were killed and 1,248 reported injured. No bottles and stones were thrown, no mine officials were imprisoned, there was no arson. All the violence came from the police. Smuts 'was not unduly concerned'. Agitators were responsible, they were trying to lead the country to destruction. Paton's position was not so very far from that of Smuts.

It is John Kumalo who defends the strike – in English, of course – saying that history teaches the need for collective action and justifies withdrawal of labour. His defence of industrial action, it is implied, is an act of racial hatred.

Paton rehearses in a quasi-magical way the persons, the values, the conclusions desired by the enactor. He seeks to secure propriety and the safety of the group by imagining a history, creating a myth of salvation. His art has the function the drawing of a bull on a cave wall in Lascaux is presumed to have: to ensure that tomorrow's work will have a satisfying outcome, with food for all, ensuring a continued integrity for his group (not a racial group, a community of feeling and ideology). He acts the writer as pharmacist,[9] stocking and labelling the products on his shelf as poison or as cure, expelling or absolving his persons according to the rhetoric of healing *permitted* by his faith, or his ideology. His work has a lot in common with one of Doris Lessing's least intelligent stories, 'Hunger'.

11

Doris Lessing

Of the five stories in *Five*, Doris Lessing remarks that 'Hunger' 'is the failure and, it seems, the most liked'. In 1952 Lessing went to Moscow with a delegation of writers. The British writers disagreed on politics but shared certain assumptions about literature, 'in brief, that writing had to be a product of the individual conscience, or soul. Whereas the Russians did not agree at all' (*SBF* 10).[1] The group was taken to see a room full of presents for Stalin. Lessing leaves the others and sits outside thinking of how simple was Dickens's morality, and yet how great a writer he was. After all her experience of an unjust society, 'Why, then, could I not write a story of simple good and bad, with clear-cut choices, set in Africa?' (*SBF* 10).

But, 'It wasn't true', she says of 'Hunger', and she does not mean that the events described are not plausible, or representative of life in Southern Africa. It isn't 'untrue' because of its moral simplicity, though it is something to do with the way in which the morality of the tale is managed. It creates a false relationship between the writer and her rhetoric which Dickens, too, fell into sometimes.

'Soul' is a private shorthand; if it means the same as 'individual conscience', that's not really missing, just made uninteresting by being forced into a mode of *statement*, expressed in such a way as to demand no effort or search from the reader. Lessing doesn't often in her short stories lose that mood which Conrad perceived in *Heart of Darkness*, 'no longer a matter of sincere colouring. It was like another art altogether . . . a tonality of its own, a continued vibration.'[2] She loses that in 'Hunger'.

The tale resembles *Cry, the Beloved Country* in its simple and exhortatory relationship to the soteriology at its centre, as well as in many parallels in its plotting. There are evocative images, especially at the very beginning of the tale, when Jabavu holds on avidly to sleep: 'He leans greedily towards it as towards a warm drink on a cold night. He drinks it, guzzles it, and is sinking contentedly into oblivion when words come dropping through it like stones through thick water' (*SBF* 208). Here and there a sentence or two like this, not seeking particularly for what Conrad calls 'sincere colouring', strikes out after a common truth of puzzled experience which lies between the words. In this case it poses an enigma of the meaning of 'hunger', whether in the title of the tale or in the experience of the sleeper, to be solved by the tale as a whole. It touches what is always there in the best of Lessing's stories, a caution, an ambivalence of meaning, a withdrawal from explanations, which provisionally redefines 'truth'. The reader is invited to participate, to contribute to an understanding which may have to be won at some personal cost.

This commonly involves a relationship which is never fully made clear between the narrative events and the consciousness of a perceiver. It's not an easy matter to define, which is why Lessing finds herself resorting to phrases like 'individual conscience' or 'soul'. It is partly a matter of absences – absences of explanation which are controlled and made potent for us as readers by a sympathetic (or wary, or disabused) relationship with the perceiver at the core of the tale. Absences are defined by what is present, and may function by inviting a reader to construct for himself or herself what lies at the core. The story issues an invitation to sympathy or antipathy, fosters a willingness to assume an understanding on the basis of information which is partial, ambiguous, or even assembled from what is most signally absent.

'Hunger' is an experiment in abandoning these subtle relationships between writer and reader. The fact that Lessing cannot do it successfully does not mean that it can't be done. It looks more difficult because the alternative mode of writing seems to belong to that terrible blind fugue in Eurasian history, ideology, and consciousness which we associate with the name of Stalin. Lessing, with appropriate irony, describes the plot of 'Hunger': 'Only one possible plot – that a poor black boy or girl should come from a village to the white man's rich town and . . . there he would encounter, as occurs in life, good and bad, and after much trouble and many tears he would follow the path of . . . ' (*SBF* 10).

With certain elaborations it is the plot of *Cry, the Beloved Country* too. Paton's work centres around the corrupted innocent's father rather than the boy himself, thus inviting the reader to sympathize with what Paton projects as African *traditional* values. Lessing, on the other hand, centres her story around Jabavu, the young and not entirely innocent African who suffers both the corruption and the liberation of urban life.

Lessing, like Paton, makes her hero inhabit a Manichaean universe of good and evil. In Paton's novel evil is the *tsotsis* (urban African gangsters) and the black politician. In 'Hunger' the good politicians, the Samus and the Mizis, occupy the world of light. The *tsotsis*, led by Jerry, live in a world of drink, sex, theft, and treachery, occupying a hell made by the capitalist system and a racialist government. In Paton's novel the son, Absalom, mourned by his father as bitterly as his namesake, has one set of choices which Paton's rhetoric urges as typical. 'Hunger' is dispensed in a different pharmacy.

The debate between the two fictions (I think Lessing intends one) becomes an argument about future paths. Lessing centres that debate on the pronoun 'We', which becomes a powerful nostrum in the terms offered by the text.

The last sentence of the letter Tennent brings to Jabavu from Mizi is 'We greet you.' Earlier in the story Jabavu has impulsively given his last, his only, shilling to Mrs Mizi for the cause. The letter returns him to that redemptive sense of solidarity: 'Jabavu lets the paper drop and stands staring. The word that has meant most to him of all the many words written hastily on that paper is *We*. We, says Jabavu. We, Us. Peace flows into him' (*SBF* 330).

In *Cry* the one-ness of Jarvis and Kumalo is seen as moral, religious, and traditional, co-opting both the tribal and the liberal European past into its notion of rightness. In 'Hunger', with a certain crudeness, the tribal past is drafted into the rhetoric of socialism against the greedy individualism of a capitalist world. Jabavu's instinctive hunger is not the same craving as that of Hardy's Jude; he does, and does not, crave the right to be 'I', an individual. He grows to recognize a need to rediscover *collective* purpose. The abandonment of this has led to

> a harsh and ugly time when there was only the word I, I, I – as cruel and sharp as a knife. The word *we* has been offered to him again, accepting all his goodness and his badness, demanding everything he can offer. *We*, thinks Jabavu, We . . . And for the first time that hunger in him, which has raged like a beast all his life, wells up, unrefused, and streams gently into the word *We*. (*SBF* 330)

In its choice of stylistic device 'Hunger' has one resemblance to Cary's *Mister Johnson* – it is written almost entirely in the present tense. Lessing would not have offered Cary's explanation, that the present was chosen because the African in the narrative 'lives in the present, from hour to hour'. And yet it is something to do with the fact that, unusually for Lessing, the perceiving consciousness is that of a tribal African experiencing the alienation of urban life. Against all her instincts as a writer, Lessing accepts a convention which has the effect of severely limiting the world of her character, to a simple present without memory, reflection, or anticipation.

The present tense also manipulates the way in which the reader responds to the fiction, limiting the ways in which he can find an understanding of its persons to a restricted mode of consciousness. As Joyce Cary puts it, the present tense may carry the reader along in an unreflecting mood, illuminating 'a very narrow scene', and sometimes, 'that sudden feeling of insecurity . . . when he feels all at once that not only has he utterly lost his way, but also his own identity' (*MJ* 10).

'Hunger' is uncharacteristic, but it will help to identify the ways in which other short stories by Lessing achieve their success. In the first place, her radicalism, in feminism or in socialism, remains circumscribed whenever she writes within a European tradition of realism. The circumscription offers its own freedom and flexibility to establish delicately balanced mutual understandings, unspoken agreements about what might be left unsaid, which may work upon our assumptions in a subversive way, questioning and redefining attitudes which appear to be unchangeable. But it seems necessary for this kind of success that the writer keeps at a certain distance from a mode of *statement*, treating her subject sceptically, hinting at the greater value of suggestion, ironic in the very essence of its method.

It also seems to be necessary for this kind of ironic realism that events should be related reflectively, with the space and power to organize given by the past tense. For this kind of success, the consciousness at the centre of the narrative should have a 'believable' relationship, in terms of culture, history, personality, with the writer, and, equally important, with the implied reader. Simple as the idea of 'believable' seems, it's really very complex. The 'implied reader' is ultimately a fiction of the author's invention. The *real* reader is encouraged to find a foothold in the fiction through a kind of shadow-twin, a mediating presence which offers a relationship, complicit or hostile, with the central consciousness. And thus the 'believability' of the central consciousness is in part a function of the degree to which the real reader is able to accept and take seriously his own 'implied' function. The ambivalence is one of the ways in which Lessing is able to explore the strangeness of relationships between individuals in human society more interestingly than in 'Hunger'.

Throughout her *œuvre* Lessing returns in differing ways to conflictual impulses. There is the impulse to what, in one of its modes, is felt as conformity, in others is felt as liberation in solidarity or collective purpose. The countervailing impulse is equally complex – individual freedom, selfishness, rebellion, perhaps even 'soul'. The complex, with all its contradictions and complementarities, is alive (sometimes especially alive in irresolution) in Lessing's responses to all the great themes she deals with – the political consciousness, the issues of women's rights, race relations. Indeed it is in a sense more important for her work than the issues themselves, either separate or compounded.

There's one more element which has great importance in Lessing's fiction, and it seems to be a major factor in what Lessing gestures towards in 'the individual conscience, or soul'. There is, in the very heart of Lessing's fiction, a sense of evil. In 'Hunger' this is displayed with all the simplicity of emblem; elsewhere it's obscured by introjection. Accompanying this, there is a melancholy awareness of the way in which, throughout their lives, her major characters, or many of them, undergo an education in human-ness, coming to terms (or failing to come to terms) with what is imperfect, hypocritical, hateful, just plain wrong, in themselves and in their society. It would be too easy to mark this as a puritan sensibility and pass on.

In Lessing, as in the American settlers, the puritan spirit contains a marvelling love of the abundance and fertility of the land. For the Americans, some of them, this joy was guaranteed by the belief that the land was an earthly paradise, God-given, so that they might praise Him all the better. Afrikaner nationalists have a similar tale to tell sometimes. Lessing has a different story. The title *This Was the Old Chief's Country* refers to the awareness that the land is purloined from others; the dramas of her sparse, inward-looking white communities are therefore acted out in a milieu which corrupts the land, the society *and* the individual.

It is a consequence of all this, I believe, that Lessing's best short stories are not usually those which tackle the obvious social and political issues directly. A story like 'Old John's Place', for instance, has nothing to say directly about racial prejudice or economic exploitation. Instead, it focuses sharply upon the miniature society of a group of white farmers, their wives and children, in a now-vanished world – Southern Rhodesia in the early 1930s. The social conventions of respectable settlers, the subtle subversions of those unspoken agreements by intrusive strangers, the silent understandings concerning sexuality, the mechanisms of social acceptance and rejection, the veiled evasions which carry with them an indistinct but potent corruptiveness, are observed by a young girl, become part of her growing up. And it is not simply a process of *accommodation* to an adult life with ready-made game-structures which Kate Cope experiences.

It is formally interesting, too, in that it makes no obvious effort conventionally to *shape* sequences of experience, to stress the climax or turn of event in the way that the generality of fiction writers in the European-American conventions often do. The mode, which is characteristic of many of Lessing's stories, seems to be controlled by subtle processes of discovery in the act of writing rather than by initial decisions of intent. It can sometimes produce a first, disconcerted, reaction in the reader that the text moves without restraint. But the real restraints, less visible than those of more conventionally organized narratives, tend to be discovered in retrospect, after one has read the story.

In a way what Lessing describes in 'Old John's Place' is the acquisition of a writer's consciousness, the ability to stand at a tangent from other people and even from oneself, by defamiliarization to understand and analyse experience to the point where equivocation and silence become better tools than clarity. It discovers an obliquity of consciousness as the only kind of consciousness, perhaps, which will enable the European writer in Africa to deal with the peripherality of a settler society. It gives the space needed to observe and silently assess, withdrawing from any overt judgement, the strategies of settlement, the patient creating of an alien illusion of 'home' by a network of trivial proprieties from which unwelcome intruders are condemned to be excluded as vagabonds.

The 'Old John's Place' of the title is a farm which has never had a permanent owner, but has been owned in turn by temporary settlers who have never been accepted fully by local whites. The story opens with the farewell party of the Sinclairs, intruders who have admitted their inability to belong to the closed group of settlers in the district, but are tactful in falling in with the customs of the country, permitting the party to proceed according to protocol, in tacitly agreed stages. First, the men and women sit separately, the women covering their glasses and protesting that 'they couldn't drink another mouthful' (*OCC* 126). Then, as the inhibitions go, the party advances by regulated steps from embarrassed propriety to rashness and danger. The Sinclairs indulgently foster (but control) the development of these adult games, while Kate, the child, wanders between the group of men and the group of women, too old to be put to bed with the infants, too young for the rituals of the adults, 'unable to do anything but loiter on the edge of each group in turn, until an impatient look warned her that something was being suppressed for her benefit that would otherwise add to the gaiety of the occasion' (*OCC* 127).

The hints and signs which accomplish the child's alienation are reminiscent of the processes which R. D. Laing records as the ways in which the young are taught to be schizophrenics by their families. With Kate it doesn't go that way. She recognizes the decorum demanded by a narrow society even in these strange rites; Kate records, analyses, learns to be true to her name and *cope*.

She observes the second stage, where the men and women mingle, but still decorously, wife and husband together, until dancing begins, and, in the third stage, the pairs dissolve into discreet saturnalia. The 13-year-old is precociously initiated into the anthropology of her own tribe: the permitted but unadmitted adulteries, the secret system of treachery on which the security of a community depends, so fragile and elaborate are its mores. It's as if a veil is removed from daytime life, revealing a truth underneath 'that was bare and brutal. Also quite irrevocable, . . . for nothing was more startling than the patient discretion with which the whole thing was treated' (*OCC* 128). During the third stage, Kate has learned, she must disappear from view. Though she knows well enough what is happening, she must wait and dread the arrival of the fourth stage – not always reached, but when it is, a matter of quarrels and ugliness.

The Sinclairs are replaced at Old John's Place by the Laceys, who belong as little as the Sinclairs and lack their diplomatic skills. The first sign that they are 'not quite right' is that it is rumoured they breed horses; the second that, as well as Mr and Mrs Lacey and the baby, there is a Mr Hackett, and that the three together have already tried farming in England, the Argentine, and the Cape. Kate is fascinated by Rosalind Lacey's flair and her baby, but torn, 'for the Laceys, she knew, were to be resisted; and yet she was being carried away with admiration' (*OCC* 135). Mrs Lacey has the kind of taste which outrages the settler community, with her bold interior decorations, glass walls, and

> fifty yards of light transparent material that looked like crystallized sunlight. . . . It was a room which had nothing to do with the district, nothing to do with the drifts of orange dust outside and the blinding sunlight, nothing to do with anything Kate had ever experienced. (*OCC* 135-6)

Rosalind has strange modern ideas about bringing up children, too, full of discipline and hygiene. Kate is allowed to take the baby out for walks, but never to pick it up or cuddle it; its human contacts are regulated by the clock just as its feeding and sleeping are.

Inevitably, the Laceys give a party; inevitably, it is *different* from other parties and we are made aware of young Kate understanding the significance of the altered design. It's 'a planned compromise between the family pattern and the thing she intended should grow out of it. Husbands and wives were put together, yes; but in such a way that they had only to turn their heads to find other partners' (*OCC* 140). Something terrible is happening; something which cannot be understood without the secret knowledge of that adult world, isolated as it is in the middle of a continent that covers Rosalind's carefully constructed environment, her white carpets and oyster satin drapes, with the pervasive orange dust of an alien soil. In a society struggling to reassure itself of its coherence, its *respectability*, even with the sacrifice of a little virtue, someone is *letting the side down*. Kate struggles to understand what 'stage' has been reached. But there are no stages any more: 'Mrs Lacey had fused these people together from the beginning, by the force of wanting to do it. . . . she was flirting with everyone, dancing with everyone. Now there was no criticism; they were all in love with her' (*OCC* 144).

Eventually Kate sees Mrs Wheatley, who had always maintained a discreet equanimity at parties when her husband flirted, in a strange panic: ' "I want to go home, I want to go home," she was saying, her tongue loose in her mouth' (*OCC* 144). It's more terrible than stage four had been in the old order. Rosalind, with the seductive force of her will, has ruptured the cherished bonds of deception. The community is in a state of fission, and Kate sees Rosalind dancing alone, ignorantly glamorous,

> down the dim shadowed space, weaving her arms and bending her body, and leaning her head to watch her white reflection move on the polished floor beside her. 'Who is going to dance with me?' she crooned. 'Who is going to dance?' (*OCC* 145)

Kate is taken to another party at the Laceys, despite her parents' misgivings. This one ends with a fight between Mr Lacey and Mr Hackett, the two men in the *ménage à trois*. The episode is a critical one in a rite of passage, Kate's entry into an adult world of artifice and illusion. She asks what Hackett and Lacey were fighting about, and gets no satisfactory answer. With a sudden oblique insight into the adult world, her wonder crystallizes as last into an exclamation: ' "But they are so much alike!" She felt as she would have done if she had seen a little girl, offered a doll, burst into tears because she had not been given another that was identical in every way' (*OCC* 153). Kate's sense of the frailty of this adult world focuses on the disciplines Rosalind forces upon her child. They seem another evasion of spontaneity, replacing emotion by more ritual. Towards the end of the story Kate gives the baby to Mrs Lacey and watches the mother's alarm and embarrassment at its instinctive joy. This prompts her to hurt Rosalind, using both the convention of youthful innocence and her own arcane knowledge, without deliberation, but with spontaneously inspired malice: ' "Why did they say the baby is exactly like Mr Hackett?" she demanded, without knowing she had intended to speak at all' (*OCC* 159). But whilst the society throws out Sinclairs and Laceys centrifugally, it draws in Kate with centripetal force. She is shown to be conscious of joining a conspiracy:

> 'Well, we have all got to go on living together, haven't we? I mean, when people have *got* to live together . . . ' She looked at Mrs Lacey to see if she had understood.
> She had not.
> Kate had, for a moment, a vivid sense of Mrs Sinclair standing there beside her; and from this reinforcement she gained new words: 'Don't you see? It's not what people do, it's how they do it. It can't be broken up.' (*OCC* 160-1)

Loss of innocence as the child enters into an adult society, the need to repress communal secrets, shared guilt, are recurrent concerns in Lessing. For instance, William MacGregor in that splendid little tale 'Flavours of Exile' embodies the compromises of the *rites de passage*. The point might be made about any society, but is made with special force by exploration of that alien society, linked or separated by loyalties acquired far away, in England, Scotland, South Africa. A society above all whose true but displaced centre is strenuously and consistently denied, for the very existence of these farms depends upon the expropriated labour of the black worker.

The complexity of 'Winter in July' lies largely in its apparently loose, exploratory structuring. Its title deserves comment. In the southern hemisphere if there is a winter it *is* in July. And yet, for a European living in the southern hemisphere the title would not necessarily have the redundant quality of, say, 'Winter in December' for a Briton. For a settler encamped in a European literary culture, it would describe something paradoxical, something slightly wrong: whether it is Africa that is wrong or the visitor is another matter.

Like 'Old John's Place', the story has at its centre a *ménage à trois*. The sole woman has drifted in an absence of love, a weariness of emotion, from continent to continent, to find herself at last sharing her life with two half-brothers. She has travelled to Africa – and this becomes crucial to the moral economy of the tale – as the result of a critical experience:

> There was one morning when she had a vision of evil . . . it might have been almost any city, on a bright warm day, from a hotel window, with the people blowing like leaves across her vision, as rootless as she, as impermanent; their lives meaning as little. (*OCC* 199)

The story takes on a profounder pattern from this vision of evil[3] – a signal that Julia, for all her coldness and rootlessness, has a capacity to discern dizzying moral perspectives in life, while spending much of her energy in denying their reality. Anyone who attempts to read Lessing's African stories as social commentary is faced by problems here – the sense of evil clearly originates in a less public level of consciousness than can be discussed in that way. And yet, once again, in a white writer, the experience of Africa brings with it the necessity to face an unnamed horror. The difference between the form the experience takes in a visitor like Conrad and the form it takes in a white African like Lessing might be suggested by saying that Lessing is capable of projecting it into patterns which share a great deal with some distinguished narratives by black writers like Bessie Head, Ayi Kwei Armah, or Dambudzo Marechera.

Inta Ezergailis, following Annette Kolodny, speaks of ' "the amputated self-perception" that characterizes many female protagonists in the work of contemporary women writers'.[4] Ezergailis gives reasons why such division should be a particularly powerful theme in women's writing. There are reasons, too, why it should occur strongly in the literature of Africa, black or white, amongst those who experience strongly the fissiparous pressures of divided societies. But it is significant that the realization of internal mutilation and division should come about in Julia's relationship with men. The relationship between the two half-brothers, Tom and Kenneth, has an indecipherable quality of intimacy, in which affection and malice blend in a way which even Julia cannot read. Tom goes off to the war, leaving Kenneth and Julia together, and the change in the household leads Julia once again to confront the insecurity and the vacancy of her inner self. The whole pattern is part of a private myth perhaps. But, on one level, it comments upon a relationship between person and place which is characteristic of that now-dead society. She misses the peace Tom gave her, the ability to let the 'restless critical part of her die . . . to enjoy the physical things slowly, without haste':

> – learning all this had, she imagined, healed her. And now, without Tom, she was nothing. She was unsupported and unwarmed; and she knew that marrying had after all cured her of nothing. She was still floating rootlessly, without support; she belonged nowhere. (*OCC* 206-7)

The passage might recall the lines in Milton in which Satan discovers Eve in the garden of Eden, alone for once, without the succouring presence of Adam:

> Herself, though fairest unsupported flow'r,
> From her best prop so far, and storm so nigh.[5]

There's a concealed feminist charge in the argument, touching the way in which society (with Milton) assumes that a woman can fully exist only in relation to a man. In this story the love relationship with Africa has something in common with marriage. Africa becomes a kind of sensuous Eden, an invitation to leave behind the restlessness and critical intelligence, and yet, when Julia wakes up from the lotos-eating dream, she finds that, really, she has nothing to do with Africa. The unreality of marriage and the illusory promises of Africa to the settler lie in parallel with each other. Both offer the apple of temptation in the pretence of one-ness, when there is only one reality of existence for Julia – her selfhood in separation.

A different relationship develops with Kenneth, based upon a mutual consciousness of the lies within them. If Tom is an Adam, Kenneth is the serpent. Both Kenneth and Julia are conscious of the hypocrisy, the lies, behind the war which Tom is fighting, behind the life they are living. The relationship is all the stronger because of its implicit hostility, because of its foundation in irony. Eventually Kenneth – still ironic even in this – arranges to get married to a nice young girl of twenty-three from 'home'.

The sensuous relationship with the African Eden becomes central in a passage just before the marriage takes place. As so often in Lessing, the celebration of Africa is tied in with a sense of the character's inevitable exclusion from it: it has some of the lamenting, elegiac power of a Wordsworth, and yet it is also, patently, the writing of a farmer's daughter:

> Around her the skeleton of rock showed under the thin covering of living soil . . . the grass – the long blond hair of the grass – struggled always to heal and hold whatever wounds were made by hoof of beast or thoughtlessness of man. The sky, the land, the swirling air, closed around her in an exchange of water and heat, and the deep multitudinous murmuring of living substance sounded like a humming in her blood. She listened, half passively, half rebelliously, and asked: 'What do I contribute to all this?' (OCC 220-1)

The imagery of the body presents a romantic, organicist view of man's or woman's relationship with the earth, the paradise which surrounds and yet eludes the weary, only to define the nature of separation. The body of the earth, so subtle, alive, forgiving, should be felt as her own, but it is not.[6]

Julia's discovery of an emptiness at the core of her own existence, her relationships with Tom and Kenneth, her experience of Africa, point towards the displacement, physical, moral, spiritual, of the settler community, but without leaving the solid specificity of the fictional case. Through a system of subterranean allusion, it hints at a twentieth-century African version of paradise lost, in which an Eve perceives her loss in her sin. The story ends with Julia going to Kenneth's room, talking about the pretty young girl he is going to marry, knowing that she cannot heal Kenneth, and, while she ponders the girl's vulnerability,

> the knowledge came to her of what word it was she sought: it was as though those carefully smiling lips formed themselves into that word.
> 'Do you know what we are?' she asked Kenneth.
> 'Not a notion,' he replied jauntily.
> Julia accepted the word evil from the humourless, homeless girl. Twice in her life it had confronted her; this time she took it gratefully. After all, none other had been offered.
> 'I know what evil is,' she said to Kenneth. (OCC 229-30)

This pervasive sense of evil is again and again defined in terms of the white perceiver, adult or child, in an African landscape. There is always a paradox, a misfit – it is as if both the sickness and the beauty of Blake's rose are seen only by the cankering worm.

In 'The Old Chief Mshlanga' the bounty of Africa is distorted by a child's eye. In Lessing childhood isn't a guarantee of innocence. Even in childhood the learned alien culture may corrupt, disabling rich experience with frozen metaphor:

> a fine lace of red-starred witchweed would summon up a black bent figure croaking premonitions: the Northern witch, bred of cold Northern forests, would stand before her among the mealie fields, and it was the mealie fields that faded and fled. (*OCC* 13)

In this story, Lessing fulfils Grotowski's prescription: 'First, *confrontation* with myth rather than identification.'[7] It is about the child's inexplicable panic when visiting the old chief, her discovery that, 'if one cannot call a country to heel like a dog, neither can one dismiss the past with a smile in an easy gush of feeling, saying: I could not help it, I am also a victim.' There is loss at the heart of the tale, the alienation of a fertile land. The old chief and his people are turned off their tribal lands for the white settler, and the girl goes to see the village again. There is almost nothing left but mounds of mud and rotting thatch. Only 'pumpkin vines rioted everywhere, over the bushes, up the lower branches of trees so that the great golden balls rolled underfoot and dangled overhead: it was a festival of pumpkins' (*OCC* 24).

There are no Hallowe'en witches to peer with candle-flame eyes through the pumpkins: the child learns to see with eyes which are less disabled by a set of alien myths. But the celebration is at one and the same time an elegy. If a new kind of ironic pastoral is again and again part of the response of white fiction to Africa, it is often based upon a grossly simplified view of the past and of possible futures. Lessing just escapes a sad reductiveness by hinting at a positive renewal.

The title of Lessing's first novel, *The Grass is Singing* (1950), alludes, of course, to T. S. Eliot's *The Waste Land*. Allusions in titles act as extended metaphors, deflecting the track of the mind, obliging it to re-interpret the evidence of a given experience in an alternative framework. In this case the allusion serves to express a region of the mind rendered arid by disconnection and anxiety. But in Lessing's epigraph there is the suggestion of a turning point:

> Only a cock stood on the rooftree
> Co co rico, co co rico
> In a flash of lightning. Then a damp gust
> Bringing rain

In Eliot the sunken Ganga awaits the rain, the end of the desert time in a change which is both ominous and refreshing in the authoritative power of its declaration: 'Then spoke the thunder.' In her chosen title Lessing suggests the way in which the action occurs in what that fine poet and novelist Mongane Serote describes as 'a dry white season', always with the implicit promise, or possibly the threat, of rain to come.

We have noticed the skill with which Lessing identifies the secret protocols, the self-sealing protective mechanisms, the conspiracy of unspeakable understanding which marks the settler communities. Mary Turner has been murdered, and Moses, the houseboy, has confessed to the crime. The neighbours know enough about what has been happening in the Turner household to know that they should treat it as being an affront to their codes. Charlie Slatter, a neighbour himself, becomes the central figure in the investigation, shielding his society from the real danger – the revelation of a knowledge which they share, fear, and detest. 'The most interesting thing about the whole affair was this silent, unconscious agreement. Everyone behaved like a flock of birds who communicate – or so it seems – by means of a kind of telepathy' (*GS* 10).[8]

The outward form of the novel – the investigation of a murder – maintains an ironic relationship to the detective story. But it is about the operation of the law in a more profound sense than this would suggest. There is a more useful comparison to be made with Greek tragedy, in this respect, that, like Sophocles' *Antigone* or Aeschylus' Oresteian sequence, it counterposes differing notions of law and justice.

Tony Marston, the trainee farm manager, fresh out from England, discovers his concept of justice is totally inappropriate in the context of the community's sense of propriety. Such is the view of law and order shared with such *gravitas* by Slatter and Sergeant Denham that Tony is obliged to be like Pontius Pilate (a foreigner too, faced with a community of belief) and 'wash his hands of it'. A third sense of justice and the law is ascribed to the murderer himself. The question of why Moses did not attempt to escape is raised, and one answer is offered by the District Native Commissioner, holding forth at a sundowner party. According to him, the man's acquiescence in his arrest is to be explained by the conventions of the tribal laws as Lobengula administered them. A man who has offended will submit fatalistically, saying 'I have done wrong, and I know it, therefore let me be punished' (*GS* 13).

Lessing meticulously casts some doubt upon the reliability of this 'expert on the native mind'. Nobody actually knows what tribe Moses belongs to, Lobengula of the Ndebele was long dead; the murderer's motives, and his internalized version of law, are allowed to remain uncertain. The fact that he chooses to wait for his arrest by an ant-heap (which figures in the Commissioner's account of Lobengula's favoured punishments) might suggest some memory of old ways of justice. But his name, Moses (though a mission name) might also suggest a stern understanding of justice and punishment.[9]

Last, near the ending of the book, there is a more complex notion of justice, arising out of Mary's own dark experience, as she awaits Moses' return, and the end which she knows will come. It is composed of two moments; first, one of compassionate release, imaginatively experienced, as she looked down on her farm,

> filled with a regretful, peaceable tenderness. It seemed as if she were holding that immensely pitiful thing, the farm with its inhabitants, in the hollow of her hand, which curved round it to shut out the cruelly critical world. And she felt as if she must weep. (*GS* 202)

The second moment complements this note of compassion with an awareness of evil like that of 'Winter in July'. The sense of herself as a distant judge returns: 'It was a torment to her, in that momentarily pitiless clarity, to see herself. . . . I don't understand, she said again. I understand nothing. The evil is there, but of what it consists, I do not know' (*GS* 207). It is in a merging of these two moments that Lessing urges the reader to find whatever blend of compassionate understanding and consciousness of evil one can bear. It is, I fear, one of those few cases in which obliquity doesn't add a toughness to Lessing's ethical analysis.

I have remarked that the best of Lessing's short stories are not those in which she faces the problems of race relations directly. In *The Grass is Singing* there is space to stalk the quarry, preparing the confrontation. Images of abundance, such as those which surround the children of 'Flavours of Exile' or 'This was the Old Chief Mshlanga', are absent. Instead there are the tobacco farmers, like Charlie Slatter, who destroy the land with a hungry monoculture. There is nothing to oppose their creation of a waste land except for the inadequate Dick Turner, with his schemes for improvement which never come to anything, but who cares for the land enough to vary his crops and to plant a stand of trees on some of his best soil.

Mary Turner, another inadequate, habituated to a superficial life in the town, is coerced into marriage by those crude and subtle social forces which insist that women exist only in terms of marriage. Mary and Dick's mutual inadequacies drive them deeper and deeper into failure. So far the foreground is occupied by social, economic, and personal problems which seem to have little to do with race. But both the use of the land and the role of women are questions which are linked, implicitly and explicitly, with racial questions, particularly with the management of labour. Slatter's active exploitation of land is mirrored in his relations with labour; Dick Turner is as racist as anybody else in his language, but achieves a measure of co-operation from his workers by persuasion and by some attempt at understanding. Mary, seeing this as a weakness in her husband and the cause of all their troubles, uses such power as she has over him to persuade him to coerce not just his labourers but his land, to abandon his mixed farming and take to tobacco like his neighbours. It becomes a question of power for her, and she compounds Dick's failure while he is ill by crude coercion of his workers, many of whom leave Dick's employment. In the process she whips Moses with Dick's *sjambok*.

All the time, it is made clear, there is an imperfectly repressed physical side to her reactions. Her trust in the effectiveness of force is symptomatic of her own insecurity and that of her settler community. The more enthusiastic the resort to force, the greater the sense that it is only this which holds the line between the enforcers and those who submit. In Mary, impatience with Dick, fear at the way he shares understanding, habits, motivation, with the workers, leads her to internalize the problem of power. Trained as she is by her world to concede power to the male, the use of force causes in her problems of gender which become linked with her conventional racial attitudes. There is a sexual undertow in her resentment against Dick's black workers:

> She hated their half-naked, thick-muscled black bodies stooping in the mindless rhythm of their work. . . . and she hated more than anything, with a violent physical repulsion, the heavy smell that came from them, a hot, sour, animal smell. (*GS* 122)

She whips Moses with a *sjambok*, watches the trickle of blood from the wound, and becomes conscious, in that special sensuous way permitted to the prejudiced, of physical power. 'He was a great hulk of a man, taller than any of the others, magnificently built, with nothing on but an old sack tied round his waist' (*GS* 126).

It's a reference both to a romantic stereotype and to a sexual/racial stereotype. But its embodiment in the text has none of the fulsome ease and simplicity with which writers of popular romances from Haggard to Wilbur Smith have used it. Mary is a reader of romances. The passage which describes her first, violent meeting with Moses is subtly and economically charged with the oblique sexuality which is associated with the *genre*, but displaced by terror, by that racial fear which revels in suppressed attraction. Later he pulls her out of a depressive apathy into hyperaesthesia: 'for the first time in months seeing the ground she walked over, and feeling the pressure of the sun against the back of her bare neck, the sharp hot stones pressing up under her soles' (*GS* 153).

Throughout the text there is a subterranean pressure to see Mary, the individual, as enacting something present in the whole community. She submits (and the hidden knowledge of that submission touches a fear and desire in every white for miles around) to a strength which, throughout her life, she has been taught to crave. Moses' tenderness involves power. For Mary his sympathy becomes, equivocally, sexual seduction – the text is tacit in a calculated way, hinting at a state of mind in the community and herself – a rash relinquishing of that formal authority which maintains the fragile power of her community.

He persuades her that she must rest on the bed, reluctantly pushing her towards the bedroom. It is like a nightmare, 'the touch of this black man's hand on her shoulder filled her with nausea; she had never, not once in her whole life, touched the flesh of a native' (GS 160). Later, she wakes up 'moaning out loud, as if she had been touched by excrement' (GS 161), and yet progressively strays further into something which she 'would have died rather than acknowledge – of some dark attraction' (GS 164). Her state of mind is an echo of something profoundly implicated in the structure of authority and self-consciousness in a racial society: an occulted masochism to complement the sadistic public face. In Mary this coheres around another sensuous image. In a state of threatened insecurity she detects in Moses 'not the native smell, but the unwashed smell of her father'; as he comforts her she feels the consolation, but at the same time the incestuous threat: 'it was her father, menacing and horrible, who touched her in desire' (GS 175).

It's not easy to guess from the text the state of mind in which Moses kills Mary Turner. We may speculate about Lobengula's justice, or that of Moses' biblical namesake, but both of these provide frames of reference which contract the man into the executioner of a vengeful code, and the story of his relationship with Mary, if it can be made credible, betokens a very complex and surprising man. The episode in which Tony Marston discovers Moses dressing Mary Turner does not greatly exaggerate the way in which settlers place their servants in intolerably humiliating situations, doing violence to a decent pride. But Moses' satisfaction seems not to be simply the satisfaction of charity or personal power. He is described as being like a father tending a child, but that hint at Mary's quasi-incestuous compliance in tender violence doesn't seem to cover his role. It is rather a complicity in Mary's fantasy world, a second reversal of the power structure in which, complaisantly, he permits himself to be shaped by her dreams. One might suggest, even, that Lessing is, in an unexpectedly artless way, being drawn in by the melodramatic form to give too great a power and substance to fantasy – that the formal effect eases the way to a kind of lie at the heart of the fiction.

In this sense the act of murder followed by the rain, the fulfilment of the promise given by the epigraph from Eliot, has a representative rather than an essentially truthful quality. It is prolepsis to the moment of a liberation, in which suffering and punishment, even death, are necessary to the solution of a complicit madness in which Mary and Moses share, a folie à deux. This shadows forth not a political or social change, but a solution to that moral and spiritual foreboding of evil which we have met before in Lessing.

My deepest uncertainties resolve around Moses, and the paradoxes that accrete around his role. Comparison with the role of Gregory Rose in The Story of an African Farm will not get us far. Schreiner's character is a servant to sentimental tragedy. The reversal of gender roles is implicit as a possibility throughout the fiction. He acts out of affection acquired through long acquaintance with Lyndall, with no racial or social barriers, only Lyndall's contempt, to discourage him.

Moses is the proud individual who renders the service of a slave; the servant who becomes a master; the pitying friend who becomes a murderer;

the condemned who judges himself and by doing so defies the law. He is offered as a tragic figure. But he is not an Othello. Othello's blackness is a difference within a sameness. He aspires to live within a society which admires him, but rejects him. He is part but not part, and the spectators who first saw the play must have found their attention suspended between knowledge and mystery. Moses exists in the fiction only as worker-servant and fantasy lover. We have no space to build a person to inhabit the contradiction.

The fiction permits us to see these paradoxes as paradigms of the relationship which white settlers in Africa created – whilst describing the blacks as children they made blacks into nursemaids for petulant adults; whilst exercising a lazy and contemptuous power over their servants they became obsessed with the postponement of a vengeful future, a holocaust leading to the death of every white, the fear sometimes taking on the character of suicidal wish-fulfilment. Perhaps this is the sting in the tail of the conflict, so powerful in Lessing, between collective and individualist ethics. The quarrel between the two rages in the self-conscious imagination of the European. But even in the kind of narrative which loves to exhibit the emergence of the individual from the mass – and Lessing excels at that – it proves too large a task to present an African as individual. Moses *represents*, and, inevitably, what he represents is an aspect of the doubt, the fear, the guilt, the rage of the European overlord.[10]

The Second World War changed the world irrevocably; it was a time for reassessment, both on a public and a personal level. Doris Lessing might have stayed in Rhodesia and attempted to find a suitable role for a radical in the minority community. Instead she elected to come to Britain in 1949, where the field of choices changed. Much of her best writing since that time has recorded and explored the consequences of that change.

In 1949, in South Africa, the Nationalist party had been in power for a year, the ANC had begun to take its modern form, and the Communist Party was entering into its most influential and most persecuted period. By contrast, the left in Rhodesia was an ineffective side-show. In the 1967 postscript to *Going Home* (1957) Lessing says that they 'weren't Communists at all. . . . They were a couple of dozen people scattered about the country who were inspired in the long, thankless, draining battle against colour bars and white supremacy by the glories of the Russian revolution' (*GH* 312-13).[11] But things were beginning to happen, even if that was not clear to Lessing.

In 1949, for instance, Robert Mugabe, then 25, was awarded a scholarship to Fort Hare. This was the University College of Mandela, Tambo, and others, for instance Robert Sobukwe (the founder of the Pan African Congress in South Africa) and Gatsha Buthelezi, now the leader of Inkatha and chief minister of KwaZulu. In his last days at Fort Hare Mugabe joined the ANC, and later in Rhodesia continued his political education, reading Marx, Engels, and Lenin. In 1949 James Chikerema, who had been expelled from

South Africa a year before for his Communist activities, was already working in Harare, the township satellite of Salisbury. In the 1950s in the Copper Belt of Northern Rhodesia the Congress movement was developing under figures like Nkumbula and Kaunda. A Lithuanian refugee, Simon Zukas, a friend of Lessing's, was co-operating with black workers to develop an effective trade union movement there. By 1956, however, Lessing had become full of ideological unease, saying that she would probably not have been a Communist if she hadn't lived so long in Africa, looking forward to a time when the Communist countries would be freer in every way than the west. 'If I did not think this I would not remain a Communist' (*GH* 102).

The move from Africa to Britain blurred the political choices for her. At the time of *Going Home*, the context of political thought for the left throughout the world had changed with the revelations of the Twentieth Congress of the Communist Party of the USSR. Communist Party members throughout the world were forced to recognize the fallibility of the Party and the dubiousness of their own roles within it. While Lessing was preparing *Going Home* for publication in 1957 the invasion of Suez and the Soviet invasion of Hungary took place almost simultaneously.[12] This prompted Lessing to add a note at the very end of the text which reveals yet more about the crisis of reassessment she was going through. She recalls her remarks about Communism and democracy, and adds that the intervention in Hungary has changed things: 'It is a crisis in the battle of truth against lies, of honesty against corruption, of respect for the goodness of people against cynicism' (*GH* 297).

The problem, writes Lessing, was 'not Hungary, but Hungary coming so soon after the Twentieth Congress . . . if the Russian troops had gone into Hungary as they did before the Twentieth Congress, it would have been shocking but no more than could have been expected' (*GH* 312). The Twentieth Congress raised the acceptable threshold of morality for a socialist regime. It did not require one to expect higher standards for the British, French, or Israeli governments – Suez might still be 'shocking but no more than could have been expected'.

Lessing's attitude was, I suspect, complicated by a certain relief. It enabled her to disburden herself of loyalties which had become embarrassing, and gave her the chance to reappraise all the political dilemmas raised by her changed position. If Margaret Drabble's characterization of Lessing as 'Cassandra in a world under siege'[13] is apt, it is partly because of this freedom from old loyalties, partly because of those insights brought by the 'colonial' into a culture which assumes her peripherality and its centrality. Peripherality to the international community of socialism, peripherality to self-consciously metropolitan British culture, both are turned around, becoming means towards the search for an alternative centre. As Jenny Taylor remarks[14] of *The Golden Notebook*, 'the novel is the stage where the formal and ideological contradictions of both realism and liberal humanism are most explicitly acted out.' But in place of a centre, we are led into a disassembling, an analytic subversion, of the conventional senses of self and credo which underlie the familiar structures of narrative.

Lessing describes the sequence *Children of Violence* as a *Bildungsroman*, and says that, although the form may be old, it is none the worse for that. But every artistic form implies, invites, and shapes, attitudes to what it embodies. The *Bildungsroman*, as a *genre*, emerges from German romanticism, and it implies a view of the individual, and his/her relationship to the world around her/him, which has been possible only in the last two centuries, and is, in a profound sense, romantic. The enterprise of *Wilhelm Meister*, for instance, has something in common with the artistic autobiography, *Dichtung und Wahrheit*. Goethe describes how, in presenting

the inner motives, the external influences, and the stages of my progress in theory and practice, I was carried out of my narrow private sphere into the wide world. . . . to exhibit the man in relation to his times, and to show to what extent this environment was inimical or propitious to him; how he evolved from it a philosophy of the world and of men, and in what way he, in his turn, if an artist, poet, or author, reproduced this philosophy in concrete form. Anyone attempting to write his own biography in this sense requires – what is hardly attainable – a knowledge of himself and of his age: of himself as the factor which has persisted under all the variations of circumstances; of the age as the force which hurries him, whether willing or unwilling, along with it, guiding him, moulding him.[15]

Like Wordsworth in *The Prelude* Goethe chooses the path of seeing the whole world as means toward projecting an idea of the self. It is not difficult to see that this strategy can be described outside-in – that it involves the projection of an idea of the world as a product of the self. It is the triumph of the egotistical sublime to reshape the universe in its own image. So the word *Bildungsroman* ('shaping fiction', or 'forming novel') can be read as an account of the formation of a self by a world outside it; simultaneously it can be the shaping of an idea of the world to confirm, or justify, the writer's invention of a self, or of transactions between versions or fragments of self.

Something of the sort is going on in both *The Golden Notebook* (1962) and the *Children of Violence* sequence. In both, the process is complicated greatly by the way that each converts historical and autobiographical actualities into the structured coherences of fiction. In these books the dimensions and perspectives are constantly altered by an implicit invitation to the reader to seek interfiliations between fictional moments, cross-references between fictive and fictive, fictive and factual. Lessing foregrounds the acts of writing and of reading, inviting us to speculate about the changing relationships between facts and fictions in the writer's, the reader's, or in any mind. Hegel observes that the *Bildungsroman* characteristically ends in ratification of existing values:

For the end of such apprenticeship consists in this, that the subject sows his wild oats, builds himself with his wishes and opinions into harmony with subsisting relationships and their rationality, enters the concatenation of the world, and acquires for himself the appropriate attitude to it.[16]

Lessing may be freed from the charge: she questions and subverts the existing relationships of society and the values and assumptions they bring with them. There is a certain note of desperation in her adumbration of alternative structures and values, particularly in *The Four-Gated City* (1969).

The Golden Notebook – neither a *Bildungsroman* nor a *Dichtung und Wahrheit*, but teasingly related to both modes – becomes even more complex in textual and narrative structure because it is filled with the anxiety of narrative, the retroflexive commentary upon the unstable nature of the text in relationship to the self (or selves, shifting as the text shifts underneath them) which authors it. The first section of 'The Black Notebook' in *The Golden Notebook*, for instance, is concerned with the reflections prompted in 'Anna Wulf' by an invitation to film her book, *The Frontiers of War* (it has a place in Anna's experience somewhat similar to *The Grass is Singing* in Lessing's, though it is not that book).

First there is her self-conscious parody of the book in a synopsis for the film – not only a parody of the book, but of the productive processes behind inventing lives for fiction while living within fact – making fiction out of life, films out of fiction, writing synopses for the industrial processes of film and so forth. Then there is Anna's attempt to recover the life buried underneath the fiction, or at least to build a narrative, fictional or factual, that is tectonically honest to the life in the way it constructs, reconstructs, redirects, but never quite reaches completeness. Constantly she dramatizes the sense of veering away from honesty by the intrusively wrong voice, the cynical dismissal or the nostalgic self-indulgence in sentiment of the writer in relation to her own text.

In this, Lessing's experience of Africa becomes secondary: ' "Even the best of you use Africa as a peg to hang your egos on." To this crime Mr. Van der Post is open. So are all the rest of us.'[17] The search is not for Africa, or even remembered experience; it is a search for some adequate idea of truthfulness, artistic, political, or personal, or, in that all these are related, an integration. 'Anna Wulf' herself is a product of these deliberately unstable textual processes; her projection as the narrative voice in the fiction might be seen as fulfilling a defensive role in relation to the author's sense of self (selves), but defence, as so often in the literature of an ironic age, is a means towards a kind of discovery. Towards confession, if one leaches that word of any suggestion that each detail of the life described is the author's, Lessing's own, the authorized version. It is confession in its formal choices, in its flaunting of the inadequacy of the formal means available: it is confession of the elusiveness of language, of memory, of self, of art, taken either together or each separately as a medium for presenting the others.

Even after the narrative of the first 'Black Notebook' is completed, the text draws attention to its own felt inadequacy and to the estranging distance of the self the text holds, complaining in a note 'some months later':

> It's full of nostalgia, every word loaded with it, although at the time I wrote it I thought I was being 'objective'. . . . the 'Anna' of that time is like an enemy, or like an old friend one has known too well and doesn't want to see. (*GN* 154)[18]

Dennis Potter once remarked in a television interview[19] that nostalgia is a second-hand emotion. Like Potter himself Lessing approaches nostalgia – for Africa among other things – with an ironic energy generated by the complementarity of first and second hand in a consciousness fully alive to its own dissonant complexity.

Perhaps the sharpest way in which the whole process of reassessment is expressed is in the tentative exploration of an aesthetic which comes early in the first 'Black Notebook', where Lessing begins by internalizing the sense of *division* which she sees as becoming, increasingly, the subject of fiction:

> The novel has become a function of the fragmented society, the fragmented consciousness. Human beings are so divided, are becoming more and more divided, *and more subdivided in themselves*, reflecting the world, that they reach out desperately, not knowing they do it, for information about other groups. . . . It is a blind grasping out for their own wholeness. (*GN* 68)

It may be that an acute consciousness of the bold divisions within such a society as the old Rhodesia can divert attention from the crises of a psychic fragmentation. It may be that in that milieu one's energies are channelled into acting for a public cause so manifestly strong that personality problems, and the failure of personal relations which may grow from them, can be seen as relatively unimportant. Moving from an Africa so depressing in its injustices and suffering, but at least clear in its political issues, deprived Lessing of the fullest sense of the efficacy of an external political focus and forced her back into the private dilemma, into a grasping for wholeness, a consciousness of fragmentation. The loss shows through here most clearly in the artistic dilemma of 'Anna Wulf':

> Yet I am incapable of writing the only kind of novel which interests me: a book powered with an intellectual or moral passion strong enough to create order, to create a new way of looking at life. It is because I am too diffused. (*GN* 68)

Paradoxically, through 'Anna Wulf' and her failure, her sense of the loss of appropriate creative energy or concentration, Doris Lessing in *The Golden Notebook* approaches closer than any other writer of her time to making 'a book powered with an intellectual or moral passion strong enough to create order'. In this, too, she continues a remarkable habit in the romantic tradition of constructing the most powerful work out of a sense of the failure of vital powers, and out of a collapse in idealistic political and philosophical foundations.

Lessing solves the problem formally by offering parallel and almost incompatible narratives (sometimes containing deliberated contradiction within a single narrative line) in the same name, that of Anna Wulf (or through fictions-within-fiction, like 'Ella'). She retains control over the process in such a way as to argue how dense the population of a single mind may be, while at the same time maintaining openly the fictionality of that complex personality. Jenny Taylor argues that the book isn't explicitly feminist, that ultimately Anna 'loses individual female selfhood through the breakdown of individual subjectivity, and the acceptance of mythic archetypes'.[20] The experience is not exemplary in that way: its montage structure hampers, it seems deliberately, any assertion of a coherent identity, coherent in the sense, at least, that our expectations of fiction would lead us to require. 'The intellectual or moral passion strong enough to create order' is a centre *in absentia*, the invitation to the reader (should one accept it) to dismantle the elaborate pretence that it may still be there in the forms, the institutions, the ideologies which entrap individual consciousness.

We are constantly made aware of how the parallel enterprises of the various notebooks and the 'Free Women' narratives all relate to each other, to Anna Wulf, to the time and space of the novel. We might describe the method of *The Golden Notebook* as metaphoric, building an account of the conflictual, self-aware, self-revising, self-inventing personality in a narrative stratification where each layer overlays, augments, and subverts the others. It would be tempting to describe *Children of Violence*, following Jakobson, as metonymic, referring to the way in which the shifting essays in personality which compose 'Martha Quest' follow each other in a sequence, articulated by succession rather than by superimposition.

But, just as in *The Golden Notebook* a structure of sequence in time runs through the book, giving it another level of organization, so in *Children of Violence*, particularly in the last volume, *The Four-Gated City*, a metaphoric strategy becomes important in the discourse. It is another expression of the perception behind *The Golden Notebook* of the progressive fragmentation of human beings, the 'blind grasping out for their own wholeness'.

Division and wholeness are given contexture by her epigraphs to the volumes in the sequence. The first, *Martha Quest* (1952), has an epigraph from Olive Schreiner: 'I am so tired of it, and also tired of the future before it comes.' The last volume, *The Four-Gated City*, has, as 'Dedication', a dervish parable[21] about a fool who, in his anxiety to keep his purchases of salt and flour separate, loses both the flour and the salt. Part One of the same book begins with an epigraph from Rachel Carson about the ways in which coastlines are constantly changing processes, frequently living processes, by which the land is built. Thus, in *Children of Violence*, the formal historical sequence becomes an ambitious argument for a change in consciousness, a fulfilment in altered terms of the naïve idealism of 'I' becoming 'We' in 'Hunger'. In this sense it is a philosophical enterprise, an attempt to fulfil what 'Anna Wulf' longs to create in *The Golden Notebook*, 'a book . . . strong enough to create order, to create a new way of looking at life'. But, in its narrative mode, and in its apprehension of order or disorder, there is a shift which is only fully accomplished in *The Four-Gated City*. In 1957 Lessing had expressed her continued attachment to nineteenth-century realism as 'the highest form of prose writing'.[22] The earlier volumes are in contact with realism, the last projects beyond it. One may read the shift as consummation or flight. It certainly signals dissatisfaction with accepted modes of understanding and perception, either inside the novel or outside it.

It is interesting, then, that there is a current of allusion to a nineteenth-century writer whose anguish with the limitations of her own society is combined with attempts to escape from the dominant form of realism. Apart from being an interesting novelist, Olive Schreiner is that most interesting kind of heroine, an imperfect, an unfinished one. She emerges from the period of the brutal and cynical colonizing of Africa, and from a period in which the subjection of women was almost as complete, as universal, and as unnoticed, as the subjection of non-white races, and the mechanisms of class-subjection were only beginning to be widely understood. If she had been re-born in southern Africa in the 1930s, all her work would have to begin again, and she would have had good reason to have little enthusiasm for the future. It is a kind of half-accepted destiny for the rebel farm-girl 'Martha Quest', born into a thin and superficial community of invaders, peripheral both to the rich life of Africa and to the dominant pride of Europe, to challenge once again the structures of power and culture which nurture her. And to fail again.

What Lessing hopes to do is to project the curve beyond predicted failure, to find a way of succeeding, or of perceiving success in terms which are quite different from those available to Schreiner. A search for wholeness, even through what is, in common understanding, personal disintegration, madness, might at last be a way of breaking through a global collapse of false orders into a new history. The hint is that there may be some who already form, as it were, the coasts of a new world of intelligence emerging from the failure of the old. It cannot be part of this chapter to examine this prophetic reach. But it does write large, in a metaphoric way, transition to a new continent.

12

Nadine Gordimer: The short stories

Throughout her career Nadine Gordimer has become increasingly interested in history and politics, but in her art, even when it deals with political matters, there is a focus on the uniquely personal experience. It is a tension in which an element of detachment is seen by Gordimer as necessary for art. It may be that it is also a strategy for coping with a destructive and divided society.

John Cooke suggests that part of the disease Gordimer identifies in her own society is a voyeurism which enables South African whites to 'keep their fellows at bay by turning them into observed objects'.[1] The perception needs modification. From the early stories onwards there is a concern with the distance between the observer and the observed. But there is often an ambivalence in the record of the observing, which casts doubt upon the life, or the reality, of the observer, endowing life upon the *other*. If it is a voyeurism, it is one which may so question the integrity of self that it partakes of the death wish. A good part of the peculiar intensity Gordimer brings to her work lies in her capacity, or her compulsion, to view human life as an alien to life might. There's what seems to be a clinical element, but with that, expanding it, elements of wonder, fear, disgust, and fascination with the strangeness of living and of death.

Gordimer has written freely for magazines like *Harper's*, *The New Yorker*, *Atlantic Monthly*, *Cosmopolitan*, and *Playboy*. Such outlets make implicit formal demands upon a writer, and form is never completely innocent. There is a broad convention of story writing, involving, as the crisis around which the tale is constructed, a Joycean epiphany, open or veiled, which becomes crucial in the construction of a life's experience. Gordimer takes the expected shape and adapts it to unconventional purposes, collaborating but simultaneously subverting assumptions concealed in the pattern.

Gordimer said of her early stories[2] that they are constructed sensuously, out of images, in contrast with the later fiction, which concerns itself with ideas. But instead of sensuous images becoming constructions of a life's experience, luminosities which hint towards understanding, they suggest the points at which understanding contracts or dissolves. The important moments are those where we understand that we fail to understand, moments where we are made to glimpse a way of meaning which is hinted by the *other*.

In failure to comprehend an echoed life which is not their own, her *personae* become the aliens, and there is pressure upon us, the readers, to sense that alienation in ourselves.

So, in 'The Soft Voice of the Serpent', we have a man in a wheelchair in a garden, a sort of ironic Eden. He is trying to reconstruct his life, his consciousness, after losing a leg, working systematically towards his own rehabilitation, accustoming himself to physical damage whilst delaying the full impact of the psychic loss. A locust settles in the garden, and the man is drawn to its strangeness, but, as we all do, he attempts the familiar anthropomorphic tricks, the Aesopic or Disneyesque strategies to accommodate it, seeing its face as 'like some little person out of a Disney cartoon'. But the creature's body can't be made akin to man; it is 'flimsy paper stretched over a frame of matchstick, like a small boy's home-made airplane' (*SVS* 9).[3] It, too, has a leg missing, but the mutilation is described in such a way as to set its strangeness yet further away from the perceiver, complicating an attempted sympathy with a quasi-scientific detachment, as if a machine is being described with an engineer's precision: 'Only the long upward shaft of its left leg remained, with a neat round aperture where, no doubt, the other half of the leg had been jointed in' (*SVS* 10). The man is encouraged, delighted, by experiencing a proper sympathy for something other than himself. But suddenly the locust, which had seemed, like the man, to be immobilized by its disability, asserts its difference by using wings, flying away, and the man is left without comfort.

The same kind of delicate defamiliarization of experience presides over several of these early stories. There is a deliberate indeterminateness in the opening of 'The Catch'. In this story, for a little while, the subjects, the centres of consciousness in the story, seem as if they might be sea creatures, if it were not for the inexplicable replacement of the word 'sea' by 'city':

> His thin strong bony legs passed by at eye level every morning as they lay, stranded on the hard smooth sand. Washed up thankfully out of the swirl and buffet of the city, they were happy to lie there. (*SVS* 13)

Like 'The Soft Voice of the Serpent', the story has an elusive family resemblance to the Kafka of 'Metamorphosis', and yet estrangement has not the same seismic centrality as it does in Kafka. In Kafka the shock of imagining oneself totally altered in physical body bullies us into becoming aware of the relationship between body and mind, self and the society of men, self and the world of objects. In the Gordimer story we are seduced into recognizing the strangeness of seeing, particularly seeing those who are 'different'. Vicariously we experience a cold access of knowledge, an awareness of detachment-from-life.

The pleasure of a holiday by the sea becomes itself a kind of alienation, a retreat from 'the human insect noise of thousands talking and walking and eating at midday'. Even the experience of time, something which uniquely defines our human-ness, modulates, becoming tied to the regular passing presence of this man who walks by, this Indian fisherman.

At the same time the whole experience is insignificant, a measure of the arrogance with which we appropriate other people to become accidental appendages of our own life: 'He was "their Indian". When they went home they might remember the holiday by him as you might remember a particular holiday as the one when you used to play with a spaniel on the beach every day' (*SVS* 16). The anthropomorphism which had tempted belief in 'The Soft Voice of the Serpent' is now reversed; the fascination with the *other* becomes reductive, a possessive condescension. The paradox is deepened by the hint that the Indian suggests unwelcome knowledge, the fearful access to areas that their superficiality denies. They see the ocean as

> a great plain of heaving water, empty and unreadable as infinity; but *he* saw a hard greedy life going on down in there, shining plump bodies gaping swiftly close together through the blind green, tentacles like dark hands feeling over the deep rocks. (*SVS* 17)

This is in part a gesture towards Freudian or Jungian abysses of consciousness, but it can remain just that only if one maintains the kind of white innocence that belongs to the holiday couple. The uncomfortable world which lies beneath the surface of their comprehension, in another sense, is the world he *lives* in, and they are protected from. It is an abyss in the Conradian sense; the experience might become just another chronicle of darkness, a terrified surface view, if the experience is left to what *they* see. But, as in Conrad, we can't pretend to leave things to what the teller sees: in the telling of it there is an abyss, a *mise en abîme*, a black hole of marvellous gravity.

The Indian catches a great salmon, a wonderful thing that is photographed with its captor, something that comes from that ocean where texts of Melville and Hemingway swim like great mind-whales. It is tamed, made into a voyeuristic fetish by the camera. But later, the young people pile into a car to go to Durban, and on their way meet the Indian, disconsolate, the fish still unsold. Self-consciously they give him a lift, and the narrator remarks 'So your big catch is more trouble than it's worth.' The Indian repeats the phrase. Her emotional response to this echolalia comes from a deep sense of the failure implicit in the whole episode, her failure to catch, not a fish, but something which he, the Indian, meant, and, by the same token, what she might be or mean: 'She felt a stab of cold uncertainty, as if she herself did not know what she had said, did not know what she had meant, or might have meant' (*SVS* 26).

Once again, it is through failure to understand that Gordimer catches at an otherness, and a self, indistinctly surfacing. There is a complex habit of consciousness here – we should resist calling it 'a theme'. Let us call it the tenor, to indicate simultaneously a drift of argument and an ethos of intelligence, with, perhaps, a metaphoric suggestion of a persistent melody. But it is not only Cooke who discovers an inhuman coldness in the music; in Dennis Brutus's words 'the kind of impersonality you find in a microscope'. The *other* in this view becomes an object, and it is almost a matter of indifference whether it is locust or human, Indian or salmon. Brutus finds a link with her society, saying that Gordimer, however sensitive she is as a writer, is also an instance of 'how dehumanized South African society has become – that an artist like this lacks warmth, lacks feeling, but can observe with a detachment, with the coldness of a machine'.[4]

Brutus (who is not white) points to an aspect of the white South African consciousness which borders upon the schizoid. There is a flaw-line in the consciousness of many in the white society, a habit of alienating everything which exists outside a narrow range of consciousness, withdrawing into an enclosed world which desperately redefines itself in evasion of the unknown. Gordimer may dramatize the sickness, define it, move towards the under-standing of it – at all events she doesn't bear the simple relationship to it of an ignorant sufferer.

Cooke suggests that Gordimer's approach to the public themes of South African society is connected with her own early family problems. In more than one interview Gordimer has told of how her mother used a mild disorder of the child's heart to keep her child at home, preventing her from dancing. In several of her novels, the central female character has to learn that 'complete liberation from private, familial restraints requires challenging the dominant political order as well'.[5] In Helen Shaw (*The Lying Days*), particu-larly, this leads to an awareness, which is not without alarm, that there is a life beyond what the subject can directly perceive. The *subject* is always in danger from this perception – there is violence at the heart of experience which might work against the *other*, or against the *self-as-other*, indifferently, even that such destructive violence might be welcome. The personal fear, or desire, lies in parallel with one aspect of the white South African com-munity's idea of itself.

These matters come together in another way in 'The Kindest Thing to Do'. Like the other two stories we have looked at, this opens in an atmosphere of deeply compromised consciousness. It's another garden, on a soporific Sun-day afternoon, a lotos-eating demi-paradise, pre-Raphaelite in its jewelled stillness. A girl is reading, and her mother calls to her:

> Her head, drooping near the drooping, bee-heavy, crumpled paper chalices of the poppies, lifted half-protestingly, her lazy hand brushed the grey specks of insects which flecked the pages of Petrarch's 'Laura in Death'. (*SVS* 28)

The family has found an injured dove, which they had hoped to nurse to recovery, but the dog has seized and worried it. The girl finds it near death and realizes the need to kill it, 'the kindest thing to do'. But more powerfully she realizes its life. It is another serpentine moment, expressed with an intensity which betrays Gordimer's early interest in D. H. Lawrence:

a dark knowledge came to her. She felt it open, a Lethean flower of knowledge, that she feared and did not want, chilling her soul with a strange, cold sap. It came coldly because it was a dreadful cold thing, the understanding of the fulfilment of the will to kill. (*SVS* 33)

This detachment-from-death, as terrifying as detachment-from-life, elsewhere takes the strange turn into affection for death as a knowledge which completes and encloses life, taking on the simplicity of art, offering the most perfect detachment.

In 'A Company of Laughing Faces', a story written more than a decade later, the affection for death is prominent again. Kathy Hack, 17 years old, is alarmed by a first, insensitive sexual contact, and turns to brief friendship with a 9-year-old boy, who disappears by the sea. She finds him, lying staring at her, a foot beneath the surface of a rock pool: 'What she felt was not shock, but recognition. It was as if he had had a finger to his lips, holding the two of them there, so that she might not give him away' (*NPL* 245).[6] The experience of the thing *seen*, and the *seeing* of things, is as vital to this incident as the encounter with death. But Gordimer has the knack of turning the voyeurism round, making us, the readers, see Kathy Hack as *other*, as disjoined from living. We have the sense that it is the dead boy who sees. The fascination with *thanatos* reveals another reach of Gordimer's sensibility.

In *Beyond the Pleasure Principle* Freud proposes a complex relationship between the death wish and the compulsion to repeat. Compulsion to repeat is 'more primitive, more elementary, more instinctual than the pleasure principle'.[7] It negotiates and reinforces the interfiliations between instincts which are apparently incompatible. Freud was himself deeply uncertain of the validity of the theory, but it might be used here with caution. There are other stories which exhibit a repeated rehearsal of death, or mutilation, or panic fear of death. In the later stories and novels the thematic channelling of the private imagination is made more complex by mutation into public themes, which nevertheless draw much of their force from their obedience to the compulsion to repeat.

In 'Treasures of the Sea' the central *persona*, who grows from child to adult in the story, has that lack of specificity and yet suggested fullness of inward understanding which signal a fiction which is in some way close to the author's experience. But it is set at a distance in a parallel world of fable. Very early in the story Gordimer establishes the sense of the marginality of the human presence in an abhuman complexity which is represented by the beach and the sea. The world of humans is something like Conrad's Congo company, waving the flag to assert possession. Sea and beach were

the real, the supreme here; the light dabs of human feet had not stepped out a beautiful background for a frieze of figures, running, cavorting, and clowning, but had merely succeeded in feeling lightly over one curve, one convolution of a composition so enormous that they would never be able to feel out the whole of it. (*SVS* 64)

There's a lightly traced but influential subtext here which refers to the marginality inherent in another white 'supremacy' (the obsolete word draws attention to itself), but the story is not primarily about race. It's about a phase of experience behind political and social awareness, an awareness of marginality. The scene is a beach again, verging upon a sea which is filled with evidences of a more perfect and comprehensive organization, an aesthetic rightness which is denied to its human visitors. The child grows to be a woman, retaining with her this appetency for the sea, though she becomes acquainted with the pleasures of the great cities of Europe and America. The sea which she remembers, the sea which gathers into itself all the unimaginable experience beyond the range of the eye, is the one which lies off the south coast of Africa, and at last she has the chance to return to it. Her new husband gives her a ring, and she chooses a big pink pearl for it, a kind of delayed betrothal to the real bridegroom, the sea.

She wakes from a light sleep to see, 'from the corner of her eye, something pinkish move on a rock just across the pool from the one on which she lay'. It isn't clear what it is, though it is the colour of the pearl. 'The water glittered up at her. The brightness was replaced by blackness. Dizzy, she caught out at what seemed to be a point of rock, a piece of triangular dark' (*SVS* 69). And she falls. The colour symbolism of the pink and the black still contains a hint of the subtext of marginality, working obliquely at a submarine level, returning the pinkly vulnerable body to a dark death. As she dies, a drop of her blood 'stained the water faintly like a tiny drop of cochineal' (*SVS* 70). Once again a myth of self-realization is fused with one of self-immolation.

All the terrors which are trained into the awareness of a white child in South Africa are present in the ironically titled 'Is There Nowhere Else Where We Can Meet?', but so, too, are more ambiguous motives. The *other* which figures in the story now is a black attacker who lies in wait for a girl crossing a piece of open land. It's a pervasive myth in a racialist community, and, like many such myths, it has a sexual undertow. It's a version of the old panic fear, and the deep fascination of Pan has always lain in his threat, or promise, of sexual theft, a rape which mimics death. The atmospherics are handled beautifully from the beginning, preparing us for ambiguities which are not just in the sky: 'the air was like smoke. In that reversal of the elements that sometimes takes place, the grey, soft, muffled sky moved like the sea on a silent day' (*SVS* 85). Against the monochrome, grey sky, grass burnt black or dry-bleached into platinum, white flowers on dark shrubs, white-splashed stones, 'all merging, tones but no colour, like an etching' (*SVS* 85), she perceives a dot of red, anomalously vivid. It's a hat worn by a black waiting on the path. It is seen as an artistic design, a figure in a landscape rather than a man, a special use of colour rather than a piece of clothing.

Gordimer's aesthetic detachment is there in the frame, but the girl walks into the picture, into unwilling or willing involvement in violence. As she walks she fingers some pine needles, and the way she handles them, sensuously, signals a private ambivalence, a secret place in which fear and pleasure, pain and desire, are not incompatible. There is a hint of the anxieties and comfort of masturbation as she rubs them against her thumb:

> Down; smooth and stiff. Up; catching in gentle resistance as the minute serrations snagged at the skin. He was standing with his back toward her, looking along the way he had come; she pricked the ball of her thumb with the needle-ends. (*SVS* 85-6)

It is a tale with in-weavings of sexuality as profound as any child's fairy story: it has half-fulfilled overtones of 'Little Red Riding Hood', though the red velvet cape in the Grimm version and the *chaperon rouge* of Perrault's version are worn by the girl herself, not the wolf-attacker. The thinly disguised sexual *motif* of the needle pricking the thumb is best known as part of 'The Sleeping Beauty', but Grimm's *Sneewittchen* seems to be the text affiliated here. The recollection is part of Gordimer's irony, for in that story the pricking leads to the marvellous birth of the child (Snow White), who fulfils her mother's wish for 'a child as white as snow, as red as blood, and as black as the wood of this window frame'. It's a curious translation of the middle European tale of winters, snows, and deep forests into a world of racial fear, in which black, white, and red have different meanings: 'For a moment it was Fear itself that had her by the arms, the legs, the throat; not fear of the man, of any single menace he might present, but Fear, absolute, abstract' (*SVS* 86).

This quasi-mythical binding of fear with infantile sexual anxieties touches on something very profound in racialist psychology. But fear of the dark rapist may merge into a mood which mingles desire with the death wish. There are two instants in the tale where, ambiguously, the experience becomes a longed-for surrender: 'she heard him draw a deep, hoarse breath and he grabbed out at her and – ah! It came. His hand clutched her shoulder.' And a little later, the violence is complicated by a hint of a beauty in threatened destruction of the self. As she struggles, the man jerks her head back, and she sees 'the waves of a grey sky and a crane breasting them, beautiful as the figurehead of a ship' (*SVS* 87).

A story of the seventies, 'A Hunting Accident', meets head-on the matters of voyeurism, detachment, death, and the artist. Christine meets Clive, a photographer whom she takes to a house party. She romanticizes the landscape they are in, using a conventional literary shorthand – it owes much to Haggard – 'that endless plain with a single hill peaked up here and there casting its single blue shadow – it's exactly the imaginary country old maps call "Land of Prester John" or "Kafferland" ' (*SE* 57).[8] At the same time she shows a taught awareness of the deforming conventions of that white, male society, which even Ratau, the black host, adopts. When Ratau asks if Clive will be one of the guns, she laughs, because Ratau was 'so unconsciously male in his natural assumption of what she had been taught, at her progressive school, was the conditioned male role of killer. "Shoot with his camera," she said' (*SE* 58). In the hunt a hartebeest cow is slow to die and has to be shot a second and a third time. Christine is embarrassed and concerned about Clive's reactions: 'how horrible this was, he would be thinking, he who had not taken any part, active or vicarious' (*SE* 64).

But Clive responds in an unexpected way, guided by a different code. As everyone else turns away in the shame of decency he walks up to the beast, photographing it repeatedly, gazing through the lens into the beast's dying eyes, 'absolutely intent on the techniques he was employing; there was a deep line she had never seen before, drawn down either side of his mouth from the sucked-in nostrils' (*SE* 65).

Next morning he is gone. At the end of the story Christine goes into a garden, among bauhinia trees, 'and blood-tendoned bones and tufts of hide, dragged from the yard overnight by dogs, littered the oval of ashen winter grass' (*SE* 66). In this mixture of beauty and death she appears to be attempting to find some kind of a meaning, piecing together as much as she can. Overhearing old men of the village in their council, she 'hung about, not too near, as if she had only to be able to understand, that's all, and the speaker would have something to say, for her' (*SE* 66).

Cooke comments that Clive's behaviour is made to 'seem an act of violence, even of torture'.[9] I am unconvinced. Clive does not speak for himself; we are left to interpret his actions. Others carry their guns and are embarrassed at the terminal agonies of the beast; Clive uses impersonal technique to re-present fact, his expertness inseparable from the absence of any sign of sentiment. He then leaves the party as quickly as he can. It may be that Gordimer is sketching, in fictional terms, an aesthetic and an ethics for a time of violence.

Her own collaboration with the photographer David Goldblatt has produced some of the most powerful indictments of violence in South Africa.[10] Vietnam and Ethiopia are two of the many places where the work of the photographer has had more influence over generous feeling in the world than words: as Gordimer and Goldblatt themselves write, 'the image and the word give back what is behind the face and place'.[11] Christine sees landscape in terms of conventional images; faced by death she can find no way to react but a convention of decent concern. Her way is contrasted with that of a dedicated professional image-maker. We live in a culture in which actual experience is massively affected and constructed by a fracturing process which disjoins and isolates the icon. We learn to see through and in the mechanical device. In such a world we may need the artist-as-voyeur to mediate. It may be that he is the only one still able directly to see.

Buried within the text, and powerfully guiding it, we may detect Gordimer's own anxiety in relation to the image. Here we have, not the technical skill of the photographer-as-artist, but intensity and excellence of a different kind which is powerful in proportion to the personal equation. Death and violence light up Gordimer's writing: she is a poet of death and violence.

Gordimer remarks that 'there was always commitment in my writing without my really being aware of it. I think it first came into my story "Ah, Woe Is Me", which was saying something about the uselessness of white gestures. I wrote it when I was about 18.'[12] If it was written by a girl of 18 in 1941, it is far-sighted in its criticism of charity in a divided society. But, even in the 1950s, her comments on the attitudes of the white community are somewhat bland in their optimism:

> And here, too, are the whites in all stages of understanding this inevitable historical process – some afraid and resentful, some pretending it is not happening, a few trying to help it along less painfully. A sad, and confusing part of the world to grow up and live in. And yet exciting.[13]

The skill of writing in a committed way without labouring or patronizing comes relatively slowly. 'Some Monday for Sure', for instance, captures a new atmosphere – that of the period after Sharpeville – with great skill. By this time a new generation of black writers was becoming prominent in South Africa, with Peter Abrahams, Ezekiel Mphahlele, Richard Rive, and Alex La Guma, among others, making urban black experience far more accessible to a white writer.

It must be said that the tale remains a construction of the mind, lacking that rich, full, accidental life which is given to the best of the early stories. It is only in the 1970s and 1980s that Gordimer discovers the ability to fuse the sensuous immediacy of her early stories with a consciously analytic mode. Some of the old patterns re-emerge, for instance the uneasy consciousness of the *other*, half glimpsed beyond the margins of understanding, in 'A Lion on the Freeway', and even more strongly in 'Something Out There'. The first of these stories is very short, perhaps 1,100 words long, but its poetic structure potentiates a great suggestiveness. Like 'Is There Nowhere . . . ?', it is about panic fear. The poetic power of the earlier story depends upon the utilization of a very particular kind of nightmare, re-dreamed under profound psychological pressure by almost every growing girl in South Africa. And yet it describes a possible happening. 'A Lion on the Freeway' deliberately moves in closer to the nightmare, recalling states of half-sleep, white nights, dreams of anxiety. And once again there is a powerful sexual undertow. It begins with a terse little inner dialogue which mimics the alarm of a distant or imagined noise in the middle of the night, and continues:

> a breath is taken and it gasps once; pauses, sustaining the night as a singer holds a note. And begins once more. The panting reaches up up up down down down to that awe-ful groan –
> Open up!
> Open up!
> Open your legs! (*SE* 24)

It is a calculated crudity, making the story, for the time being, a complaint of sexual frustration and weariness, merging libido with anticipatory affection for violence and death. But in the end of the story Gordimer links the menace of the lion and the importunity of the sexual instinct to a public, prophetic theme. The lion becomes the people, roaring for freedom, on the march at last, a terrible parturition.

'Something Out There' is some 40,000 words long. It demands this space because it unifies the two broad modalities of Gordimer's short stories, the private and public, the sensuous and the analytic. The 'something' is another version of that *other*, glimpsed with terror from the corner of the eye, the ever-present danger which may in the end turn out to be desired. It takes the form of a chacma baboon, puzzlingly at large in the white suburbs of Johannesburg. The story alternates between evidences of the creature's movements, disturbing irruptions into the lives of ordinary whites, and the story of four people preparing sabotage against a large power station. The parallel develops a telling metaphor.

Over sixty years ago, one of South Africa's most interesting poets and thinkers, Eugène Marais, wrote a study of a group of chacma baboons, which was lost, but surfaced, mysteriously, in 1968.[14] The disappearance of *The Soul of the Ape* robbed him of a crucial role in the history of science, in which he might have rallied the opposition to behaviourist psychology. Marais argues the case for there being two kinds of memory, individual causal memory and, as Marais calls it, *phyletic* memory, which governs instinctive behaviour. His ideas have a relationship with those of Freud, but go further in a direction which was not to be picked up for many years, until the work of Tinbergen, Lorenz, and Ardrey. As Ardrey puts it:

> Freud, with lesser luck, had only theory. Eugène Marais . . . with all his complexities of inner pain and overwhelming insight . . . could gain from long, direct experience materials for his basic conclusion that the human psyche, like the human body, has evolved from the world of lesser animals.[15]

Marais stresses the baboons' extraordinary adaptability; forced to migrate by human appropriation of their land, they survived the virtual destruction of their normal habitat. Their fate had much in common with the way in which the Afrikaners were treated by the British after the Boer War. The chacma's natural diet is fruit and insects, but Marais's refugee hill troops adapted to flesh eating. When men were in the vicinity they would go thirsty for days, showing ingenuity in harvesting water-rich bulbs and devising elaborate means of collecting rain water. Marais comments 'it needs no wide systematic knowledge of animal behaviour to recognize the great difference there is between habits such as these and the greatest adaptability conceivable in animals below the primates'.[16] Marais is observing an intelligence common to baboons and man. The prejudiced white will sometimes insult those of other races by talking about them as baboons. Marais and Gordimer find a way of twisting around the slur, making the *chacma* into a metaphor for a persistent thrust towards freedom in Man, rather as the hardy scrub, or *maquis*, was used to describe French resistance in the 1939-45 war.

In 'Something Out There' the career of the chacma through white society alternates with, and echoes, the activities of the resistance group. If there is one complex image which focuses the whole pattern, it is the one where an ageing white woman lies in her bath reviewing her dying body, and then, suddenly, becomes aware of the baboon, who has even managed to penetrate this private experience, staring through the glass wall of a tiny courtyard no bigger than an airshaft: '*Looking at the woman in the bath. Seeing what she sees*' (*SOT* 165).[17] Elsewhere, in *Burger's Daughter*, Gordimer uses similar images of ageing, palpating the breasts in obedience to medical advice, becoming more and more aware of the withering self instead of looking 'out there'.

Voyeuristic anxiety is being exploited here, too. As Cooke points out, the story begins with photography 'and returns again and again to anxious attempts to reduce the thing half seen to a verifiable image'.[18] Now the unverifiable and half-seen becomes that which is tangibly there, becoming the *seer* behind the glass. The private image of decay becomes linked to the very powerful image of a force at work for millennia in African history. Gordimer recalls 'the dog-faced ape of ancient Egyptian mythology, Cynocephalus, often depicted attendant upon the god Thoth, which she has seen in museums abroad' (*SOT* 164).

There is a sense in which the glimpse of 'something out there' is not just a threat to peace of mind, disturbing a habitual engrossment in self, foreshadowing the end to a blind and childish security. It becomes, as well, a first meeting (terrifying enough to be repressed) with a fundamental part of oneself. The point is made by van Gelder, the golf-playing aesthetic surgeon, whose life it was to disassemble and to reconstruct human faces, to break and piece together the bone which underlies the being the world sees. He reflects upon that fleeting glimpse of the baboon (Marais is worth remembering here): 'he had looked back into a consciousness from which part of his own came. There were claims from within oneself that could materialize only in these unsought ways, in apparently trivial or fortuitous happenings that could be felt but not understood' (*SOT* 176).

In each of these tales the self confronted by the *other* is put into contact with something neglected, but vitally important. There may be an element of wish-fulfilment, but in the end Gordimer is talking about revolution, approaching it through the viscera, tying it to sexuality and to death wish, to the ageing of the body and the terrors of dream. Her characters look over the edge and see 'the horror', pointing into the infinite recessions at the centre of the text in such a way as to draw the reader clean through, beyond the text. In that respect her engagement is complete. But her characters frequently remain as far as ever from a satisfactory meeting with the *other*: the other remains an effect of the psyche, a projected image. Gordimer foreshadows the sickness of anticipation, the reluctance of vision, in a community which refuses to know *others*, and so cannot fully tolerate self.

13

Nadine Gordimer: The novels

In Gordimer's first published novel, *The Lying Days* (1953),[1] a young girl grows up in the narrow world of a mining town, self-absorbed, registering every moment in terms of immediate sensation. A series of relationships enable her to grow beyond her sensuous self, until she begins to become alive, tentatively, imperfectly, to the world outside. She begins to experiment with protest movements, though as spectator only, not as actor. The *other* of so many of the stories mutates in the first alarming invasion of a political and social consciousness, gained through a painful process of dissociation from family and home. 'Helen Shaw' becomes a way of constructing an enabling role, a means of marking out a possible independence, or qualified autonomy, from the structure of relationship which is home as starting-place. In the later novels, near the surface or in deep structure, there are versions, mutations, extensions, of this changing awareness, rites of passage from the common myth (Ben Jonson's common moth)[2] of security and self-satisfaction which binds the white community.

The picaresque structure of *A Sport of Nature* (1987), Gordimer's latest novel, has been commented on by reviewers. Throughout a career in which the heroine, like a Thomasina Jones, breaks all the rules, her rightness is guaranteed by a sensuous understanding which goes out to other people, giving full weight to their needs and desires. The name of the heroine, Hillela, recalls the Rabbi Hillel. When a proselyte promised to accept Judaism if it could be taught to him in the time in which he could remain standing on one foot, Hillel said 'What is hateful to thee do not do unto thy fellow. This is the great foundation; the rest is commentary. Go now and learn.' Hillel's 'Golden Rule' is in parallel with the second commandment of the New Testament.

More than thirty years separate the two works. The changes in ethical concerns, in fields of vision, modes of analysis of the world, of perception, of human relationship, are as great as the reach of time might suggest. The continuities are equally strong; the relationship between the continuities and the change is so complex that it can emerge only through close reading.

It is not surprising to find Gordimer placing herself in the Judaeo-Christian tradition of the Golden Rule, but I am not proposing a formally religious

Gordimer, any more than a Marxist one. One can not be easy, either, about the idea of a neo-Freudian Gordimer, but there is an element of dialogue with the later Freud in her fiction. In *Civilization and Its Discontents*, Freud argues that the evolution of civilization 'must present the struggle between Eros and Death, between the instinct of life and the instinct of destruction, as it works itself out in the human species'.[3] The essay was written as the menace of National Socialism grew in Germany; the post-war history of South Africa can be seen as a continuation of the psycho-social problems of Europe between the wars. There is a clue in this passage from *Occasion for Loving* in which Jessie Stilwell thinks about the difficulties of retrieving the early experiences locked in her mind:

> There were signs that it was all still there; it lay in a smashed heap of rubble from which a fragment was often turned up. Her daily, definite life was built on the heap, but had no succession from it, like a city built on the site of a series of ruined cities of whose history the current citizens knew nothing. (*OL* 25)[4]

Cooke refers to the archaeological discoveries of the 1960s unearthing evidence of ancient kraals which disproved conventional wisdom about Bantu demographical history. But Freud uses the metaphor of the city in arguing against Romain Rolland's conviction that the source of religious experience is an 'oceanic feeling', in which the individual personality merges into a boundless experience. Even Rome, the eternal city, constantly changes, destroying the old and replacing it with the new. In the psychical entity of the mind all past experience may be co-present: 'it is rather the rule than the exception for the past to be preserved in mental life'.[5] Freud dismisses Rolland's 'oceanic feeling' as the persistence of an early phase of ego-feeling, one in which the child attempts to appropriate everything outside itself.

As is to be expected, the deep motivating structures appear in different ways in different novels, and there are distinct changes in the way they occur between the earlier and the later works. *The Lying Days*, for instance, is divided into three sections, of which the central one is 'The Sea'. It is the section in which Helen Shaw experiences sexuality for the first time, moves out of the domination of the family and the mother, out of the self-absorption of the adolescent and of the white community, and attempts to experience the reality of others.

Helen has been kissed (perhaps, the narrator herself confesses uncertainty, for the first time) by Ludi, a man ten years older than herself. They return to the beach, accompanied reluctantly by Ludi's mother, who agrees to come after brief argument in a passage which associates the sea, and Helen's adolescent sexual eagerness, and death. She coaxes her mother with her voice, but wills her not to come:

> She hesitated still. 'You could sit under the funeral tree.' (It was a dark and mournful tree that hung unexpectedly over a dune.) Trembling with

the guilt of my desire to prevent her, I could have gone on finding reasons for her to come. (*LD* 67)[6]

It is a baptism by total immersion as Helen enters the water without a bathing cap (a small, but conscious, gesture of risk) (*LD* 67-8). The self-absorbed, almost solipsistic physicality of the adolescent girl is referred and transferred to the sea, converting the girl into the object of thrusting, probing, shocking, hands, tongue, membrane of the towering sea, aided, as if by appropriated limbs, by her own wet hair which touches cold fingers, and which blinds and clings. The subtext is patently sexual, but more subtly masochistic, suiting the dreaming anticipation of sex by an adolescent girl in a society which demands the girl's submission to male power. The imagined life, and the self-centred play of the adolescent imagination which prospects it, are summarized:

> I let my hair into the water, dipping and spreading it in a solitary game. . . . I played in the water and thought of Ludi swimming back to me: it seemed to me, as I imagined a woman in the complacency of marriage, that it was wonderful to think of him removed from me, simply because he would come back. (*LD* 68)

Her imagination bears no relationship to the actuality. Ludi fails to give her her first experience of intercourse in an ambiguous episode which damages the cosy mythology of sex for her. But he does break down the adolescent narcissism with a sense of *otherness*:

> my hand came into contact with his jaw and I felt the wonderful shock of a burning warmth other than my own flesh; I rolled over to bury my face in the angle between his neck and the cushion. (*LD* 80)

The experience of the other in racial difference is touched upon in Helen's relationship with Mary Seswayo. In *The Lying Days* this is as limited, as much a matter of the bound imagination, as Helen's reaching towards sexual knowledge. What is missing in Helen's approach towards overcoming exclusion through racial fear is the certainty that the author, a woman of thirty, is able to push aside the limitations of Helen and say what she is unable to imagine or know. The indeterminacy is a rare kind of critical honesty, a truthfulness to the disabilities of the writer as well as her subject. Helen sits in the train and attempts to imagine a woman working at a sewing machine in a black township, repeatedly revising imagination in her anxiety about condescension:

> Probably she chattered while she sewed. No, probably that was wrong too; native women are always far more gay or far more serious than white women, so one mustn't try to visualize their moods from one's experience of Europeans. . . . There was no way of knowing, no way of knowing. . . . I had grown up, all my life, among strangers: the Africans, whose

language in my ears had been like the barking of dogs or the cries of birds. (*LD* 186)

Helen's experiments in imagining this 'world of strangers' culminate in an incident of central importance. She becomes involved, tentatively, fearfully, in a protest (an actual, historical event, on May Day, 1950) against the Suppression of Communism Act. From an immobilized car she watches as a rioter is killed. Clingman remarks that the episode signifies Helen's marginality as spectator rather than actor in history.[7] One might add that exclusion from history is in parallel with failure in personal relationships, that each has a metaphorical relationship with the other, and that in this intimate binding, ethics, phenomenology, and political consciousness have no clear dividing lines.

The title of *A World of Strangers* (1958) suggests the ways in which Gordimer continues to pursue a concern opened up in *The Lying Days*. The central experiences of *otherness* are in Toby Hood's relationships with a black friend, Steven Sitole, and a radical woman, Anna Louw. Toby is the alien here, and to believe in his psychological and emotional progress we must accept that he is entirely an Englishman of upper-middle-class origin. Toby is made as complete an outsider to South Africa and as naïvely apolitical as Gordimer can make him. He is offensively sardonic about 'the world of victims we now know', and determined, before he comes, not to play the role his liberal family has prepared for him, 'a *voyeur* of the world's ills and social perversions'. His languid detachment is broken by the experience of South Africa, though it offers him sufficient possibilities of elegant carelessness in the world of High House and Cecil Rowe (her name barely conceals a reference to Cecil Rhodes). His friend Steven, whose detachment from responsibility is of a different kind from Toby's, embittered and reckless, is killed in a car crash after a police raid. If Toby initially is suspended between the uncaring and selfish Cecil and the careless Steven, Steven's death propels him towards the caring commitment of Anna. But Gordimer detaches the novel from the real political possibilities of the South Africa she describes by making 'Anna Louw' a disillusioned Communist. The qualities which link Anna with Gordimer's close friend Bettie du Toit were, in that historical context, inseparable from the kind of commitment which only membership of the South African Communist Party (or, after its banning, a continued loyalty to its principles and programmes) could signify. Gordimer, perhaps, offers an illusion to liberals, or respectability to her publishers and reviewers.

There is a strangely gratuitous-seeming *introit* before the beginning proper in 'Part One'. It is as if many of the pressing personal themes are confined to an ante-room. The ignorance of what surrounds and supports every moment of her own life to which Helen Shaw admits is reflected, as in a distorting mirror, by Toby's account of his first meeting with Africans. The very first words of the novel, 'I hate the faces of peasants', introduce Gordimer's essay in the transposition of a complete home-grown emotion into the haughty language of an uncomprehending alien culture, deeply affected by class distinction. The trouble is that the words don't at all fit Toby's English culture of class.

One of the things which this annexe to the fiction does do is to show, in a pleasantly satirical manner, the way in which some English settlers, with far greater possibilities of understanding Africa than Toby, know just as little about it, have lived in Africa simply without *seeing* it, so that Stella Turgell hates Africa (England too) and loves Italy. Her husband, she says, adores Africa, because he loves rushing about doing things. But for her, Africa is nothing but ugliness: 'Beauty is *the* most important thing in life, *don't you think so?' (WS* 16).[8]

It's fair satire, and yet there is an abstract, willed character about her portrayal. One of the functions of satire is quasi-magical, a means of dispelling unwanted feelings or attitudes by embodying them in a person or action, to be cast out of the tribe or the city. Stella's attitudes are self-consciously literary. She cannot recognize 'beauty' until it is determined for her, at second hand, by literature. Toby verbally exorcizes her, embarrassed by her feeble aestheticism. But he himself cannot think of alternatives except in aesthetic terms:

> Stella's passion for Italy was nineteenth-century Byronic. . . . she saw everything like one of those young girls in Forster's early novels about the English in Italy, girls who marry the libertine sons of dentists in places with names like Poggibonsi, or whose lives are changed irrevocably after being spectator to an Italian quarrel in an Italian square. The Italy of Moravia and the realist films did not exist for her. Her way of talking about Italy embarrassed me. (*WS* 15)

The Woman of Rome and *Bitter Rice* replace Stella's Forsterian virgins and Byronic heroes; satire on Toby's aestheticism covers satire on Stella in a double perspective. But perhaps the real secret underlying the text is that Toby himself is drawn from literature (and perhaps film) rather than life. His scorn of the peasantry and his embarrassment with English romanticism cover an inability to engage with the actual, an aesthetic voyeurism, as gross as Stella's. But his horrified reaction: 'Were these the sort of people Africa gets? Christ, poor continent!' (*WS* 27), forcefully satiric as it is of some kinds of pretension, is burdened by a para-text of anxiety in the artist. It is a palimpsest in which Toby's embarrassment with Stella echoes Gordimer's uncertainty about the role of art – like hers, a sensuous, personal, 'detached', and very European art – in Africa.

The insecurity parallels the political, social, and historical insecurity of the whole work, an insecurity admitted in such a way as to leave the way open for reassessment of the significance of the fiction and its possible relationships with history. Its optimism is provisional in a self-critical, even a self-mocking way[9] and, characteristically for Gordimer, it echoes in a final meeting with an other, Sam Mofokenzazi. At the end of the novel Toby promises to return in time for the christening of his friend's child. Sam replies ' "Maybe you won't come back at all. Something will keep you away. Something will prevent you, and we won't –" the rest was lost as we disappeared from each other down our separate stairways' (*WS* 266). Clingman draws the parallel with the ending of Forster's *A Passage to India*, and comments that Gordimer's ending is 'at a higher and more demanding level'.[10] If it is so, it is not because of any greater coherence; quite the contrary. It is because the implicit tenor of the whole fiction is to concede the inadequacy of an aesthetic reconstruction to the historical moment.

Occasion for Loving (1963) was published after Sharpeville, when opposition movements which had hitherto kept to a policy of passive resistance and non-violence were driven to experiment with violence, in particular with sabotage. It was a time when anyone who took the idea of love as the motivation of social or political action had to look hard and carefully at what that implied. The epigraphs combine to make a link which, perhaps, none of their authors would have made, but which charts the leap which has to be made if a liberal conscience is to transcend its own limitations: 'We have all become people according to the measure in which we have loved people and have had occasion for loving' (Boris Pasternak); 'In our time the destiny of man presents its meaning in political terms' (Thomas Mann); ' . . . servitude, falsehood and terror . . . these three afflictions are the cause of silence between men, obscure them from one another and prevent them from rediscovering themselves in the only value which can save them from nihilism – the long complicity between men at grips with their destiny' (Albert Camus).

The story is of a triangular relationship between an English woman, Ann Davis, an African artist, Gideon Shibalo, and Ann's scholarly husband, Boaz, who is wrapped up in his study of African musical instruments. Boaz doesn't protest at the relationship as he might have done if Gideon had been white; the reader is at liberty to take this silence as indicating that Boaz is unusually sensitive in suppressing personal feelings in face of an obscene law, or, in a contrary way, that his liberalism makes him a subtle kind of racist. Equally one might find it difficult to determine whether Gideon is an oppressed artist of attractive personality or an unscrupulous manipulator. There seems to be less doubt about Ann. Her entry into the affair seems insensitive, her exit from it has the callousness of panic. But there are ways in which her experience might be seen as being deeper and more positive than those of other characters. The complexity is caused, brutally and tragically, by an external circumstance which has all the distortive effect upon human relationship which, in Greek tragedy, is motivated by Fate. But here what Fate operates through is not a god-given dispensation of *themis*. It is 'a line in a statute book', the act which forbids sexual relations between people of different races, 'naming' a crime as awesome as parricide and incest were to the Greeks, though often committed in secret. Ann's rashness must be seen in the context of a far deeper insensitivity. And, however the affair started, it becomes something more than the escapade of a silly adventuress.

The central character is Jessie Stilwell, and the opening of the book displays some of Gordimer's most personal concerns. It begins with an ambivalence – an episode of reflection which occupies a twilight between waking consciousness and the dream. It begins by marking once again the insecure status of *home*:

> Jessie Stilwell had purposefully lost her way home, but sometimes she found herself there, innocent of the fact that she had taken to her heels long ago and was still running. Still running and the breathlessness and the drumming of her feet created an illusion of silence and motionlessness – the stillness we can feel when the earth turns – in which she had never left her mother's house. (*OL* 9)

It is not, as we might have expected, a description of a sleeping dream-state, rather of one of those moments of sudden abstraction in which buried states of mind break through into routine activity, and advise us of myths we have never really forgotten and which still direct some part of our lives: 'There was nothing peripheral to it; she had never been out of the garden, or challenged the flaming angels at the gates' (*OL* 9). The internal world to which we are introduced here is integral to the total effect; the whole enterprise depends upon the way in which the intensely private Jessie observes and engages with the lives of others; the way in which private and social worlds do or do not mesh.

In the latter part of the novel Jessie lives in a house by the sea, where Gideon and Ann take refuge with her. The sea evokes deep levels of consciousness; at night she imagines hearing 'in the sound of the sea the voices of argument and the cries of children teasing one another' (*OL* 185). And yet it is not the house of her childhood, the place from which she has been running all her life, nor is it her married home, the centre of present reality. It is, once more, Gordimer's version of the 'oceanic': 'She listened and there was nothing but the sea; all voices were its own, all sounds. The sound was an element, like its wetness' (*OL* 185).

It is this defamiliarizing sense of alternative life which gives the sea and its margins the power to suggest changed perceptions of the forms of order, the topologies which govern our lives. The minute forms of life in rock-pools and crevices give, not the anthropomorphic pleasure of a more developed being (perhaps a locust or a lion), 'with an existence that a human being always guesses at in simplified terms of his own, but the pleasure of pure form. Volute, convolute, spheroid, they were order, perfect order at the extreme end of a process' (*OL* 195). The sea is present as an obverse of everyday reality, guaranteeing it as death guarantees life, from early stories like 'The Catch'. It is sometimes presented as the estranging container of dangerous and confusing mysteries. Here it takes on a mathematical simplicity of great purity, the wish-fulfilment of a desire to evade a human complexity.

There is, significantly, a point at which Ann signals emotions of which she is not entirely conscious. Gideon has disappeared. Jessie assures Ann that he will come back soon. Ann's expression is nervous, evasive, guilty. Jessie asks 'But what *could* happen to him?', and Ann fails to answer for a moment, in deep confusion. ' "Well . . . he wouldn't just walk out into the sea . . . ?" The moment it was said she was smiling at the absurdity, the preposterousness of it' (*OL* 261). Later, as Jessie talks of Ann and Gideon, Tom becomes aware of the way in which Jessie, too, is being shocked into new awareness:

> 'She's in love with him, there's no getting away from it, whatever we thought about her before. . . . But I don't know what she wanted . . . '
> 'Wanted him drowned . . . you said so.'
> 'Being in love with him isn't simple; I mean, the whole business isn't. . . '
> (*OL* 271)

Death by water becomes more and more a pointing to that recession into the abyss, that dis-covering of a resolution of experience under experience, perhaps a reconciliation of Thanatos and Eros; or, perhaps, a recognition of the abyss in Derrida's sense, of inexplicable chains of reflexivity finally defeating meaning. There's a paralysis at the centre of the book in which Gordimer, through the distorting medium of Jessie (a character who parallels her own life and personality in multiple ways) identifies the barriers which face Eros in a world dominated by Thanatos; identifies, too, the attractions of a defection from humanity, defection into a sea-death seen as attractive in its formal simplicity.

The Late Bourgeois World (1966) sustains the terseness of the short story mode for 30,000 words. It begins with the apparent suicide of Liz Van Den Sandt's husband Max by driving his car into Cape Town harbour. The incident is announced to a cold and angry Liz in a telegram read over the remains of a late breakfast with her lover Graham Mill. It remains a contexture for the whole action of the *novella*, providing occasion for the plot and simultaneously a descant of death by water controlling the subtle connections between public and private scores.

The public theme is given by the experiments in sabotage which have been mentioned above. The armed wing of Congress, *Umkhonto we Sizwe*, had been silenced for the time being by the Rivonia trial; Poqo, the PAC equivalent, was destroyed by mass arrests; and the ARM (African Resistance Movement), an amateurish and less coherent body, had been completely crushed as well. Gordimer writes that '*The Late Bourgeois World* was an attempt to look into the specific character of the social climate that produced the wave of young white saboteurs in 1963-64.'[11]

Max was an ineffectual revolutionary. He had failed in violent resistance, he had betrayed his colleagues, and his suicide isn't seen as an act of expiation, or of justification, or even an appeal for sympathy. Liz comes close to saying to Graham that he did it to spite her, but one senses more attentiveness in her curt words to Bobo, their son: 'He must have driven his car into the sea. He was never afraid of the sea, he was at home in it' (*LBW* 16).[12]

Max's bungling idealism is contrasted with Graham's convincing and inactive liberalism, with a fine irony. Graham

> doesn't act, that's true; but he doesn't give way, and that's not bad, in a deadlock. . . . When I talk with him about history or politics I am aware of the magnetic pull of his mind to the truth. One can't get at it, *but to have some idea where it is*! (*LBW* 37)

The mind is linked to the body of the man in a description of Graham's magnificent but mechanical efficiency as a sexual partner. But Liz is conscious of the latent power being hers, a power of life and death, or rather of death: 'while we lie there silent . . . I am the one who has him helpless. If I flex the muscles inside me it's as if I were throttling someone' (*LBW* 38).

Graham is a liberal lawyer with professional courage. Such people do magnificent work in relieving the personal consequences of a devilish legal system. They also test the law for the law-makers, discover its inefficiencies, help the rulers refine its cruel force. Liz's job is one which curiously parallels Graham's. She works in a medical laboratory analysing stools and blood. 'Neither of us makes money out of cheap labour or performs a service confined to people of a particular colour. For myself, thank God shit and blood are all the same, no matter whom they come from' (*LBW* 37). Both of them, she remarks wryly, keep their hands clean.

Max's sexuality, on the other hand, is destructive:

> With every orgasm I used to come back with the thought: I could die like that. And of course that was exactly what it was, the annihilation, every time, of the silences and sulks, the disorder and frustration of the days. (*LBW* 49)

Graham does everything that is required of him: he is as safe and effective in conducting a case as he is in bringing a partner to orgasm. Max's intellect appears to be as passionate, dangerous, and uselessly self-destructive as his sexuality: his theoretical work on the methodology of African socialism is doomed from the start. But in his death he reveals a depth in Liz, 'A vision of seaweed swaying up from deep underwater. Not asleep but awake in the vision, as I opened my eyes in the room. . . . the rippling distortion of the great stems, brown thrashing tubes that sway down, down' (*LBW* 38-9). As she imagines Max's death she becomes aware that the 'flowers had stirred and opened. . . . I lay quite still and felt myself alive, there in the room as their scent was' (*LBW* 39). His death, like that of the boy in 'A Company of Laughing Faces' or that of the bird in 'The Kindest Thing to Do', generates awareness – a sexually charged awareness – of life, just as Graham's resolute sexuality and intellectualism makes Liz contemptuously aware of death. It is perhaps the most powerful pursuit of a disturbing private myth in Gordimer's *œuvre*.

The whole thing leads to another paradoxical connection between sex and death, though it does not result in a sexual act or in death. Luke Fokase, a member of a black nationalist armed resistance movement, tempts Liz into a dangerous involvement in arranging supplies of money for sabotage. The sexuality of their relationship is obvious, though it never goes beyond the first stages of a highly formal erotic game, a political seduction. Liz is persuaded to help Luke with an illegal transfer of money from abroad, which can only lead her to disaster – a long prison sentence on a charge of treason or complicity in acts of sabotage. Sexually and politically, Liz is invited to employ her power as dangerously as Max ever did. She knows a way of transferring funds for Luke through her senile grandmother's bank account: 'And while we talked, the thought was growing inside me, almost like sexual tumescence' (*LBW* 86).

It may be dangerous, but Liz retains her sense of humour, her awareness of the act (sexual, political, and suicidal), in its reality and simultaneously its theatricality. In her grim ironic reference to Greek myths she retains her sense of Luke's cynical detachment, and her own:

> And so he's gone, my Orpheus in his too-fashionable jacket, back to the crowded company that awaits him somewhere in the town-outside-the-town. In a way it must be a relief to leave behind pale Eurydice and her musty secrets, her life-insured Shades. . . . Only the flowers, that are opening their buds in water and will be dead by Monday, breathe in the room. I put my face in among them, ether-cool snowdrops; but it is a half-theatrical gesture. (*LBW* 89)

The title is given meaning. The death around which it is constructed is not that of Max, nor is it the complex intimations of death contained in Liz's sexual life. Liz as Eurydice is prevented from leaving a dead world, a Dis or Hades securely cocooning her, the late bourgeois world of the title. The wry gesture of the tragedy queen burying her face in spring flowers (ether-cool, the anaesthetic consolation of beauty and of art) is as self-referential for the artist as it is for Liz her character. It's a question about the validity of the artistic gesture, a wry half-admission that as sexuality can mimic death in its passion and intensity, so may art, excluded from its consummation in a world of reality. And, it's implicit, the suicidal gestures of such as were involved in organizations like ARM were ineffective art.

A Guest of Honour (1970) is not likely to find favour with the powerful in some African countries, not because it is unsympathetic to the problems of newly independent nations, but rather because it is very acute in identifying the problems of neo-colonialism. It relates the problems of a public world to those of a private world in the character of Colonel Bray, a man who has identified with the cause of independence before it was achieved, and who is now invited back to help build the new African nation. There's a wry authorial joke in his name: unlike the Vicar of Bray he doesn't compromise his principles to remain what he is. He is committed to freedom whatsoever authoritarian may rule. He fails, he dies, and though the problems are related to the thematic matters we have been discussing, they are so related in a less direct way than in the case of other novels by Gordimer.

Bray's death is referred to in the title, I believe by means of a quiet allusion to W. H. Auden's 'In Memory of W. B. Yeats (d. January 1939)', in which the third section begins: 'Earth, receive an honoured guest'. Auden's poem, written in the confused and menacing days when Europe awaited its terror and disgrace in the Second World War, identifies behind all Yeats's human and political failings a redeeming quality of truthfulness. It is this same quality which makes Bray 'a guest of honour'. His sexual infidelity to Olivia in his affair with Rebecca parallels his changing allegiances in the rivalry between Mweta and Shinza, an apparent treachery which contains within it a deeper honour. The later stanzas of Auden's poem are deeply relevant:

Intellectual disgrace
Stares from every human face,
And the seas of pity lie
Locked and frozen in each eye.

Follow, poet, follow right
To the bottom of the night,
With your unconstraining voice
Still persuade us to rejoice

In their timeliness, their capacity to identify the historical moment, Auden's words define a mode of poetic authority towards which Gordimer turns increasingly, seeking the kind of poetic responsibilities which Auden celebrates when he enjoins the poet 'In the prison of his days/Teach the free man how to praise.' In deep structure they are parallel in developing an ethic, an aesthetic, and ways in which the two are indivisible, fit for the responsible artist then in Europe, now in Africa.

The conservation movement is strongest in the 'market economies', and yet there is a conflict between the philosophy of the market and that of conservation. Again and again we hinder the increase of the earth by multiplication of profits. The name of the central character of *The Conservationist* (1974), Mehring, is a word-play on the German verb *mehren* or *vermehren* (to multiply, increase) which touches ironically upon this problem. More deeply the irony penetrates problems suffered by the wretched of the earth, destroying their land to find fuel, grow cash crops, and feed a rapidly growing population.

It is easier to be a conservationist if you don't need to grow your own food on a meagre share of land. Mehring is a dealer in pig-iron, at the heart of the international trade in raw materials. He is also a weekend farmer with a conscience about the preservation of wild guinea fowl and their eggs. The wanton destruction of a clutch of eggs is linked at the beginning of the novel with the discovery of a dead man, a black stranger, a wretched castaway on the third pasture of Mehring's property. The *otherness* of this intruder becomes more and more important in the coding as the novel proceeds. And, in his death, he becomes increasingly a trope for growth and fertility, like the guinea fowl eggs, a vehicle for conservation and for *Vermehrung*.

The land has been in drought for years. No rain can be expected for months, the river's 'too low to be seen or heard'. Nobody knows how the man has died: he is face-down in the river mud, as if he has drowned in the midst of the deep drought. The police, to avoid the paper work involved in the death of another *kaffir*, bury him there, in the river bed. Mehring thinks of protesting to the authorities, but it is no good: there is no escaping what lies under his land, waiting for the rains to return and the river to flow. The body and the land are Mehring's property only in the sense that the whole nation is *property* to the white man; ownership depends upon the burial of something, burial by the forces of 'justice'.

Mehring has the conviction that he is the custodian, the steward of the land. It's an ethical position which is compromised by this burial. The pastoral sentiment, one which so many return to for comfort in a world which they destroy, becomes powerful in its irony. Man remains what Andrew Marvell saw him as, the mower who destroys his own paradise, exiling himself by pursuit of a petty triumph.

At the same time, Mehring does exhibit in his deepest reactions a vital – the word might equally be *mortal* – commitment to the earth which seems so superficially his. He returns from Tokyo, thinking wryly of his boastful pride in talking about *his* land to customers on the other side of the globe, goes to sleep on the grass of his farm, and wakens, 'aware of breathing intimately into the earth'. He doesn't know where he is for the moment, but recognizes something in the situation, 'staring into the eye of the earth with earth at his mouth', which is strongly familiar to him, something already inhabited in imagination (*TC* 41).[13] There is a hinted level at which Mehring's real connection with the land is one in which the black *other* under the drought-parched river bed is in some way himself.

Mehring isn't a fool. He knows that the system under which he lives is rotten, and he knows his own rottenness in accepting what it gives him, choosing carefully where to exercise his conscience. He is aware that what he is obliged to ignore in order to preserve this balance is the essence of the matter. At this level he is 'the conservationist' in apathy, burying knowledge to conserve a comfortable world: 'To keep anything the way you like it for yourself you have to have the stomach to ignore – dead and hidden – whatever intrudes. Those for whom life is cheapest recognize that' (*TC* 79). The familiar Gordimer paradox which associates, as two sides of the coin, the vital and the mortal, can be spun and land on the obverse. Mehring is, in a sense, already dead, lying with the black body in the mud.

But at last the rain returns, the body surfaces, and with it the rotten stink of a world of vegetation. As he waits at the traffic lights, travelling to the city and his own death by violence, Mehring remembers the corpse, in terms which are drawn from riotous abundance of life; 'the mealies have stored sweetness of lymph, human milk and semen, all the farm has flowered and burgeoned from him, sucking his strength like nectar from a grass straw' (*TC* 251). We move here from a pastoral mode into a mythical one, or, perhaps, since the pastoral mode has always verged upon the mythical, exploiting its energies, we return to the roots of the mode. The black *other* has become an Osiris figure, buried as the fourteen pieces of Osiris were, to guarantee the annual miracle of the return of the flow of the Nile, with its life-giving mud. And, as Newman[14] and Clingman[15] demonstrate, there is a powerful subtext in Zulu mythology, gathered from Gordimer's reading of *The Religious System of the Amazulu*, which the Reverend Henry Callaway compiled in 1868.[16] In Callaway's account the ancestral spirit returns to claim the land for its descendants. As Clingman remarks, there is a psychological corollary, in that the buried corpse also becomes a point of repression within the mind of Mehring. This subtly controls the inner monologue and creates a tropistic tension betwen the rhetoric of conservation and the mythic anticipation of the return of the land.

The Conservationist could be seen as Gordimer's version of *The Waste Land*, and it's fitting that the narrative is constructed, not as history, but as inner monologue, focusing, sometimes with suffocating intensity, upon the inventions of a mind intent upon itself. One is aware of history as one reads – Mehring himself is the new South African, the enlightened businessman who combines a relentless pursuit of profit with an expansive sentiment for the land. But history is half-occulted by the tissues of subjectivity. *The Conservationist* shares with *The Waste Land* its underlying structure of an arid and dispossessed land being restored to life by the return of the rain, the life-giving properties of the burial of the dead and death by water. But the magical properties with which Mehring endows the corpse in his land: 'That corpse you planted last year in your garden,/Has it begun to sprout? Will it bloom this year?', are given it by a European mind – by his fictive imagination, by Gordimer's mimicry of a representative consciousness. It is a way of disturbing resonances in the reader's mind which come to their full potential only when the rising of the corpse to the surface of the earth and water is echoed, distortedly, by the manner of Mehring's death (or does he die?). In this the ironies of Mehring's name come into full play: in the increase, the multiplication of the land Mehring himself meets death (or something like it), not in a reed-bed or in good earth, but between the cyanide-rich mine dumps which surround exhausted gold workings on the Witwatersrand. He is inveigled there by a woman of indeterminate race, who leads him to murderous accomplices. His funeral is not recorded. Even the fact of his death on this poisoned ground is not made certain. But it is revealed, wryly, that Mehring is associated with the *possession* of the burial ground: 'he's on a Board with the chairman of the Group this ground still belongs to' (*TC* 264-5).

In a final brief epilogue the black stranger is given decent interment by the people of the farm: 'They had put him away to rest, at last; he had come back. He took possession of this earth, theirs; one of them' (*TC* 267). The text just beneath the surface, in the dry river bed of South Africa's recent history, is in the language of liberation politics. 'He had come back' recalls an old liberation cry of the ANC:[17] at the Congress of the People in Kliptown on 25-6 June 1955, each item of the Freedom Charter was adopted and acclaimed by the cry 'Afrika!' and its response, 'Mayibuye!' – 'Let it come back!' Among the most prominent items of the Charter is the declaration of the common possession of the land and the mineral wealth that lies beneath it, the return of the land to the people, and its people to their land.

There is a certain presumption in the writing of *Burger's Daughter* (1979), in that it offers to deal, at the most intimate level, with the lives of an extraordinary group of people, white Communists and their families. Gordimer has known such people; with one of them, Bettie du Toit, she was in close daily contact for several years. But she has always remained at a distance from their political activities. Gordimer takes the case of someone in the second generation of such a family, Burger's *daughter*, someone whose name is in itself a kind of dedication to an austere and painful life (not that such people are masochists, without joy or humour). There are two halves to Rosemarie Burger's given name: the first, Rosa, is in memory of Rosa Luxemburg, the charismatic leader of the failed German Communist revolution, who died a martyr to the cause of the people. The second half, Marie, which is more often than not suppressed, but is always there, links her through her solid aunt Marie to the Afrikaner *volk*.

Gordimer has described how the germ of the novel came in the realization that much of our inner life is conducted in unspoken conversations with absent friends or relations. In the three sections of *Burger's Daughter* there are three such imaginary auditors. Conrad is an ex-boyfriend, marginal to Rosa's family and to Rosa herself: his importance lies much more in his being the listener-in-the-mind than in anything he has done or said. Katya, the internal auditor in the second section, is Lionel Burger's ex-wife who has left the world of politics, to which she belonged only in a fragile way, retiring into a pleasant self-indulgent life in southern France. Lionel himself takes on the listening role, posthumously, in the third section, as Rosa returns to be gaoled in the very prison where she visited him as a schoolgirl before his death.

Conrad's value as an auditor for Rosa lies in his marginality: 'When together they met friends of the Burgers she seemed pleased and animated to chat, and forgot him in his presence; his name was Conrad Something-or-other' (*BD* 39).[18] But there is an obverse to this insignificance. In the inner monologue, like Katya, and like Lionel Burger himself, Conrad becomes, not just the addressee of an autobiographical letter, but an *alter ego* as well, a focus for a possible life, for an alternative self. Rosa, being a Burger, is formed in the presence of an ideal of service and of self-sacrifice. Conrad, in his secret, condemned house that no longer has a postal address because it is due to be destroyed to make way for a freeway, offers her escape into something like anonymity. It is Conrad who draws attention to that aspect of personality which remains locked within quasi-Freudian complications. He gives access, as it were, to one of the driving forces behind Gordimer's work, the intense, narcissistic concentration on the private world of the senses which is the starting-point of the early fiction, and is now absorbed in a larger programme. His name, Conrad, and his research into the new wave of South American novelists (Gordimer herself has expressed great admiration for them) suggest a pull towards the aesthetic life. At the same time Conrad prompts, forces almost, an enquiry into the immediate personal realities which a Rosa Burger, surrounded and formed by a family tradition of political responsibility, might neglect. Conrad sees only two realities, sex and death. He confesses to strongly Oedipal feelings towards his mother (*BD* 44); somewhere at the root of the problems of Burger's daughter there are complications in her relationship with her father which resist resolution. Conrad admits to motiveless fascination with power and with suicide, some of the subjects which invest many of Gordimer's stories with power to disturb, and which are intimately a part of her view of adolescence. '– Didn't you ever imagine killing something, just because it was small and weak? You know how you're obsessed with the possibility of death when you're adolescent' (*BD* 46).

Conrad is caustic about the kind of life which is lived according to an ideal, dedicating oneself to the future, living 'lives you can't live, instead of your own'. He uncovers an area in Rosa's life which she recognizes as real:

> my father's daughter. And now he is dead! Dead! I prowled about that abandoned garden, old Lolita's offspring caught Hottentot Gods in the grass that had taken over the tennis court, and I knew I must have wished him to die; that to exult and to sorrow were the same things for me. (*BD* 63)

When Conrad and Rosa finally part she recognizes that their relationship too 'had become incest' (*BD* 70).

For Rosa, Conrad is a way of examining the self or selves enclosed within sealed identification of name and family. Rosa recognizes this in an ambiguous phrase: 'whatever can be done . . . will be done by people who, far from poring over the navel of a single identity (yes, a dig at you, Conrad), see the necessity of many' (*BD* 112). There are alternatives in the syntax: the many selves are aspects of one person, or the single self can only be fully itself by recognizing others. The whole thrust of the novel is towards Rosa's rejection of a singularity, her recognition that only by admitting the many, and thus becoming manifold, can the self fulfil itself.

The relationship with Conrad has its contrary in Rosa's relationship with Noel de Witt, whom she visits and writes to in prison, fulfilling the obligations of the family in a relationship which can have no physical expression. It is one of the contrasting relationships which define the emerging manifold of Rosa's personality: though there can be no physical contact, there is a strength of feeling in the relationship with Noel which can't be matched by her relationship with Conrad.

The death-by-water motif which is so prominent elsewhere in Gordimer's work returns in the imagined death which summarizes Conrad's role in the fiction: 'At sea, at sea; to circumnavigate is to end up no farther than you started. The world round as your navel' (*BD* 192). This guessing of Conrad's death prompts Rosa to discover in which ways she is unlike Conrad, like her father. Like her father 'I can take from people what I need' (*BD* 192). Thus Conrad acts as a contrary to Lionel Burger as well as to Noel de Witt. Rosa, like Lionel, lives by interaction – if need be by manipulation of other people. Rosa's realization of this parallels a development in Gordimer's own work as an artist. *The Late Bourgeois World*, *A Guest of Honour*, and *The Conservationist* have plotted an increasing concern with history, society, and politics. After Soweto, after the death of Biko, the manifest function of art is in interaction with history; though the artist may still claim detachment, it is one of limited autonomy rather than independence.

The 'death' of Conrad occurs at a time when Rosa accepts the need to manipulate others. She has approached Brandt Vermeulen, the sinisterly sophisticated *verligte* who has influence in government circles. Here is another contrary: Brandt and Lionel Burger both have recognized their likenesses to each other, and each shares the illusion that the other would have held the same view as himself but for minor accidents of history. But they are very different. Gordimer registers perversion of intelligence in Brandt Vermeulen, the intellectual defender of *apartheid,* by an aesthetic failure, an offensively obscene plastic statue (*BD* 181-2). Taste and morality, politics and aesthetics, remain closely related in Gordimer's discourse.

Conrad's imagined death by water is paralleled by an incident which takes place before the beginning of the novel, but is alluded to several times in a way which gives it resonance throughout the fiction. Rosa's real brother has drowned in a swimming-pool accident. The matter is first mentioned after the sentence of life imprisonment is passed on Rosa's father:

> I know those hours afterwards. After someone has been taken away.
> After my brother drowned. After arrests. After my mother died . . . (*BD* 28)

One of the strings which this memory sets vibrating is supportive of Conrad's sensuous fatalism. Tony's death is alluded to in connection with another death, the death of a meths-drinking white down-and-out on a park bench where Rosa ate her lunch. It acts as a reminder that political or public action cannot achieve everything, that it will not eradicate suffering, pain, death (*BD* 80). But while it defines limits to collective action, it is one of the ways in which Rosa is shifted out of self-absorption.

There is another brother-figure, someone who has shared in the experiences of Rosa's childhood, and offers another twinning of contraries. He is black, and he is known to the reader, as he is known to Rosa, as 'Baasie', until she meets him in exile in London. This kind of relationship is not unusual in a South African childhood. The pet-name 'Baasie' (little master), a playful and condescending reversal of the situation the child will have to accept when he grows up, suggests the harsh understanding that the offer of friendship covers.

It is a relationship that must change. And the realization of that change, terrible in its emotional implications for Rosa, becomes the turning-point of the fiction. Rosa meets 'Baasie' accidentally in London, and he telephones her in the middle of the night. He has very harsh things to say. But the first thing he has to say is that he is not 'Baasie'. His real name, *which Rosa has never known*, is Zwelinzima Vulindlela. 'Zwelinzima', a name which is surely suggested to Gordimer by that extraordinary play *Sizwe Bansi is Dead*, means 'Suffering Land'.[19] In *Sizwe Bansi* it is the identity which Sizwe Bansi takes from a murdered man to enable him to stay in the city and to work despite the white man's pass laws. In *Burger's Daughter* it becomes part of the system of contraries by answering and questioning the values suggested by the name Burger.

Zwelinzima represents an aspect of the Black Consciousness movement: the challenge to the white liberal who speaks in a facile way about the black as his brother to recognize how deeply he is implicated in the system of privilege and oppression. Zwelinzima protests about the way in which the world is interested only in the imprisonment and death of Lionel Burger, not in what has happened to so many blacks, including his own father. He isn't even interested when Rosa tells him of the death of Tony. The power of the change effected by this encounter is brought home, once more, by a reference to drowning. In previous references to Tony's death Rosa has recalled the 'chlorinated water with flecks of his pink breakfast bacon in it that I saw pumped from my brother's mouth when he was taken from the pool' (*BD* 79).[20] After 'Baasie's' phone call Rosa

> ran to the bathroom and fell to her knees at the lavatory bowl, vomiting. The wine, the bits of sausage – she laid her head, gasping between spasms, on the porcelain rim, slime dripping from her mouth with the tears of effort running from her nose. (*BD* 323)

The episode becomes the death of a possible Rosa, the Rosa who takes refuge in Europe, in exile, in detachment from all that 'Baasie' forces upon her, the death of a Rosa whose reactions may remain on a personal level, rather than as part of a broader duty, responsibility to a 'suffering land'.

The change from Conrad to Katya as auditor is marked by another episode of pain in which Rosa watches helplessly as a black man beats a donkey; the torture concentrates her sense of human cruelty. 'Not seeing the whip, I saw the infliction of pain broken away from the will that creates it; broken loose, a force existing of itself' (*BD* 208). She does not act because she realizes that to do so would be trading on her own whiteness, but also because the episode is an intimation of the deep structure of violence which guarantees her white authority. It is a trauma which produces a first reaction of bitter irony against the self: 'So a kind of vanity counted for more than feeling; I couldn't bear to see myself – her – Rosa Burger – as one of those whites who can care more for animals than people' (*BD* 210).

The confession marks Rosa as somebody trapped fast in a form of race consciousness. Rosa acknowledges this: 'After the donkey I couldn't stop myself. I don't know how to live in Lionel's country' (*BD* 210). It also describes a distinct leap forward in the consciousness which is shaped or constructed by the fiction. I use the awkward form of words in order to view Rosa as an artefact arising from Gordimer's imagination rather than as what the fiction pretends she is. The passage might be treated as a dramatization of the problem put to the white progressive by the writings and career of Steve Biko:

> no matter what a white man does, the colour of his skin – his passport to privilege – will always put him miles ahead of the black man. Thus in the ultimate analysis no white person can escape being part of the oppressor camp.
>
> There exists among men, because they are men, a solidarity through which each shares responsibility for every injustice and every wrong committed in the world, and especially for crimes that are committed in his presence or of which he cannot be ignorant.[21]

The Rosa who talks to Conrad attempts to live a sealed-off life in a South Africa distorted by cruelty. Such a Rosa might exist, but the inner knowledge which goes into this fictive consciousness is that of someone not educated from birth into an awareness of the cruel foundations of that society. A Helen Shaw, a Nadine Gordimer, might certainly have had to climb in this way, a way which involves repeated reconstructions of the self, prompted by many personal revelations. In the fiction the drowning of Conrad becomes a provisional conclusion to that aspect of awareness. Rosa realizes: 'I may have been talking to a dead man: only to myself' (*BD* 210). But the whole thrust of the discourse also touches another stage in the continuous reawakening to the responsibilities of art which sustains and refreshes Gordimer's work.

Life with Katya, then, becomes a further stage in the realization of the limitations bred into a 'Rosa'. Rosa sets out the experiment in these terms:

> I wanted to know how to defect from him. The former Katya has managed to be able to write to me that he was a great man, and yet decide 'there's a whole world' outside what he lived for, what life with him would have been. (*BD* 264)

There is a substantiality to that world which is expressed in part by Rosa's affair with Bernard Chabalier, an intellectual who is working on the influence of the *pieds-noirs* in French life and culture. The subject has its irony: Rosa, the Afrikaner girl, can never 'return' to Europe as the *pieds-noirs* did from Algeria. Europe, and Chabalier, can only be an exile from Lionel Burger and Noel de Witt. The role of Chabalier is once more expressed in contraries. His Mediterranean sensuousness and physicality are in themselves fulfilling to a degree. Addressing Katya, Rosa speaks of her 'French' self, in terms which suggest the cost as well as the ease, as 'a young woman in perfect lassitude and carelessness of sensuality'. She reports Bernard comparing his role to that of Noel de Witt: 'It has nothing to do with passion that had to be learned to deceive prison warders; and you're no real revolutionary waiting to decode my lovey-dovey as I dutifully report it' (*BD* 279).

There is the growing awareness of something in Rosa which goes beyond the lotos-eater's life of a Mediterranean paradise and Bernard Chabalier's arms. It is something which Katya is particularly able to see through her own knowledge of Lionel. She looks at Rosa, remembering,

> under an attention beyond desire, a passion beyond theirs on the bed, the passion-beyond-passion, like the passion of God, although for him there was no such concept: he was on his own; a frightening being . . . (*BD* 284)

Here Gordimer reveals one of the strongest motivations of the novel – a sense of the strangeness, intensity, and dedication of the revolutionary. Katya, and Gordimer too, are obliged to use the language of religion to express Lionel's personality, while recognizing that he would reject such language. The puzzlement signalled by this surfaces again in a sense of the deviousness which goes with the personal warmth and the forceful ideals. Chabalier is sensitive to a most complex pattern, and a subtle distance behind the close-ness, in Rosa's body, recalling as it does (for whom? not for Chabalier, directly)

> the touch line of her father's chest, warm and sounding with the beat of his heart, in chlorinated water. Her eyes (the colour of light, creating unease; Boer eyes, *pied-noir* eyes?) – moved above his head among trees, passers-by and – quick glance down – in a private motivation of inner vision as alert and dissimulating as the gaze her mother had been equally unaware of, looking up to see the daughter coming slowly over the gravel from the visit to her 'fiancé' in prison. (*BD* 290)

In the near-overloading of the prose at this point one may glimpse a great effort, not just on the part of a fictional Chabalier, but also on the part of the artist, to grasp the elusive. If Burger represents a security which Rosa inherits, living beyond her brother's drowning and her father's dying im-prisoned, it is a submarine depth of a kind that can be possessed only by those who continually risk drowning.

Nadine Gordimer is far too subtle a novelist to be unaware of the problems implicit in her fiction. There is a sense in which the whole fiction is designed to point out of itself, out of the whole protocol of European fiction, to a historical reality which finally engulfs it. In this sense the reproduction of the Soweto Students Representative Council leaflet (*BD* 346-7) is the section upon which the whole book pivots, together with a brief reminder on the succeeding page of Rosa Luxemburg: 'The real Rosa believed the real revolutionary initiative was to come from the people; you named me for that?' (*BD* 348). The choice of this dictum is a significant way of placing the unreal Rosa. Rosa Luxemburg failed in her initial objective of the creation of a workers' state in Germany. The 'heroes' of the South African revolution have so far failed if this narrow definition of aims is the one that must be adopted. Rosa attributes the knowledge to her father, quoting Lenin, once again pointing out of the fiction to history:

> You knew it couldn't be; *a change in the objective conditions of the struggle sensed sooner than the leaders did*. Lenin knew; the way it happened after the 1905 revolution: *as is always the case, practice marched ahead of theory*. (*BD* 348)

The question that is raised is a tediously familiar one for the white progressive in a black society: what does this leave for a 'Rosa', real or fictional, to do?[22] As it is presented here, it seems to provide a choice between being a leader, adept in theory but in practice unable to initiate, or one of the people, who sense the practical conclusion without a need to know the theory. And, if this is the choice, it seems unlikely that the European can either be fully part of 'the people', or be effective as a leader.

There is a kind of answer given in the text. Rosa reflects on what she has done, and what her father's colleagues in the liberation movement expect of her still:

> The course of action I have duly fulfilled, with consequences for me some of which were self-evident, foreseen and accepted, just as theirs were, is part of a continuing process. It is complete only for Lionel Burger; he has done all he had to do and that, in his case, happened to imply a death in prison as part of the process. It does not occur to them that it could be complete for themselves, for me. (*BD* 113)[23]

It is an expansion of a dictum Gordimer has already used – 'Nobody can defect.' The problem for Rosa is, at root, not the choice between a personal life and a public duty, or between theory and practice. It is the relationship sought and achieved between the individual and the process, and through this the discovery of a condition in which theory and practice are at one.

July's People (1981) might be described, in a loose sense, as an apocalyptic novel, in that it deals with a future of terrifying changes. But there is a more restricted sense in which the term might apply. It deals with a revelation of the unknown. It is a strenuous attempt to deal with the area of blindness which lies behind the experience of the 'first world'. It is set in a revolutionary future, in which the cities of South Africa are battlegrounds for black revolutionaries supporteld by Cuban advisers against white South Africans and mercenaries. Bam and Maureen Smales and their three children are given temporary refuge in an African village by their servant, whom they call July.

The Smales family are 'liberals', accepting the usual enlightened doctrines, and they treat July with what passes for generosity. Their attempt to cope with life in the kind of hut which is normal for a rural community of Africans, without electricity or piped water supply, supermarkets, baths, and all the rest, makes them an uncomfortable family of Crusoes. But Defoe's Crusoe, deprived of the benefits of society, sets about providing substitutes. His isolation is filled by a busy competence which a society of traders and businessmen might admire. He adopts Friday with the confidence that he can give Friday the two most necessary things – trousers and a God.

But if July is a 'Friday', he is one who offers the Smales an established context – the life of the majority. Gordimer uses the anomalies, not just to write about survival, but to map the changing relationships, the understandings and the failures of understanding between the races on which 'normal' white life is built. This revelation of the unknown is what gives the novel its apocalyptic character. Gordimer creates a denseness of texture, verbal and emotional, without linguistic self-indulgence. I'll have to gesture towards the beginning and ending to illustrate. The epigraph is from Gramsci's *Prison Notebooks*:[24] 'The old is dying and the new cannot be born; in this interregnum there arises a great diversity of morbid symptoms.' The epigraph might be taken as a reference to the fictive future of the novel. It might also be taken as referring to the actual present in which it was written, the South Africa of the very early 1980s. But beyond these two possibilities, the epigraph can be taken as a way of placing the discourse of the novel, and the actual world to which it refers, in the context of a Gramscian view of history and society. The point would take more space to develop than I have here. But one indication is the way in which the last words, describing Maureen Smales running towards the helicopter which offers her return to a 'safe' white society, draw the contrast between survival and responsibility:

> She runs: trusting herself with all the suppressed trust of a lifetime, alert, like a solitary animal at the season when animals neither seek a mate nor take care of young, existing only for their lone survival, the enemy of all that would make claims of responsibility. She can still hear the beat, beyond those trees and those, and she runs towards it. She runs. (*JP* 160)[25]

A Sport of Nature has a curious relationship with *Burger's Daughter*. As in the earlier novel, history is woven, intertextually, into the narrative, the ANC and the PAC, Nelson Mandela and Verwoerd, Sharpeville and the Rivonia trial entering into the discourse without any sense of dislocation. Rosa Burger herself is mentioned (*SN* 33) rather in the same way, giving an extra sinew to the interrelations of texture and signification.

If *Burger's Daughter* attempts to define one kind of heroism, the career of Hillela (complemented by that of Sasha, her cousin) essays an alternative. Rosa Burger swings out from the centre, discovers that nobody can defect, and returns by centripetal attraction to her father's cell. Hillela, in her centrifugal energy, in her generous, spontaneous way travelling the continent and the world, is no less defined by a centre. Rosa's name indicates the power of an inheritance to hold, even in the discovery of freedom – the vision of a dead German revolutionary, the integrity of the Afrikaner *volk*, the civic responsibility of a citizen – and her father's image shadows her whole career. Hillela's name, with its recollection of a liberating and humanizing strain in Jewish thought, is no less a recognition of inheritance, but it is one which opens the way to rediscovery. Rosa Burger is a thoroughbred, Hillela a 'sport of nature' – the epigraph cites the *Oxford English Dictionary*: 'a spontaneous mutation, a new variety produced in this way'. *A Sport of Nature* is buoyed along by a note of celebration, the sense that history renews itself all the time, thriving upon freedom of imagination, whereas *Burger's Daughter* is never far from elegy, from the sense that history (or family as vehicle for history) may confine or entrap. A note by Sasha points the implications of the title:

> *Instinct is utopian. Emotion is utopian. But reformers can't imagine* any other way. *They want to adapt what is.* . . . *It will take another kind of being to stay on, here. A new white person. Not us. The chance is a wild chance – like falling in love.* (SN 217-18)[26]

Hillela's relationships with her own family provide in their several ways the measure of how far she travels politically (instinctively, emotionally) from even the most enlightened elements of her own society. Just before Sasha writes the note above, Pauline, the aunt of progressive views, is described: she 'lifted her head, two streaks of grey, now, at the hair-line, like Mosaic horns, to challenge' (*SN* 217). The originality of Hillela's rabbinical near-namesake is in the paring away of the Mosaic doctrine, with all its negative injunctions, to a golden singularity. Apart from Sasha (the cousin with whom she has an early incestuous affair) it is only Ruthie, her mother, whom she meets in Angola after twenty-nine years of separation, who can understand the golden simplicity of Hillela which makes her a sport of nature.

Burger's Daughter addresses the problems presented by the Black Consciousness movement. There is a sense in which it doesn't answer them. Steve Biko asks himself the question whether he is against integration, and answers that if integration means 'a breakthrough into white society by blacks', yes, he is against it, and against the idea that white leaders are a *sine qua non* for progress. If on the other hand integration means 'free participation by all members of a society, catering for the full expression of the self',[27] he is in favour. In a letter written in his prison cell, Sasha records his perception that *'Even the white communists, people like Fischer and Lionel Burger, hadn't recognized quite that degree of initiative in blacks, before, they'd always at least told blacks how they thought it could be done'* (SN 371). The coupling of the historical and fictional figures once again signals the degree to which *A Sport of Nature* deconstructs and reconstructs the argument of *Burger's Daughter*, answering to the way in which black politics have re-formed white; it isn't that Bram Fischer and his fictional counterpart couldn't have integrated into the kind of society and culture which is intended by Black Consciousness, they weren't free to take the chance, history hadn't reached that beachhead of imagination. Hillela becomes an essay in defining such a freedom, as it might emerge, still against long odds, in a white South African now.

Once again the shoreline, with its complex connotations, is important in the structural geography of the work. The first station in her journey away from the involutions of white society in South Africa is Tamarisk Beach, the meeting place, and sometimes the home, for political outcasts. Once again the place signifies a marginality, but now it is no longer the marginality of the self-indulgent white playing in the surf with her back turned on an indecipherable continent. The margins are those of a beachhead for transition, for change from one state into another. In exile, Hillela is in a chrysalid state from which she emerges, eventually, as the widow of Whaila Kgosana, a black revolutionary, and mother of Nomzamo, named after Nomzamo (Winnie) Mandela.

The state which precedes the transition is defined, once again, by family. Pauline finds that the only advice to be got out of Black Consciousness was 'Work to change your own people, not us.' She refuses out of a 'vanity that would accept black rejection only as some schism within the central movement towards liberation' (*SN* 323) and they leave Africa for London, while Hillela becomes more and more deeply involved in the life of black Africa. On the other hand Sasha stays, works for black trade unions, and in doing so defines a route for action which remains real in its effectiveness, though not new. '*It was done before we were born or when we were little kids by people whose names I've learned*' (*SN* 350), and he ends up in a detention cell, with a bible and a sanitary bucket, like Rosa Burger, like her with a sense that white roles have changed, but perhaps perceiving that change in a different way. There's a sense of tentative complementarities of role here, in the search for an emerging identity.

Gordimer's fiction steadily moves away from chronicle, with its dependence upon actual historical event, to prophecy, the attempt to capture and direct a future. A leap of imagination begins to border upon dabbling in magic. There's a simplicity about the rhetoric which sets *A Sport of Nature* apart from *The Conservationist* or *Burger's Daughter*, with their profound ironies. The technique – omniscient author, third person, past tense, written in an undeclared time – has that reassuring conventionality which allows rapid unobstructed narrative and absence of risk, in sympathy with the heroine. It's an easy ride of a kind we are denied with Rosa Burger, Mehring, Liz Van den Sandt, or even Colonel Bray. And it ends, with the patness of a fable, with Hillela, now wife of the black chairman of the OAU, present at the ceremony which transfers power from the Republic of South Africa to the new black state – Azania? – it isn't given a name. The picaresque allows such simplicities and such celebrations; for once in a while Gordimer permits a happy ending. It is precisely, I suppose, *because* the discourse depends upon the renunciation, on behalf of the white population, of the power and the glory, that in this one work she can avert the instinct for tragedy.

14

André Brink

The first time I set foot in South Africa, nearly thirty years ago, was in Cape Town, and one of the first things we did was to go to the cinema to see a Soviet Russian version of *Othello* (Sergei Bondartchuk, 1955). Our curiosity (which seems, in retrospect, deplorable) was gratified. The first embrace of Othello and Desdemona was greeted by shouts of disapproval. At least one person was asked to leave the cinema. This was the first time I had occasion to think seriously about the political and social power of art in a divided land. I am not sure to this day how to assess that power. But I am sure there is something odd when Bondartchuk, Olivier, or Welles can play Othello, but not John Matshikiza, John Kani, or Alton Kumalo.[1]

Theatre in South Africa has changed in the intervening years. There is a flourishing black theatre now, which often works under appalling difficulties. Some of the disadvantages may be turned to advantage. Grotowski's concept of a 'poor theatre', which divests itself of any but the simplest properties to concentrate on the vital relationship between actor and spectator, is both necessary and liberating in the new wave of South African drama.[2] The tensions of South Africa urge this theatre to become, in the sense that Artaud meant it, a 'theatre of cruelty' too.[3] It draws upon deep reserves of pain and anxiety, reaching the endemic, the metaphoric, state of plague of which Artaud wrote, encompassing actor and spectator in a community of enactment and dis-ease. Brink's *Looking on Darkness*[4] addressed these problems at a time when the flowering of this theatre was only just beginning.

Joseph Malan, the central figure in the narrative, is a 'coloured' actor. The South African system of race categorization is absurd. The concept of 'white' or 'European' has enough problems. Using biochemical tests E. D. du Toit has established that an average of more than 7 per cent of the genetic material in 'white' South Africans in general could come from no other source than 'non-white' ancestors.[5] South African law retreats into subjective and social criteria for its 'definitions', so that a 'white' person becomes someone who: 'a. In appearance obviously is a white person and who is not generally accepted as a Coloured person; or b. Is generally accepted as a white person and is not in appearance obviously not a white person.'[6] The classifications 'Bantu' and 'Asiatic' are also fraught with difficulties: for instance 'Asian' covers the descendants of Indian and Chinese indentured labourers, but *not* the descendants of workers imported from Indonesia, often called Cape Malay (classified Coloured) and *not* Jews (classified White). Visiting Japanese businessmen are 'White' too.

So we come to the 'Coloureds'. Take the whole population of South Africa, deduct all those you have decided to call 'White', 'Bantu', or 'Asian'. 'Coloured' is what remains. Like all other human groups the group carries a variety of genetic materials. It is sometimes said that they are the only group which could be considered to be uniquely native to South Africa. The statement means very little. Every individual in South Africa, of whatever classification, would probably have to be described as of 'mixed race' *if* one could in the first place devise a stable enough definition of race to know what it is to 'mix' race. We might be on slightly safer ground if we talk about difference in culture.

But the concept of 'Coloured' is so dependent upon arbitrary political decisions, restrictive social practices, and economic factors that it is even more difficult to make generalizations about the cultural identity of the group than it is to make such generalizations about 'European', 'Bantu', or 'Asiatic'. The group is defined simply in terms of what it is not, and that causes endless (and ultimately unnecessary) difficulties in saying what it is. However, the categorization distorts the lives and opportunities of the people who are so classified.

When Brink writes in the persona of Joseph Malan, a 'Coloured' actor, his attitudes are informed by the knowledge of a common culture, shared, or partially shared, between 'white' and 'coloured' speakers of Afrikaans. Miraculously, out of the genocide and the barbarous destruction of cultures, a real cultural vitality and originality has developed in the Coloured community. It has contributed massively, and in a way which often goes unrecognized, to 'white' culture. There have always been 'Whites', particularly in the Cape Province, who recognize this closeness with affection. But, more often than not the white Afrikaner is disbarred by his own heritage from any attempt at imaginative understanding of the group which is so close to his own, and which has been so decisive in his own history and culture.

Brink is consciously using the narrative in *Looking on Darkness* as a means of making good this lack. But Brink creates a cultural life for Joseph Malan which is rich in the creative imagination of Europe. Shakespeare, Cervantes, St John of the Cross, Antonin Artaud, Beckett, Brecht, Camus, Michelangelo, Aristophanes and Sophocles, Calderón, Molière, and Dürrenmatt, fleck the narrative and enter the structure of feeling. This aspect of the novel is a reflection of Brink's involvement in the spirit of the *Sestigers*, a group of Afrikaner writers of the 1960s, whose works, in his own words, attempted to free Afrikaans fiction

> from its colonial restraints by introducing trends of thought and technique then in vogue in Europe and by breaking down taboos in the field of religion, ethics, sex and even narrative technique.[7]

Elsewhere Brink compares the work of the *Sestigers* to that of the Russian dissidents, remarking that 'through their resistance to traditional pressures within their puritanical society and their revolt against obsolescence in letters and ethics, the impact of their renewal went far beyond the frontiers of literature'.[8]

There is no difficulty in believing that a Coloured actor like Joseph Malan could share that excitement. But there is a subtle rhetorical point smuggled in by the part these cultural aspirations play in the argument. They encourage the reader to see Malan's intelligence and sensitivity in terms of his grasp of European culture. Brink runs the danger of making Malan the channel through which European discoveries may be made relevant to the life of the Coloured community, rather than suggesting the way in which the Coloured community, or Joseph Malan himself, might add something distinctive to the culture of the world.

Each time the jazz pianist Abdullah Ibrahim (Dollar Brand) plays he adds something distinctively African, South African, Capetonian, to the continual re-emergence of jazz, that international art. Like jazz, the art of the actor is performative.[9] But what Joseph Malan performs is almost always 'based on' Shakespeare, Calderón, Aristophanes, or whatnot. 'Based on' is the escape clause. We are given to believe that the plays are adapted to a culture and an audience. But we cannot observe the result, and are given little guidance in what it might be. Some allusion is made to the ideas of European thinkers, such as Artaud, Brecht, and Grotowski; at other times the dramatic experience is hinted at by reference to the long history of drama and its functions in European society. Malan speaks of the way his company altered Calderón and Molière in adaptation:

> it was necessary for the *biblia pauperum* we wanted our theatre to be. So we tried to change it into what it might have been if the actors of the *commedia dell'arte* had lived in Cape Town today, and if they'd been Coloured like us: an exuberant musical with sharp but playful comments on the political scene. (*LD* 238)

The prescription for a theatre is interesting, but it's difficult to erase the suspicion that it is parasitic. Malan is made to found his strategies on ancient or modern solutions which have been tested in a European centre of cultural power – the condescension of the Catholic church to the illiterate poor implicit in *biblia pauperum*, or the stylized convention given life by a peculiar experience of history and society in *commedia dell'arte*.

Brink does everything he can to give some notion of the complex circumstances which have formed Malan's identity. Section Two of the novel describes Joseph's family history at length; Section Three is devoted to Joseph's education in Africa and Europe; it is all an honest and determined effort to describe the waste of human abilities in a racist history. The result is shocking and truthful. But, like *Cry, the Beloved Country*, or 'Hunger', it is a typological truth, a rehearsal of rhetorical securities.

The *Sestiger* spirit demanded a transvaluation of all values in the Afrikaner community. Brink remarks that after Sharpeville 'Everything I had taken for granted had to be re-examined: tribal customs and taboos, religion, relationships with groups and individuals and with the country itself, ideas, a view of history, plans for the future.'[10] But the first product of that reassessment for Brink, *The Ambassador* (*Die Ambassadeur*, 1963), reveals something about the deep thrust of feeling behind much of Brink's writing. It certainly addresses 'tribal customs and taboos, religion, relationships with groups and individuals and with the country itself', but it does so within the boundaries set by a personal morality. What the novel really explores is the revelatory effect of an unconventional sexual relationship upon the central character, Paul van Heerden, the South African Ambassador to France. This affair contradicts the role and personality expected or required of him by his office, his nation, his society, his culture, but is presented as liberating something more genuine within himself. If there is rebellion here, it is romantic rebellion, and, even when Brink is self-consciously wary of it, his habit of mind is fixed in a romantic mode.

Technically, *Looking on Darkness* is simple. The device of the murder trial followed by the condemned man's autobiographical apologia is not new. At the centre of things is another unorthodox romantic relationship, between Joseph and the English girl whom he finally kills, Jessica. Strangely, many Afrikaans-speaking readers would be willing secretly to accept such a love affair as a valid theme for literature, even at the same time as supporting legal measures to punish miscegenation and to ban books which deal with it sympathetically.

Both *Looking on Darkness* and *An Instant in the Wind* (1976) become a kind of political pornography if one looks at the matter from the state's point of view; the effect of both books upon a naïve reader is to disassemble the public ideology, at least for the extent of the fiction, by fostering a subversive private sentiment. The strategy works by shame and conflict: shame and guilt at the abandonment of the publicly held view of racial and sexual propriety (often justified by an appeal to 'natural' difference) enter into conflict with shame at the suppression of 'natural' affinity between humans. Once again it is a confusing struggle of Eros and Thanatos for possession of the imagination.

The story of *An Instant in the Wind* is summarized on the end cover of its British edition in a way which is designed to catch an unsophisticated lover of romantic fiction:

> A white woman and a black man are stranded in the wilderness of the South African interior. She is an educated woman, totally helpless in the wilds. He is a runaway slave, the lowest of the low in society's eyes.
>
> They know only each other . . . and a long trek back to civilization.

The unsophisticated reader would not be disappointed, except, possibly, by Brink's frankness about sexuality. But beneath the self-indulgence of some of the writing there are reflections of violence, reminiscences which are there not for their own sake, but which recall a texture of history which is shared by Adam, the coloured man, and Elisabeth, the white woman, as it is shared by Brink and his South African readers. Awe and puzzlement, guilt and pride in a complex past is implicit in Afrikaner culture.

The book shares some of the aspiration towards epic or saga of naïve South African fiction, dwelling, as that does, on the heroism of the few adventuring into a dangerous land. But instead of the heroic band of white settlers repelling the black marauders with supreme courage and competence, it creates a sentimental myth of a very different kind. Erik Alexis Larssen, collecting specimens for the great taxonomist Linnaeus, and thus a representative of the highly literate, scientific competence of Europe, proves to be an incompetent coward on the veld. Adam Mantoor, the illiterate coloured runaway slave, who has spent five years acquiring the survival skills of the Khoikhoi, proves to be a more than admirable Crichton, becoming Elisabeth Larssen's protector, defender, and then her lover. In the romance of the fiction his skills are complemented by his vigorous sexuality, once more in contrast to Larssen.

Brink's affection for the land and fascination with its history shows through in lovingly rich descriptions of flora and fauna, and also in harrowing accounts of journeys on foot through arid regions. But the attempt to reconstruct the lost culture and society of the Khoikhoi suffers from the scarcity of the record. This matters, since, for all his *sestiger* interest in narrative experiments, Brink remains a realist, even a naturalist. His attempts at realism expose the insecurities and the ironies of the writer's productive activity more clearly than many a self-conscious post-modernist drawing attention to the finger on the keyboard, the mind observing itself in literary labour.

The effect may not be intended, but it is appropriate enough in a book which concerns itself with meetings between a literate, conforming society and an unlettered humanity. Interpenetrating the text there is the pastoral tradition, in which the literate writer sees himself, and his society, as lacking something, and the unlettered – the shepherds, the pastoralists, the Khoikhoi and Adam – as more capable of spontaneity and genuine freedom, capable of teaching the literate something of value. It's rather like Marlow's repeated talk about blacks being as natural and true as the surf.

Thus Adam teaches Elisabeth to live more fully, even though she can never completely resign herself to Adam's version of freedom. Their mutual knowledge is consummated only when she learns to call him by his Khoikhoi, name, Aob, and yet it is subverted by her compulsion to leave Paradise, to return to 'civilization', to the Cape. The loss of Paradise leads to Adam's – Aob's – death. Brink laconically records the transaction – 'in March 1751 he was flogged (three rixdollars) and strangled (six rixdollars)'. So Brink, the literate man, the writer, the heir to a European, Christian tradition, the Romantic, structures his nostalgia for a lost, unlettered spontaneity by means of a religious myth and literary convention, subtexts which we, his readers, can share in the common transmission of *scriptures*.

An Instant in the Wind is, perhaps, almost as deeply untrue as the multitude of novels written about the Great Trek. At times it is almost as badly written:

> With narrowed eyes and a strange, implacable smile he comes nearer. The water glides from his hips. He is lean, angular, but lithe, with a sort of cat-like grace, his body rippling with thin, tight, fierce muscles . . . she sees, from behind, across the muscles of his back, across his buttocks and his thighs, the terrible black-purple network of scars and swollen, knotted stripes.
>
> She is aware of panting through half-open lips.
>
> 'Savage!' she hisses. (*IW* 86-7)[11]

Such writing trades in dreams, and the persistent use of the drama of the present tense encourages Brink to throw away much of his customary fastidiousness in language. But at least Brink is re-dreaming the dream, attempting to put romanticism back again where it started, at the service of a serious idea of human integrity enfolded by a yet larger idea of 'natural' integrity. That may, for some readers in the last quarter of the twentieth century, be a difficult vision to take seriously. It may be seen, too, as a trading on repressed fantasies about race and sexuality which don't help to make the world clearer. But a faulty sentiment may be the most efficient point of entry for a literary cat-burglar to introduce subversive doubt. The whole thing is a lie, but lies are sometimes the allies of truth.

Brink's next novel, *Rumours of Rain* (1978), shows a high degree of consciousness of his own instinctive romanticism, to the degree that it might be read as a rather complex apologia for the romantic spirit as a life-giving thing in the context of white South Africa after Soweto. Soweto is a text concealed beneath the text, giving the narrator's changing attitudes to the process of memory and the act of writing the urgency of a discovery which goes beyond the merely personal.

Brink had shown already, in *Die Ambassadeur*, a considerable skill in the ironic use of a first-person narrative. Here he chooses as his vehicle for narrative Martin Mynhardt, a conscious anti-romantic, but one whose affections are fully engaged by the romantics who surround him, Bernard Franken, Bea Fiorini, and his own son Louis. Mynhardt is an Afrikaner businessman, one of the new breed which has completed the transit from a rural community obsessed by its own past, by its religion, by its repressive values, by its love of the land and its need for racial domination. But in Martin Mynhardt there is nothing to replace this potent complex of emotions except a thin, loveless, self-seeking pragmatism. Like Swift in *A Modest Proposal*, Brink appears at times to be using his ironic skills to give plausibility to an argument which is enlightened, if one accepts the heartless basic premisses. Mynhardt argues the value of channelling money into the Homelands with the hope of creating opportunities for financial independence there. He co-operates with plans for extending the boundaries of the Homelands, and takes advantage of ministerial corruption to make money from selling the family farm, though this uproots and distresses his mother and breaks a link which has given unity to his family for generations.

Swift chooses to satirize a real attitude by taking it to a manifestly intolerable conclusion. Brink chooses to dwell on the ironies of a view which is actually held by some of the most 'progressive' or *verligte* members of a community. As a result Brink is obliged to 'place' Mynhardt's morality, and his world-view, by setting him against other characters, and by observing his failure to engage with them, to understand their meanings.

Martin, writing in the characterless neutrality of a London hotel room, describes the weekend in which he travelled to the family farm to persuade his mother to give up the family property. The reader becomes increasingly aware that his anxiety in searching for the meaning of that weekend, his sense of its decisive nature, is bound up with his pride in the abandonment of romantic sentiment. Once, he says, he might have described it as ' "the last weekend before the end of the familiar world", or some equally melodramatic phrase. But I have shed my romanticism long ago and even my sense of humour is, according to Bea, no more than the positive side of my cynicism' (*RR* 12-13).[12]

Martin returns frequently to his early ambitions as a writer, discovering with astonishment that he may be, after all, writing the novel he had once wanted to. Meaning emerges in the self-conscious act, the present tense of writing, rather than in a recitation of memory. In the progress from 'Memo' (the businessman's brisk heading for the first section of this personal history) to the end, the aspiration of the narrative progressively moves from the recording of the fact to the imaginative re-creation of it. And as Mynhardt moves back into this Coleridgean view of truth, we are urged to believe that the level of understanding becomes greater.

Just before he sets out on the 'apocalyptic' journey Martin has attended the latter part of the trial of his friend Bernard Franken, who is found guilty of terrorist activities. Extracts from Franken's address to the court punctuate the first part of the narrative and form a powerful and dignified defence of an Afrikaner's participation in the liberation movement. This is no *roman à clef*, but there is an intended relationship between Franken and two prominent Afrikaner dissidents.

Breyten Breytenbach, another member of the *Sestiger* group, entered South Africa illegally under an assumed name in 1975, was brought to trial in extraordinary circumstances, and sentenced to nine years in gaol. In June 1977 he was tried again on charges which were shown to be ridiculous, and dismissed with a nominal fine for technical misdemeanours. Breytenbach's clandestine revolutionary organization, Okhela, bears more than a passing resemblance to Bernard Franken's 'Inkululeko' in its ideology and aims.

Bram Fischer is even more clearly in Brink's mind as he writes. His trial in 1964 bears many similarities to Bernard Franken's. There are differences.

Fischer was a member of the Communist Party, an organization which always sought a trans-racial, trans-cultural, international identity. Breytenbach and 'Franken', by contrast, set up organizations whose aims are defined in terms of Afrikaner consciousness and history. In Fischer's address to the jury he said:

> I am on trial for my political beliefs and the conduct to which those beliefs drove me. The charges arise from my being a member of the Communist Party . . . two courses were open to me. I could confess and plead for mercy or explain my belief and my activities. If I were to ask for forgiveness I would be betraying my cause. I believe that I was right and I will explain my views to the court.

Fischer's address has become a model which has inspired many who have been on trial for similar offences in South Africa. The beginning of Franken's speech is a free translation from Fischer's Afrikaans which omits reference to Communism:

> *When a man is on trial for his political beliefs and actions, two courses are open to him. He can either confess his transgressions and plead for mercy or he can justify his beliefs and explain why he acted as he did. Were I to ask forgiveness today I would betray my cause and my convictions, for I believe that what I did was right. (RR 64)*

Brink has written that 'in the evolution of my own ethical and political thinking his statement marked a turning point, a decisive moment.'[13] Fischer adroitly quoted from an address by Paul Kruger in 1881, which is inscribed at the base of the statue of Kruger in Church Square in Pretoria (right in front of the Court). So does Franken – Brink's translation is as follows:

> *With confidence we expose our cause to the whole world. Whether we triumph or die: freedom will rise in Africa like the sun from the morning clouds. (RR 136)*

Fischer was imprisoned almost until the end of his painful terminal sickness, despite the appeals of sympathizers throughout the world, and Helen Joseph expresses the effect of that death:

> So passed a great and loving man, who had sacrificed his own freedom for the freedom of others. At his memorial meeting in Johannesburg, I paid my final tribute to the man I had known and admired so much, in the last words of Julius Fučik, a Czech political martyr, 'People, I have loved you.' Bram had had the gift of love.[14]

Possibly the most distressing aspect of Fischer's trial for members of the liberation movement was the role of Pieter Beyleveld. Another Afrikaner and long-established member of the Communist Party, he was a genial and trusted man and President of the Congress of Democrats. No one has adequately explained why, after a short detention, he agreed to appear as state witness against Fischer. Similarly, the shadow of treachery hangs over Mynhardt in his failure to extend sanctuary to Franken: his behaviour in thus ensuring the arrest of his friend is given a clearer, simpler history than any that could be imagined for Beyleveld, but the deep sorrow of the betrayed is caught well enough by Franken's words. At that moment Mynhardt does not recognize a Judas in himself: to betray love one must be capable of love, and Mynhardt, the ex-romantic, has lost that capability. He can therefore remain unsure of Bernard's meaning:

> *Perhaps my arrest could have been avoided at the time it happened. But it is so easy to misjudge a situation, or a trivial detail, or a friend.*
> (Was he looking up at me when he read those words? Had he noticed me in the audience? It must have been my imagination.) (*RR* 139)

The book is a continuing meditation upon the relationship between love and duty. Martin's intimations of personal love, and his failures in love, are mainly within his own white community – his friendships with Charlie Mofokeng and Welcome Nyaluza are sufficient to suggest that for Martin, such affection as he is able to admit isn't racially exclusive. Repeatedly Brink stresses the sustaining reserves of love in a traditional Afrikaner society. For instance his father-in-law, a stern Calvinist, is described: 'there was in him an essential and unmistakable humanity, a humility which couldn't but impress one. A man of love, one might call him' (*RR* 100). Martin takes issue with the old man over his conventional view of the guilt of Pilate, and defends Pilate with an argument founding notions of duty and justice in expediency:

> To my mind it is the action of a reasonable man who has a clear view of the demands of his time and who refuses to be influenced by irrational considerations. . . . I even find a measure of greatness in such a mind. (*RR* 100-1)

Brink uses Martin's cynicism as a stalking horse, but is subtle in communicating the sense of loss at the heart of the cynicism – a loss which is eloquently conveyed by the repeated dismissive reference to his early romanticism. It's strikingly conveyed by his reminiscences of earlier times with Bernard, in particular their impulsive, dangerous, romantic journey down the Orange River, in which the depth their relationship discovers has a tender homoerotic strain to it:

> The lean, brown, sinewy back in the canoe ahead of me, speeding into the rapids, the white waves splashing over his blonde head. . . . The sort of experience no philosophy can grasp or express . . . deeper than consciousness or conscience. (*RR* 127)

In the same way Martin looks for closeness with Louis, his son, but is disappointed – the rift has become too great after his son's war experiences in Angola. His relationships with women, too, lack this dimension, at least from the time of his first meetings with his wife Elise. In all this the more intimate sin of Judas becomes the dominant one, the sin of love's exhaustion and inversion, rather than the amoral poise of a Pilate. The point is brought home, perhaps with too heavy a rhetorical persistence, by Martin's repeated recourse to a boyhood memory of his Grandpa requiring him to remember and repeat some part of the Bible after the end of each reading. The stammering child can only remember '*And have not love*, Grandpa' (*RR* 191).

The most troublesome treachery for Martin is in his manipulating his mother to sell the farm. When Martin tells her the offered sum, 'She looked at me for a long time before she asked quietly: "And every man has his price?" ' (*RR* 196). In Martin selling the farm (and himself) he sells also his father, who is buried on the land, and all that his father represents, in his obsession with the history of the tribe. The elder Mynhardt's enthusiasms, even though they lead him into the Broederbond and the Ossewabrandwag, demand to be seen as anti-authoritarian idealism not too far from that of Bernard Franken. His father, Bernard, and the Afrikaner nation, become for Martin an enigma. When he has lost his glasses and everything is out of focus he comes across his father's grave and experiences a terrible isolation, 'I felt no emotion, nothing whatsoever. And even though I'd learned to eliminate emotion long ago, nevertheless I had expected to feel *something*, to come one step closer to the enigma of my father' (*RR* 206). The richness of the book (and though the moral rhetoric is sometimes repetitive and simplistic it is a rich book) is in its keen sense of the depth of the enigma, the consciousness and conscience of the Afrikaner seen from the inside, the sense of a society rooted in its own past, for good and ill.

The most remarkable evidence of the strain of romantic sentiment is a complex of images centred around Bea, the woman who fascinates Martin, though he uses her heartlessly. Her full name is Beatrice Fiorini, and the relationship with the Beatrice of *Vita Nuova* and *Divina Commedia* is very lightly veiled. She is closely linked with Bernard. His name might recall that of Bernard of Clairvaux, another respected teacher, who gained the title of *Doctor mellifluus*. The connection between Bea and Bernard is always alive in Martin's mind, as is the web of connections between these two and all those others he has failed to love – Louis, Charlie, Aunt Rienie, Elise, his parents, Reinette. Martin has 'based his survival' on the separation of all the elements of his life – by the end of his writing he finds that 'Now it was becoming more and more obvious that there were subtle undeniable links between them, threatening me' (*RR* 435).

Bea, a Catholic, a European, an Italian, persuades Martin to take her to the festival of Calvinist Afrikanerdom, the commemoration of the Day of the Covenant at the Voortrekker Monument. She believes that it will help her to understand him. And when they leave she says, 'You know, this is my idea of hell: exactly on the scale of this Monument and this festival' (*RR* 434). Brink's *sestiger* internationalism identifies a dark side to the Afrikaner spirit.

The network which has Bernard and Bea as its centre is his only link with a figurative eschatology of light.

The apocalyptic weekend of the narrative begins with Bea pleading with Martin to delay his visit to the farm. At the end of the narrative Martin reveals the events which have led up to Bea's phone call. Her plea for help has a reason, as Martin discovers when he returns to the news that violence has broken out in Soweto. Amongst those who have been arrested is Beatrice Fiorini; it is implicit that Beatrice anticipated her arrest, and turned to Martin to give her the help he has denied Bernard, but he refuses, travelling down to strike his sordid bargain over the family farm. At much the same time we are given the details of Martin's coronary, which he has referred to several times already. His heart attack came as he was having intercourse with Bea. The incident takes on a metaphorical force, to do with his failure to love, his lack of heart.

The essential point of the novel is reached in its last section, and it consists in the recognition by the writer of the meaning of what he has written:

> Everything I've recalled through my writing surrounds me and threatens me. It wasn't an 'intellectual exercise' after all, nor 'a form of mental massage'. All frontiers, all lines of demarcation, have been destroyed. (*RR* 445)

It is the new understanding of the interconnectedness of all the aspects of his life, the impossibility of all his attempted separations, which gives Martin access to the liberating image which ends the book. It is, however, ironically impossible to decide whether the Martin who writes understands it any better than the Martin he writes about. The coming of the rain which is rumoured in the title is bound in with images of suffering. It is a flood which carries the red earth away: 'streaming endlessly, red water as if the earth itself was crying, as if the earth was crying blood. *Nkosi sikelel'i Afrika*' (*RR* 446).

For that matter it is difficult to decide what Brink intends the ringing rhetoric to represent – how much it conveys the miserable desperation of Martin, how much the inevitability of the historical process. Perhaps it is both. The last words are from the anthem of the liberation movement, and can be translated 'God save Africa.' That is a sentiment which may express the culmination of the process of self-discovery which Martin is supposed to have undergone, but it is impossible to separate the words, *Nkosi sikelel'i Afrika*, from the struggle, the suffering, the aspirations of the black population of South Africa. Brink, in his account of the dilemma of the Afrikaner, does not do enough to earn the allusion to that dimension. It is a text which is too distant and too powerful to enter into the already complex contexture, though Brink gives notice that he recognizes the need to face the challenge. As it stands, the allusion is impertinent.

If *Rumours of Rain* is written in response to the shock-wave which Soweto created throughout the world, *A Dry White Season* (1979) derives much of its power from the under-text of the Biko affair. The finding of Magistrate

Prins was that Biko died as a result of brain injury complicated by renal failure sustained as a result of a 'scuffle in the Security Police offices in Port Elizabeth' and that 'on the available evidence the death cannot be attributed to any act or omission amounting to a criminal offense on the part of any person'.[15] Jackson reveals one of the ways in which Biko's injuries might have been caused. Moke Cekisane, secretary of the Black People's Convention in Port Elizabeth, was detained at the same time and place as Biko. When Jackson interviewed him after interrogation he had lost forty pounds, had acquired an uncontrollable tremor, and had become a chronic epileptic. He told Jackson that:

> the detainees had been handcuffed to a cement wall with their foreheads only a few inches from the surface. Electrodes had been attached to the back of their necks and current applied. The intermittent shocks had caused their heads to jerk forwards against the wall. The frequency of the shocks had been increased and had produced a trip-hammer effect, so that the foreheads smashed against the wall with great rapidity.[16]

Brink began *A Dry White Season* in 1976, set it aside, and returned to the book after the Biko affair, writing the greater part of the novel in 1978-9. It is an account of a very ordinary man, Ben du Toit, and his gradual involvement in the world of Secret Police and the South African legal system. Gordon Ngubene was a cleaner in the school where Ben taught, and Ben had taken a charitable interest in Gordon's son, Jonathan (his real name is Sipho). During the Soweto riots, the boy disappears, and, with the help of a black taxi-driver, Stanley Makhaya, Gordon begins to piece together some of the facts. Eventually it is learned that the boy has died 'of natural causes' during interrogation. The story would normally have ended there, but Gordon insists on the return of Sipho's body. He is told that the boy was shot dead during the riots a month before, and has already been buried. Gordon resigns from his job to concentrate on finding the truth, and dies after arrest and interrogation. As in the Biko case Gordon's terrible injuries, which are transparently caused by violent assaults, are explained away by the findings of the inquest, which decides that he committed suicide by hanging. Ben takes over the enquiry. His marriage is broken, he loses his job, he is ostracized by the white community and at last is killed in a hit-and-run 'accident' organized by the Special Branch.

Once again the structure of narrative is founded on a reference to the romanticism of the writer. We are given to understand that the narrative is put together after Ben's death by an old university friend, a writer of romantic fiction, using documents bequeathed by his subject. Of course he is as much a fiction as the events he relates. But, just as the fictional events contain echoes, deliberately placed, of the circumstances of innumerable deaths in detention, so the mode of narrative alludes to the writer and to the act of writing, to the complex ways in which fiction transmutes events.

In *Rumours of Rain* there's a glamour attached to the heroism of Bernard, and also of Bea, which contrasts with the sordid failures of Martin. In *A Dry White Season*, for much of the action, every effort is made to present Ben as humdrum, as little glamorous as possible, driven to challenge the foundations of the state and the assumptions of his society by a simple honesty. There is one fissure in this surface. Ben has a brief affair with Melanie Bruwer, and the instincts of the romantic story-teller pull the fictional narrator, and Brink himself, into a mystical celebration of love, a glimpse of transcendence which makes Melanie, perhaps, another Beatrice:

> The final consummation would be to break right through the senses and plunge into the darkness beyond, into that love of which our passion had been but the celebration and the token. *Behold thou art fair, my love.* (*DWS* 273)[17]

And this experience of love is linked to an ethic of commitment and risk: '*Once in one's life, just once, one should have enough faith in something to risk everything for it.*' The romanticism isn't defeated, but is placed in context by the outcome. Melanie is removed from the scene, her South African passport and permission to return to South Africa denied to her, and Ben is left to follow Sipho and Gordon, murdered by the agents of the state.

There's a new access of realism too, forced on Ben, on the narrator, on Brink, by the changing political climate. For much of its length the novel has a passing resemblance to Paton's *Cry, the Beloved Country*. It's tougher, but it recognizes compassion as the principal basis for personal action. Ben is a conventional, simple, old-fashioned man, changed by the pressure of circumstances. The blacks – Gordon and Emily particularly – are such that a liberal South African reader can have sympathy for them. They are *clients* of the good white man, and this means that the sympathetic white reader can be reassured that, in the last analysis, the power remains his.

But the ethic behind this has been overtaken by history, in particular by the Black Consciousness movement. The novel contains its own revision: Jonathan's younger brother refuses to see Ben and his kind as potential allies, and goes away to train with the revolutionaries across the border. And Stanley Makhaya tells Ben that he fears the reaction of his own people to his co-operation with Ben over this matter: 'my people are in a black mood. My children too. They speak a different language from you and me' (*DWS* 287-8). This angry, self-reliant mood, stimulated by the Black Consciousness movement and by Biko's death, led to the struggles between the 'Comrades' and the 'Fathers' in the middle 1980s, and also to extraordinary experiments in self-government in the townships which are now a matter of history. Brink builds conflict into the novel, an ideological shift of attention which throws what has gone before into the uncertainty of debate. The discourse concedes its own provisionality, its vulnerability to historical process.

A Chain of Voices (1982) is set in the hinterland of the Cape in 1824-5. It is about slavery, both in the narrower sense that it tells the story of an aborted rebellion of a handful of slaves, and in the wider sense that it refers unmistakably to the continuous rebellion of the majority in the 1970s and 1980s. The title of the work, *A Chain of Voices*, refers to the structuring technique of the book, in which the narrative proceeds through many voices, each of the persons involved contributing statements, some quite long, others very brief, in a chain which enables us to see the whole action from multiple points of view. The title has another relevance. It is analogous to Blake's 'mind-forg'd manacles' in the poem 'London', in that it refers to the way in which habits of thought and speech bind humanity in a more subtle and powerful way, permitting custom to force acquiescence, than the power of the law court or the gun.

In the Act of 1807 Great Britain had abolished the slave trade, though slavers continued to avoid the embargo for seventy or eighty years. In 1833 Britain abolished slavery in the Empire, though practices amounting to slavery continued in many British possessions. In 1806, during the Napoleonic Wars, Britain had annexed the Cape. The British record with regard to conditions of subject people in the Cape was mixed. Caledon's proclamation of 1809 introduced strict pass laws for Coloureds, made registration of labour contracts compulsory, and defined conditions under which wages could be withheld against goods supplied to a servant. Further proclamations of 1812 and 1819, providing regulations for apprenticeship of free Coloured children between the ages of 8 and 18, allowed such children to be employed without remuneration. Somerset's proclamation of 1818 provided for severe punishment for white indentured labourers who left their employers. On the other hand the introduction of Circuit Courts led to partial amelioration of conditions for slaves and servants. In 1826 Bourke appointed a registrar and guardian of slaves to control the worst excesses of slave owners, and in 1828 he formally ended legal discrimination against free persons.

The end of formal and legal slavery on 1 December 1834 led directly in 1836 to the Great Trek, in which disaffected Afrikaner farmers sought to preserve their freedom to enslave others. The novel is set in the period just before emancipation, and envisages a false dawn in which a slave named Galant rises up with others against the white masters. In this desperate enterprise they are encouraged by Joseph Campher, a white foreman from Brabant, a man who is enthused by the Napoleonic ideal, but who, in the final test, proves to be a traitor.

There's a sense in which the novel might be described as prophecy. By prophecy I do not simply point to the way in which the abortive slave rebellion might prefigure the township uprisings of the 1980s. The most important function of the Hebrew prophet was to explore and define the failings of the tribe, its duty to the deity and to itself, to criticize and warn the people of Israel. Thus, there is a sense in which Brink employs the past as a text to penetrate a sense of the present. That might equally be expressed by the reverse – that the reader is bidden to bring his sense of the present to this fable of the past.

The Afrikaner nation has always seen itself as a chosen people, isolated in a hostile world, fulfilling the word of God, with the Great Trek as the equivalent of Moses leading his people towards the Promised Land. The Bible accepts slavery as a necessary and inevitable part of society,[18] and the Hebrews bought and sold humans as chattels, flogged them and killed them despite legal restrictions, and used slave women freely as concubines. In this the difference between Hebrew and Afrikaner practices, or those of slave owners in the Americas, was not great.

Of the two van der Merwe brothers, Barend and Nicolaas, Nicolaas is the less rigid in his attitudes to slaves, but it is he who fails to escape death in the rebellion. Nicolaas propounds an argument which must have been used by kindly men every time the manumission of slaves or the independence of subject peoples has been proposed in any society, that they would be incapable of surviving freedom: 'They need us even more than we need them. . . . If you treat your slaves properly they'll never abandon you, not even if the law says they're free' (*CV* 226).[19]

But as he takes back Galant, recaptured after an attempt to escape into freedom, and they stumble into a fog, Nicolaas has a powerful intimation of the forces of history that are steadily eroding what is, for him, a profound principle, and with it a 'feeling of oppression', the sense of 'a frontier world shrinking around me, a natural freedom contracting', the sense that neither dependence nor independence can be one-sided, that neither master nor slave can survive 'without this subtle and subjugating bond approved by God' (*CV* 227-8).

Once again Nicolaas's anxiety might be an echo of the dilemma of the Afrikaner in the last years of the twentieth century, awaiting the inevitable implosion of his Divine Rights and duties. But there is little more to be gained from the stranger, Joseph Campher, suckled though he is on the post-revolutionary Napoleonic dream of Liberty, Equality, Fraternity. In the last analysis, the 'subtle and subjugating bond' (or, if you will, 'a chain of voices') holds him in thrall as well. Between the oppressors and the slaves he recognizes those paradoxical beings like himself, subversive idealists for whom the only possible victory is in a defeat, leaving the unattainable ideal intact, 'And that turned us into an abomination' (*CV* 414).

For Campher, the only possible outcome of bitter knowledge such as this is betrayal. For Galant, who comes to a similar revelation, the only possible outcome is violence – a violence which might, from the outside, seem senseless, but becomes an existential assertion. He reflects upon his failure: 'what we fought for still lives on, without beginning or end, like the mountains, like fire' (*CV* 491).

'Romantic' has many meanings, but it isn't abusing the word to apply it here. It doesn't, however, meet the case of the 1980s, that of the 'Comrades' in the townships, challenging high-velocity rifles with stones picked up from the road, children of 8 or 9 being arrested for 'intimidation' of armed policemen and soldiers and suffering torture and mutilation in gaol. Those who have the reckless courage of desperation don't often compare what they fight for with mountains or fire. And Galant's hour in the loft with his white childhood sweetheart doesn't begin to sound even like partial compensation for injuries.

Constrained as he is by his vivid awareness of the dilemma of the white, and particularly the Afrikaner who understands the wastefulness, absurdity, and cruelty of the doctrines by which the South African state maintains power, Brink turns again and again to the political fable. Art becomes a surrogate action, a dream of intervention, which carries within it its own hopelessness. It is precisely this problem which Brink makes central to what is in many ways his most satisfying work, *The Wall of the Plague* (1984), his latest as I write.

The title[20] indicates the way in which the novel offers to chronicle that area of darkness which is so often at the heart of European fictions of Africa, a darkness which is within the European's sensibility rather than in the continent that evokes it. The book is set in France, and, like *Rumours of Rain*, is woven around a journey in which the central character experiences a palimpsest of present and memories of the past. Andrea Malgas, a South African Coloured, is researching the background to a film projected by her white South African lover, Paul Joubert, on the subject of the Great Plague of the fourteenth century. The wall of the title was built in Provence in a futile attempt to exclude the plague, and is now ruined. She travels with a black, Mandla, a trade union activist who is forced to evade the attentions of the South African security services.

The structure is metaphorical. But the indirectness of the fable creates more space for the argument. The argument is, in any case, reflexive: it is about what the artist can or cannot do by the indirectness, the metaphorical habit of art. And it is about the relationships between art and the actual texture of lives lived in the 'plague', the pestilence which enfolds South African history and society and destroys it from within, explored in metaphorical parallel with the bubonic variety in fourteenth-century Europe.

The names of the characters are significant in the controlling pattern of metaphor. Andrea Malgas's first name associates her with André Brink, not as an identification but as analogy or as allusion to a reach of consciousness explored by the fiction. Her second name 'Malgas' makes other associations: '("I'm a Malgas. We're sea birds." Her father's pride: that the family name means "gannet".)' (*WP* 22).[21] The image of the wanderer returns again and again. So does that of the sea, and the capacity of the wanderer to dive into it from another medium, to inhabit different worlds serially or simultaneously: 'I immersed myself in the vast French interior as if it were a sea. Mental skindiving: that is the only description I can think of for my experience during those uncounted, unmarked days of aimless travelling' (*WP* 22). 'Mental skindiving' is equally a metaphor for what the writer does as he invents narrators to carry the fictional responsibility for his narrative, venturing into areas of alien experience, as if diving into a world which might destroy.

The relation between Andrea and André is complementary to another relation – that between Brink and Paul Joubert, the Afrikaner novelist. Like Brink, Joubert made his reputation in his first novel by attacking the prejudices of his own peoples; like Brink he has changed the medium of his writing from Afrikaans to English; like Brink he has a deep affinity for French culture. He resembles Brink physically, in dress and in mannerisms. But unlike Brink he has run out of steam as a novelist, and lives on the reputation of a film of his novel, *The Survivors*, whose success was due to its director, now dead. Joubert suffers his special version of the pestilence by retreating into an arid aesthetic, alienated from Africa in the comforting, civilized grasp of Europe. His name, Joubert, points to one of the mainsprings of the novel, his search for a past in Europe. Joubert is a Huguenot name, taken to the Cape with other Huguenot refugees in the seventeenth century. Paul's descent has been in refuge from persecution, from an ancient plague, just as his present seeks refuge from the sickness of a nation.

All that Paul finds of his family in Provence is one old man, who subsequently dies, and his name, Jaubert, weakens still further by its subtle skew the connection Paul craves. Paul is on the way to failure as an artist, but he remains an idealist – indeed it may be that his failure lies more than anything else in the enervating nature of that idealism. His first name hints at the nature of the idealism. At several points a pattern of reconciled dualism emerges as an expression of Paul's aspirations – of his delusions. Andrea, trying to enter into the ethic of Paul's writing, the myth he creates of a group of people who withdraw from the turbulence of the black death into a fortress to tell stories, like the characters of the *Decameron*, finds herself sympathizing with their withdrawal. It is like her own, or Paul's, escape from the plague of South Africa to discover Paul's

> 'reassuring patterns of the eternal complements: heaven and earth, good and evil, light and dark, man and woman, body and soul – '. And yet I could not help wondering . . . whether this was really what Paul had meant to write. Was he being wholly true to his own life, or was there wishful thinking in it? (*WP* 118)

Paul's comforting ethic of complementarity has a European rather than an African ring to it, and its true roots are perhaps hinted at more strongly in Mandla's shrewd comment on a bas-relief on the Roman triumphal arch in Carpentras. It shows two figures, perhaps a Roman officer and a barbarian prisoner, it isn't clear. Mandla comments, shrewdly, 'What do we have here? Master and servant? Or Christian and Jew? Or Catholic and Huguenot? Or White and Black? . . . Have you noticed the way they always come in pairs? The one can't do without the other' (*WP* 291).

Mandla sees, not reassurance and complementarity, but duress and division. But his phrasing of it recalls most powerfully the rhetoric of Paul's namesake, another traveller, another man who bears an ambiguous relationship to his native culture, Paul of Tarsus: 'There is neither Jew nor Greek, there is neither bond nor free, there is neither male nor female: for ye are all one in Christ Jesus' (Galatians 3:28). The reassurance of Paul's epistle is in the ideality of the church, and the latter-day Paul finds similar reassurance in a liberal conscience. Mandla's sense of the recurrent division, the continued virulence of the plague, with a continuum of repressive violence from 'The spears and slings of the Gauls against the sophisticated techniques of Rome' to 'the assegais of Blood River against the guns of the Boers' (*WP* 291), it is suggested, is more true to history.

As for Mandla, his name means Power, and recalls the salute adopted by the black liberation movements in South Africa: 'Amandla!' Whether coincidentally or not, it echoes the name of Nelson Mandela, the embodiment of the African drive to freedom, as well. Mandla represents the new, hardened spirit of self-reliance in rebellion ushered in by Biko and Black Consciousness, welded together with the political toughness and vision of Mandela and the ANC. Andrea's journey through Provence, to discover the *locus* of the plague, is at the same time a movement from love of Paul to love of Mandla. In its turn this is a movement from the bland but sterile ideals of a liberal, the individualism of European humanism, the trust in art and in persuasion as effective mediums in themselves, to revolutionary self-sacrifice, which is obliged to subdue the self to a collective ethic.

The novel is a self-assessment, though not in a simple autobiographical sense. It is also, on one level, an exploration of the responsibilities and the limitations of art. Paul's sterility as an artist is not seen as a necessary condition; he has stopped writing, not because he is unable to say more, but because he has not reached the point where his next move is clear. In her valediction to Paul, Andrea says 'You've left the end of your story open. I know you hoped I would offer you a solution. But each person can only live his own story, Paul. Each has to find his own conclusion' (*WP* 399).

The reflexivity of the discourse is vital, but though it points to itself, the narrative does so in order to place the narcissism of the artist (in this context, the liberal-minded European artist) in a wider context of responsibilities. Andrea Malgas, the artist as sea bird diving under the water of an alien world, sees the problem as one of 'going back' – that is, returning to South Africa, re-entering the plague world, but gives this repeated motif a new twist by neo-Darwinian metaphor – return becomes recapitulation of embryonic transition, and thus becomes, decisively, a moving forward from the wonderful underwater world:

> But sooner or later one has to go back to firm earth, that earth where one belongs. We don't have gills, but a nose. Not a smooth oval whole of head and body, streamlined like a penis: but five limbs. We must go back. (*WP* 400)

15

J. M. Coetzee

Brink experiments with formal patterns, but remains essentially within the naturalist tradition. Though he structures with symbolic or metaphorical patterns, he relies upon density of fact, profusion of *dramatis personae* and dialogue, to carry his argument. The pattern is often richly layered and not without ambiguity, but in the last analysis Brink wishes the reader to be in no doubt about meaning. J. M. Coetzee's work is in distinct contrast.

The post-modernists will claim him for their own – his work is highly self-conscious, tersely fashioned in such a way as to draw attention to the fashioning process. He makes the decisive break from the kind of formal realism which draws the reader into acquiescence, inviting instead an uncomfortable relationship between reader and text, one in which uneasy questions must clamour without any certainty of answers.

But post-modernism is, in part, a return to an agenda which was largely abandoned during the nineteenth century. Coetzee invites comparison as much with Swift or Sterne as with Kafka, Borges, or Beckett. It is interesting that he should turn to Defoe as the kindling for a fiction in *Foe*; in all his fictions he explores the isolated, survivors in hostile environments, as Defoe does, and though the mechanisms of loneliness and survival are primarily psychological in Coetzee, material in Defoe, there is in some ways a similar vision of an unheroic human life, clinging with desperation to a vulnerable sense of self.

He has leanness of style, a savage affection for the grotesque, a satirical ability to expose the rotten roots and burnt-out landscapes of the mind. His characteristic mode is that of the ironic monologue, in which we are left uncertain whether the narrator intends defence or discovery, self-protection or shrewd attack. At his best the cool yet disturbing structure of his prose benefits from reading aloud, so critical are the internal stresses of syntax and meaning. He is frequently mannered, but the mannerisms are dramatic, as in the best of mannered comedy simultaneously revelation of folly, inadequacy, evil, and assault upon our self-satisfaction as readers. In all he writes there is a fascination with words, with their organization into structures, and with constantly changing relationships between surfaces and interiors in language.

By a sharply different route he reaches the same intensities of experience as Conrad. But Conrad is the traveller, converting disturbing experience into symbolic values which have less to do with place than with the human condition in general. Coetzee always, ultimately, roots the tale in a home ground. There is a passionate intensity in this instinctive homing, and the passion is more often than not strongly coloured by sado-masochism. This is not a comment on J. M. Coetzee's personal psychology. His subjects are of the kind which require the exfoliation of motives to the point where the sado-masochistic becomes an inevitable station.

In *Dusklands* (1974) (the title points to the continued experience of darkness), one *novella* is set in a South African past, the other, *The Vietnam Project*, in a mythic America of the early 1970s. Yet its account of a conventional man, withdrawn in contemplation of his own society's collusive violence and inhumanity, retreating at last into violent destructiveness, draws much of its energy from a white African's understanding of his own society.

The narrating persona, Eugene Dawn, is a kind of artist himself; he reports to a manager named Coetzee. The relationship is close to that of a graduate student reporting to a supervisor, but the combination of academic detachment and the anxiety of hierarchical subjugation is in the service of a project which would be unusual in a university. Dawn is preparing an analysis of the record and future of psychological warfare in Vietnam. The relationship of power between formal superiors and inferiors is more important in many ways than the details of the project which takes shape in the context of that power.

It is not simply about students and supervisors, nor simply about bureaucrats or government, where government becomes a closed activity in itself. It is not simply, either, about the Vietnam war. If anything it is 'about' meaning, about our individual and collective entrapment in the word-structures through which we project our selves. It is about the way in which every aspect of hegemonic duress, a duress more mental and spiritual than physical, distorts, dehumanizes, and ultimately destroys the individual.

Dawn argues for the exploitation of the father-myth and the father-voice as the origin and vehicle of an effective propaganda, a linguistic analogue of the B-52 bomber commanding from the sky: 'The father is authority, infallibility, ubiquity. He does not persuade, he commands. That which he foretells happens' (*D* 21).[1] The irony is that Dawn, in offering a model for his own society's domination of an alien's world, seems to be diagnosing his own relationship with a hierarchy which he fears and obeys, and thus his own alien-ness. 'Coetzee' as father-substitute (in the hierarchies of the fiction) and J. M. Coetzee (in terms of the act of literary production) become parts of this analytic process. Fiction-making therefore becomes, in a multiple and complex way, the imagining and constructing of social relations, the re-creation of 'our selves' which guarantees the continuance of a society even in a collective madness.

In a sequence of images of alienation from self, defamiliarization, and the icy madness of migration from human dignity, 'Dawn' begins in a way which at first seems like a genial exaggeration of the sufferings of the scholar bound to his labours:

> Hemmed in with walls of books, I should be in paradise. But my body betrays me. . . . my back begins to petrify in the scholar's hook. The ropes of muscles that spread from the spine curl in suckers around my neck, over my clavicles, under my armpits, across my chest. (*D* 7)

The images of the scholar and writer are vital to the narrative, continually reminding us of the provisional nature of the text. Here, the scholar who constructs a world to satisfy the powerful is himself constructed by the exigent ruthlessness of that power. He who discovers the means to control and create victims is himself victimized by his collaboration. The agents of such societies become creatures of dusk, and thus the name, Eugene Dawn (well born, a new beginning) is a withering irony.

The second fiction of *Dusklands*, *The Narrative of Jacobus Coetzee*, is offered as a scholarly translation and edition of the work of an ancestor: 'Edited, with an Afterword, by S. J. Coetzee: Translated by J. M. Coetzee'. Its relationship with the early history of exploration of the Cape is far looser than this would suggest, but there is a certain difficulty, an unease, for the reader, in assessing how far the fiction ports historical fact. The claim that it is all, as it were, in the family, adds a dimension to the fiction which can easily be caught: Coetzee is one of the names which has persisted throughout the white settlement of Southern Africa from the seventeenth century: the family name implicates J. M. Coetzee, and through him every white South African, in the triumph or the guilt of Jacobus's journey.

The period of expansion from the tiny footprint of settlement in the Cape, and the courage of the pioneer *Trekboers*, form the kernel of legend for a people fascinated with its own history. This is more potent as myth than the pioneer myth of North America – there isn't much doubt that the white Americans have won, but the descendants of the first Coetzee are still trying to subdue the enemy and force him into reservations. For most of the Afrikaner nation the pioneers are the one available guarantee of their own peculiar notion of beleaguered identity, ruggedly courageous in the defence of freedom. Part of what Coetzee does in the *Narrative* is to demythologize this consoling sense of history, dramatizing the genocide on which expansion was based, and its dehumanization of the pioneers:

> The only sure way to kill a Bushman is to catch him in the open where your horse can run him down. . . . It is only when you hunt them as you hunt jackals that you can really clear a stretch of country. (*D* 58-9)

What makes a monologue of this kind remarkable is that the reader may remain unsure of its status – it is offered as the scholarly recovery of autobiographical narrative, and the reader must still be finding his way towards deciding whether it is or is not. One is reminded once more of eighteenth-century satire, of Swift or of Fielding, except that here it is the heroes of a nation and a culture who are made, ventriloquially, to hint at the techniques of mass murder, or to recommend the peculiar sexual pleasures of the racist. It reveals the connection between racism and sadistic masculine egotism in a way which is available only to one who writes after the Nazi era, and yet reflects the equation between life and property so characteristic of an eighteenth-century colonial farming society. Dutch girls, says the narrator, are themselves property bringing with them not only:

> so many pounds of white flesh but also so many morgen of land and so many head of cattle and so many servants. . . . Whereas a wild Bushman girl is . . . a rag you wipe yourself on and throw away. . . . She is the ultimate love you have borne your own desires alienated in a foreign body and pegged out waiting for your pleasure. (*D* 61)

But demythologizing, though it may dismantle a construct consolingly offered as truth, does not commonly end up as a claim to simple truth itself. It's like the Jacobean malcontent prating in soliloquy about his cynical and evil motives. Whatever belief you accord to the speaker is in parentheses; it depends upon your collusion with a convention. In any case it doesn't matter whether you 'believe' in the reality of the speaker. He becomes a tool for probing unconfessed desires and habits, in this case attaching them to the type of a national and cultural hero. By claiming your collaboration as reader he invites you to implicate yourself, not just as a member of *that* nation or culture, but as a member of any national group which can find such heroes in its past (that's most of us).

In the Heart of the Country (1977) (the title distantly, but deliberately, recalls Conrad) is a fiction in which it is more difficult to determine meaning than in Coetzee's earlier work. It is cast in the form of a diary, or an internal monologue, the habitual mode for Coetzee, a form tending always towards the solipsistic. As in Kafka, one is aware of the suspension of multiple potential meanings within a whole, within a complex which is coterminous with the fictive persona. The word 'persona' is particularly useful here: it is not a fictional representation of a person that is intended. What the fictive narrator writes is too transparently a construct of art, and the narrator herself is too much a dependent part of that construct for one to be able to imagine her occupying any space-time except that of the narrative. There is a sense in which this is true of a 'real' diary, or autobiography, or any narrative, but here the radical unreliability of narrative becomes the foreground of the narration.

It's a magnificently sustained and at the same time frugal tale, the confessions of a bitter, lonely spinster, living in a dependent, jealous relationship with her father and an equally passionate relationship of dependence upon the farm servants. Her father is remote in his arrogant masculinity, his sexuality which is so much a theme of his daughter's rage. Eventually she kills the father and draws a coloured farm servant, Hendrik, and his wife,

Klein-Anna, into a suffocatingly intense *ménage à trois*. When this fails, the old mad woman falls into a fugue in which she listens to prophetic, hallucinatory messages from the sky.

These are the bare bones of a history which is subverted in the whole strategy of the telling. The narrative is divided into 266 numbered sections. Of these, the first thirty-five, the entry into the whole of the discourse, form a fiction as believable as any other part of the narrative. Among other things, (some of which, one could say, may be maintained as truth in so far as we may take anything in the narrative as truth), it tells of the father bringing home a new bride, the daughter's jealous responses to their luxurious sensualities, and her murdering them both, in delighted sadistic frenzy, with repeated blows of an axe. In section 36 these events are casually disowned, and we have to step gingerly into an alternative fiction, in which there is not and never has been a new bride, or a killing, but in which the murderous intensity of rage and frustration remain.

It's easy enough to readjust in one sense – we can set that narrative aside as imaginative, a dream of lust, both sexual and blood lust. But after this opening one is never disposed to place trust in the narration again. So when, in the main narrative, the father uses the servant, Klein-Anna, for his sexual pleasure, and Magda, the narrator, loads a gun, takes it out into the yard, shoots into the chamber where the father is fornicating (sections 113-23), there are long moments of doubt as to what level of belief one is asked to accord to the narrative. We *know* it's a fiction, and that knowledge already circumscribes the parenthetic faith we might spare, but we are more than usually aware that we should grudge even that allowance.

The discourse is peppered with reference to its unreliable nature, indeed, to the arbitrarily constructing and constricting nature of language itself:

> Words are coin. Words alienate. Language is no medium for desire. Desire is rapture, not exchange. It is only by alienating the desired that language masters it. (*HC* 26)[2]

> The question to ask is not, How do I, a lonely spinster, come to know such things? It is not for nothing that I spend evenings humped over the dictionary. Words are words. I have never pretended to embrace that night's experience. A factor, I deal in signs merely. (*HC* 27)

As an extension from this there is the explicit rejection of any claim for the discourse as history. This is put in Magda's mouth, but might be taken, cautiously, as hinting a provisional aesthetic for Coetzee's own work, throwing some light on the formal pretence of the *Narrative* towards the status of history or chronicle: 'My talent is all for immanence, for the fire or ice of identity at the heart of things. Lyric is my medium, not chronicle' (*HC* 71). Yes, lyric of darkness rather than chronicle, that's fair, and yet there are multiple ways in which the lyric fiction, wrapped in the generation of its own inner tensions, focusing around an increasingly solipsistic experience, alludes by inversion to an idea of society. It might even be said that 'Magda' becomes, in the end, the subtle and complex portrait of something at the heart of white South African society, particularly after the trauma of Soweto. Magda realizes that she has, by one way or another, destroyed the society within which she has existed, and discovers:

> I was not, after all, made to live alone. . . . I need more than merely pebbles to permute, rooms to clean, furniture to push around: I need people to talk to, brothers and sisters or fathers and mothers, I need a history and culture, I need hopes and aspirations, I need a moral sense and a teleology. (*HC* 119-20)

Every prophetic passion demands last words, and these are given, cryptically, to the mad old woman, by mysterious machines which speak 'Spanish' to her, a hallucinatory substitute for the society she has expelled. The *dicta* of the sky-machines are cryptic, and offer meaning on several levels, personal, ethical, artistic, social, and political; it would be difficult and tedious to expound here the relationship of every one to the fable which contains them. But among the last words the fourth offers a complex statement which has bearing on aesthetic, ethical, and psychological issues:

> *It is the slave's consciousness that constitutes the master's certainty of his own truth. But the slave's consciousness is a dependent consciousness. So the master is not sure of the truth of his autonomy. His truth lies in an inessential consciousness and its inessential acts.* (*HC* 130)

If the 'Spanish' *dicta* in some way interact with the Seven Last Words of Christ's Passion (and it may or may not be part of Coetzee's design), this reverberates intertextually with Christ's need, in the fourth of the Last Words: 'I thirst'. In any event it points to an aridity, a drought of the inward being of White South Africa.

The death of Biko occurred during the year in which *In the Heart of the Country* was published (1977). This murder and the subsequent trial are a shadow behind *Waiting for the Barbarians* (1980). The fiction is set on the borders of an Empire, unspecified, but containing echoes from many systems, from the Roman through the British to the Third Reich and the Soviet Union of Stalin's time. It's also an Empire of the psyche, dark barbarians surrounding and threatening the bureaucratic and military order of coercion. The sinister Colonel Joll (the name evades any identification of nationality, though I suppose it just stops short of being jolly) visits the frontier post, his eyes hidden behind dark glasses. He takes over from the local magistrate in investigating an old man and a boy. The old man dies, and Joll's formal report echoes the language of such deaths during interrogation in South Africa:

> During the course of interrogation contradictions became apparent in the prisoner's testimony. Confronted with these contradictions, the prisoner became enraged and attacked the investigating officer. A scuffle ensued

during which the prisoner fell heavily against the wall. Efforts to revive him were unsuccessful. (*WB* 6)[3]

Both this and the recited explanation of the guard resemble well enough the statements of Major Snyman, Warrant Officer Beneke, Colonel Goosen, and other officers questioned at the Biko trial. The passage indicates the quality of ritual that attaches to such incidents, and their conventions of report, which, in a coercive society, are made to have value in themselves, more value than direct evidence of eye or ear. What the magistrate sees when he opens the shroud is reminiscent of the death photographs of Biko (though not every detail corresponds): 'The grey beard is caked with blood. The lips are crushed and drawn back, the teeth are broken. One eye is rolled back, the other eye-socket is a bloody hole' (*WB* 7).

The magistrate is not an unkindly man, neither is he a fool. He does his duty and tries not to get involved. He is an ordinary man waiting for the time when he can draw his pension, the kind upon whom the Empire depends, just as much as upon the sadistic Colonel Joll: 'I believe in peace, perhaps even peace at any price' (*WB* 14). But he also has the saving quality of curiosity, the ability to enquire behind the ritual gesture to the substantive evidence. His own perspective upon the 'civilization' of the Empire is qualified. He is not as fully convinced of the primitive status of the barbarians as the Empire, or Colonel Joll, might like. He is an amateur archaeologist, and has investigated the remains of a complex city 2 miles away from the town where he is posted. The experience makes him acutely aware of the transient nature of systems of power, and of his own marginality too. There are echoes here of the rediscovery of African history through archaeology, and the effect it is just beginning to have upon the self-image of white culture, discrediting the old cliché of 'the dark continent'. Different echoes are evoked when the magistrate toys with the notion of genocide:

> It would be best if this obscure chapter in the history of the world were terminated at once, if these ugly people were obliterated from the face of the earth and we swore to make a new start, to run an empire in which there would be no more injustice, no more pain. (*WB* 24)

The 'final solution' attempted by Hitler as a way of preparing for a thousand-year Reich was neither the first nor the last occasion for such sophistries – one thinks of Jacobus Coetzee and the San (though there have been other such happenings in Africa). Here the magistrate rejects the sophistry, pleading a weary conservatism rather than humanity. Subsequently we follow the magistrate in a slow, puzzled exploration in which he learns more about the transience of his own group of colonists, the dignity and rootedness of the barbarian aboriginals:

> We have been here more than a hundred years, we have reclaimed land from the desert and built irrigation works. . . . but they still think of us as

visitors, transients. . . . They do not doubt that one of these days . . . their beasts will graze on these rich fields we have planted. (*WB* 51).

Technological superiority is the watchword of the imperialist. It's the superficial view of the unreflective radical, a myth that breaks down as the water, or the power, or the cash, or the military power runs out. Myths encourage counter-myths, and the magistrate's vision of a resumed natural continuity after the colonial episode draws on a pool of conservative sentiment in all of us which might be equally superficial.

Coetzee has chosen, as a first move in the strategy of his fable, a simplification. He de-historicizes. In his meeting of cultures the barbarians remain untouched by contact; they are simple nomads, and their innocence of history is not modified by the fact that there are traces of an ancient culture all over the land they inhabit. Indeed, Coetzee's magistrate makes history itself, and the time-scales which characterize life within history, a creation of 'Empire', in contrast to a 'natural' time: 'What has made it impossible for us to live in time like fish in water, like birds in air, like children? It is the fault of Empire! Empire has created the time of history . . . of beginning and end, of catastrophe' (*WB* 133).

Undoubtedly there is something attractive in this vision. It may ally the untouched 'barbarian' with children and with the natural world in opposition to the uncomfortable and destructive pursuits of an imperial sensibility. But, as soon as you begin to apply it to a real rather than a fictive pastoral world, the implications of such a world-view begin to become more serious, excluding the victims, the subjects, the enemies of Empire from its history.

On the other hand, the magistrate characterizes the disease of 'Empire' in general (and implicitly the South African regime) with great force: 'Empire dooms itself to live in history and plot against history. One thought alone preoccupies the submerged mind of Empire; how not to end, how not to die, how to prolong its era' (*WB* 133). The implied political statement is difficult to disentangle from the existential complaint. It is sometimes said, without much thought, that the condition of South African white society, and similar 'Empires', is 'schizoid'. Here Coetzee almost literalizes the metaphor. R. D. Laing remarks that the schizoid individual's whole effort is

> to preserve his *self*. This . . . is precariously established; he is subject to the dread of his own dissolution into non-being. . . . [he] fears a real live dialectical relationship with real live people. He can relate himself only to depersonalized persons, to phantoms of his own phantasies (imagos).[4]

A society which rests upon the barbarities of Biko's interrogators, or those of the fictional Colonel Joll, is sick in precisely this way. On the other hand, the magistrate struggles with his own disabilities to recapture a lost and difficult dialectic of relationship.

Like Marvell's Man (Lover and Mower), the representatives of Coetzee's 'Empire' exist in a state of war, and exile, destroying what nourishes them, ignorant of the garden around them which testifies to reality despite all their mad aspirations. In this sense 'Empire' is more powerfully a psychic concept than a political one. But the magistrate's state of mind is a complex one. He is becoming detached from 'Empire', experimenting – feebly enough – with the dialectic relationship which is forbidden by Empire. At night he sleeps with a barbarian girl who is blind, crippled, almost destroyed by the attentions of Empire. The relationship isn't consummated sexually; it is indeed almost a relationship with a phantom of fantasy. But eventually the magistrate, by making an arduous and dangerous journey beyond the frontiers of Empire and returning the girl to the barbarian community, recognizes the girl as something more than phantom. In doing so he moves a stage forward to discovering an identity of his own, no longer totally enclosed by 'Empire', closer to the kind of relationship with others which can validate a healthy self. He returns to face the official disapproval of the Third Bureau of the Empire in the form of one of Colonel Joll's inferiors, a Warrant Officer who is drawn from the living model of a South African Special Branch Officer:

> 'You have been treasonously consorting with the enemy,' he says.
> So it is out. 'Treasonously consorting': a phrase out of a book.
> 'We are at peace here,' I say, 'we have no enemies.' There is silence.
> 'Unless I make a mistake,' I say. 'Unless we are the enemy.' (*WB* 77)

It is this inversion, this perception of ourselves as enemy, which is pivotal to the economy of the fiction. It is reinforced almost immediately by a passage which prompts reconsideration of the title, even of the fiction as a whole: 'I am a free man. . . . And is there any principle behind my opposition? Have I not simply been provoked into a reaction by the sight of one of the new barbarians usurping my desk and pawing my papers?' (*WB* 78).

Trilling diagnoses a similarity and a difference between Kafka and Shakespeare. Briefly, both writers are keenly aware of 'man's suffering and cosmic alienation'. The difference is 'that Kafka's knowledge of evil exists without the contradictory knowledge of the self in its health and validity, that Shakespeare's knowledge of evil exists with that contradiction in its fullest possible force'.[5] Coetzee's universe lacks some of Kafka's concentration. Equally it lacks the populousness and variety of Shakespeare's world. Coetzee has been compared with Kafka too often, and for superficial reasons; he should be spared comparison with Shakespeare. But one way in which his fictions are comparable with both is in the way he links 'this little world of man', the neuroses of the suffering self, and the great world of history. In Hamlet, an ambiguous sickness of the mind parallels and comes to embody the sickness of a society. In *Das Schloss* or *Der Prozess*, the convolutions of a bureaucratic system project the anxiety and terror of displacement and alienation in the individual. Similarly the magistrate's sufferings, his changing relationship of complicity and denial in relationship to the rule of 'Empire', are full of refracted evidences of man's relationship to the barbarian state in the twentieth century.

But Coetzee refuses to offer us a heroic image in the rebellion of the magistrate. In the following exchange the last sentence of Colonel Joll retains an ironic force. The magistrate accuses Joll:

> '*You* are the enemy, Colonel! . . . History will bear me out!'
> 'Nonsense. There will be no history, the affair is too trivial.' He seems impassive, but I am sure I have shaken him.
> 'You are an obscene torturer! You deserve to hang!'
> 'Thus speaks the judge, the One Just Man,' he murmurs.
> We stare into each other's eyes. (*WB* 114)

The delicate suggestion of discomfiture in the magistrate is enough to warn us that his rhetoric obscures a truth of which both he and the Colonel are aware. They are locked together in the knowledge of complicity. It is a realization which is made explicit towards the end: 'I was the lie that Empire tells itself when times are easy, he the truth that Empire tells when harsh winds blow. Two sides of imperial rule, no more, no less' (*WB* 135).

So far, Coetzee's fictions have been written in the first person singular, and, except in the case of the *Narrative*, in the present tense. The favoured form has been the monologue, with its limitation of point of view, a limitation which may draw the reader into some degree of involvement with the soliloquist while at the same time giving her or him space to stand apart and enter into silent commentary. So the reader may share intense experience of insanity projected through the monologists of *The Vietnam Project*, the *Narrative*, or *In the Heart of the Country*, while retaining an ironic and moral reserve as a way of protecting the self from the dangers of dislocative emotion.

In *Waiting for the Barbarians* the central persona, the monologist himself, acquires the capacity for reflection, commentary, irony, judgement, whilst never breaking completely free from the insanity. But the centre of madness is located in the society, the 'Empire', and the character's confession of his own inadequacy is, as it were, a tribute to the power of Empire. The character's limited autonomy gives the reader far less space. The reader can be taken unawares by the persona's changing perception of things. It is far less clear what our intended relationship with the magistrate is, compared with our relationship with Magda, Eugene Dawn, or Jacobus Coetzee. What space there is left may be taken up with introspection, with considering what degree of autonomy we might claim, at what level of our own consciousness we might trust our own relationships with 'Empire'.

Life & Times of Michael K (1983) changes to the third person and the past tense. This is the combination favoured by Franz Kafka. This fact, and the 'K' of the title, may have encouraged many readers to expect a fiction so deeply influenced by Kafka as to be almost a continuation of his work. Only an insensitive reader could maintain this illusion for long. It is, like Kafka's work, spare, lucid, powerful in style. Like Kafka it treats the bewilderment of the harrassed and lonely individual in a hostile world. But it is almost as if Coetzee had chosen to use the letter 'K' to draw attention to other, crucial ways in which it is very different from the work of Kafka.

For a start, Kafka's choice of 'K' teases us with the sense of a close yet indefinable relationship, a deformed dream-identity as it were, between Kafka and K. There is a distance created between Coetzee and Michael K which is more than the fact that their initials are different. 'Michael K' is one of the dispossessed, deformed with a hare-lip, institutionalized in childhood, low in social status, of limited intelligence, by trade a humble gardener: he is 'placed' by the conventional registers of a society which (wrongly) would value more highly J. M. Coetzee, the white writer and university teacher without notable physical blemishes.

Kafka creates complex social structures in his fictions which have variable relationships to the Austro-Hungarian Empire, Vienna, or other 'realities', but in one way or another his fictions wrench the 'real' out of time, space, and familiar understanding into a hallucinatory suspension of dreamspace, dreamtime. *Michael K* deals in a real space familiar to Coetzee and many of his South African readers, Cape Town, Stellenbosch, the dry farmlands and *dorps* of the Karoo. The time is displaced from present or past, and it isn't very important whether it's a possible future. But it is recognizable as a projection of forces at work within the present. Its relationship to 'realism' is somewhat like the relation between an X-ray photograph and a colour print, a dark monochrome revelation of the bones of the present rather than its richly coloured surface. Nevertheless it uses existential desolation in such a way as to point more precisely towards a present history than Kafka.

Kafka's personae are isolates; whatever solace they find in relationships with others is impermanent and imperfect, and stresses their necessary solitude. Michael K sets out taking his crippled mother in a converted wheelbarrow back to her home in Prince Albert, dodging thieves, army, police, surviving in the chaos of a civil war, clinging to her society as long as he can.

Certainly he then becomes a solitary, and in a real way was never anything else, despite his mother. But his solitude is modified by the heroic and comic act of commitment, an essay towards permanence and love. And the drive towards survival, the pace of travelling at a walking speed through the unremarkable small towns and dusty highways, once more combine to become reminiscent of seventeenth- or eighteenth-century fictions as much as twentieth-century: *A Journal of the Plague Year, The Pilgrim's Progress*, even *Joseph Andrews* might come to mind.

In the second section, too, without knowing it, he discovers somebody who loves him – the young pharmacist[6] who sees in his refusal to live (at least in the way required of him) an affirmation within the negation: ' "It's not a question of dying," I said. "It's not that he wants to die. He just doesn't like the food here. Profoundly he does not like it. . . . Maybe he only eats the bread of freedom" ' (*MK* 200)[7]. And yet even he does not at first understand what K's enemy is, taking it to be his memory of a vengeful mother (*MK*

204-5). The enemies characteristic of an earlier age were plague, sin, indigence, hypocrisy, deprivation of human society. In the twentieth century, after Nazism, Stalinism, purges and holocausts, concentration camps, gulags and political prisons (the concentration camps of the Boer War, Robben Island, Pretoria Central among them), the solitude of the individual begins to be defined in terms of the penal institution, the labour camp, the gaol.

In *Life & Times* Michael K's life is punctuated by institutions and imprisonment, from the orphanage, through hospital, forced labour on the railway track, to the police cell, and hospital again, to the Jakkalsdrif resettlement camp, and finally the hospital of a rehabilitation camp sited on a race course in Cape Town. Even the beleaguered Cape from which K begins his run for freedom is a fortress with a large perimeter, an 'Empire' (in the sense given to that word in *Waiting for the Barbarians*) contracted in self-defence. The orientation of the solitary's life in *Robinson Crusoe* or *The Pilgrim's Progress* is towards finding one's place in a true society. In *Michael K* it is towards being *out* of place, escaping the enforced society at whatever cost. And yet there is a terrifying sense in which that society is no longer outside the experience of self. It is not simply the authoritarian state, not simply everything in the daily intercourse of ordinary lives which potentiates the deathly authority. It is, finally, the internalization of that destructive power. Michael K reflects on families, and his own childhood in the orphanage, Huis Norenius, and the camp at Jakkalsdrif, where parents brought up children on land trodden so hard that nothing would grow there again:

> my father was Huis Norenius. My father was the list of rules on the door of the dormitory, the twenty-one rules of which the first was 'There will be silence in the dormitories at all times.' (*MK* 143)

This introjection of institution and authority as the father who denies and inhibits is one element in the schizoid desperation of self. Self is to be preserved, even at the risk of the body itself being sacrificed. The shrunken, the minimal, the deprived, becomes preferable to a comparative ease that threatens selfhood, the ease offered by the regimented society.

The system of control is connected with the father, the mother is associated with the earth and growth. It is she who longs to be taken back to the farmland of Prince Albert. When she dies she is cremated, becomes a packet of ash which K carries with him everywhere until at last he plants pumpkin seeds and mealies, on land scattered with her ash and irrigated by water from the dam. ' "Where is your mother now?" I asked. "She makes the plants grow," he replied, evading my eyes' (*MK* 178).

He sees himself in terms of earth. In the arid wilderness he remembers the earth he tilled as a gardener in Cape Town, seeing himself as becoming more and more like the wilderness:

> smaller and harder and drier every day. If I were to die here, sitting in the mouth of my cave looking out over the plain with my knees under my chin,

I would be dried out by the wind in a day, I would be preserved whole, like someone in the desert drowned in sand. (*MK* 93)

In contrast, when he is in hospital a little later and an orderly brings round trays of food to everyone but himself, Michael K experiences 'the first hunger he had known for a long time. He was not sure that he wanted to become a servant to hunger again; but a hospital, it seemed, was a place for bodies, where bodies asserted their rights' (*MK* 98).

The schizoid impulse to allow the body to go may be seen, paradoxically, as a desire to *preserve* the self. On the road towards this there is the rejection of the body as part of the self. The body comes to be seen as an object. For K the sweetest moments in the Jakkalsdrif camp are when this sense is most complete, and yet when the body-as-object simultaneously becomes body-as-earth, life-giving and life-receiving in a way which bypasses human institutions to discover new self-justification. He lies so still that the children 'incorporated his body into their game. They clambered over him and fell upon him as if he were part of the earth' (*MK* 116).

Perhaps the only genuine vision of freedom which a South African white can construct is one which travels through negation, just as some mystics have found God only through suffering the *noche escura del alma*, the dark night of the soul. Coetzee makes the language of the pharmacist point the allusion. He compares himself with 'Michaels', who is so adept at escape:

> Whereas I – if one dark night I were to slip into overalls and tennis shoes and clamber over the wall . . . – I am the kind who would be snapped up by the first patrol to pass while I yet stood dithering over which way lay salvation. (*MK* 221)

To pursue the analogy with Juan de la Cruz which Coetzee seems here to suggest, the darkness on the way to 'salvation' must be that of confronting a terrible sickness of mind, experiencing a withdrawal from everything which is conventionally held to be normal. In Coetzee it involves an effort which I can only describe as re-inventing Man – and the only way the poor human imagination can manage that is by proposing something like a God, even a bungling God. It is a closed circuit: the invented Man and the inadequate Creator are cathode and anode of a literary process, the current of anxiety which gives heat and light to the spare filament of text:

> With Michaels it always seemed to me that someone had scuffled together a handful of dust, spat on it, and patted it into the shape of a rudimentary man, making one or two mistakes . . . but coming up nevertheless in the end with a genuine little man of earth, the kind of little man one sees in peasant art. (*MK* 220)

We catch the passing reference to *The Waste Land*, 'a handful of dust', Coetzee, like Eliot, discovering fear at the root of man's experience of creation. Like Eliot, too, sending his Man on a quest through a desert, eloquent of myth in his physical deformation, his sexlessness, and yet his capacity to make the wilderness bloom. Once again, like Eliot, he sets his Man on his journey against the background of a sinister history, the collapse of human institutions in anarchy and barbarism. And last of all, like Eliot, the quest is in the end towards a desperate, minimal, preservation of self amidst the ruins.

But there are crucial departures from the example of Eliot. Coetzee does not present as the centre of things an effort to maintain integrity through a cultural continuity, through failure to maintain an ideal order: 'These fragments I have shored against my ruins'. Against a background of Dachau and Hiroshima, Vietnam and Cambodia, the Gaza Strip and Soweto, integrity becomes a more earthy kind of survival, the subsistence of man despite elaborate machineries of power, duress, and destruction. His Man is a peasant:

> a creature that spends its waking life stooped over the soil, that when at last its time comes digs its own grave and slips quietly in. . . . For Michaels has passed through the bowels of state undigested; he has emerged from its camps as intact as he emerged from its schools and orphanages. (*MK* 220-1)

A highly conscious intertextuality, a frankness about the provisional nature of the discourse, a continuous, ironic awareness of the presence of the writer in the text, these are among the ways in which Coetzee disowns authority within the fiction which might parallel the authority of the state in the life of the individual. In this his strategy has much in common with many contemporary authors, as indeed with some eighteenth-century fiction writers. The form itself becomes a criticism of the 'real' world, and one of the steps towards this is to disclaim 'reality' or 'truth', for the author to show how the lie is put together. It is a sort of anarchism of literary form, by contrast, for instance, with *1984*, in which Orwell employs a conventionally structured narrative and narrative persona for his criticism of the highly structured and manipulative state. In Orwell the writer criticizes the state for being like the writer, for manipulating something called reality to serve its own purposes. Coetzee, on the other hand, though he manipulates and cannot do anything else, conducts a running analysis of the manipulative intelligence of the writer, which co-exists with and reinforces his critique of the state.

This is at its clearest in *Foe* (1986), a fiction which takes as its prime subject the genesis of fiction. That fiction is, in *one* sense, an archetype of fiction as we now understand it, *Robinson Crusoe*. Defoe's Crusoe is, at the same time, an archetype of the solitary condition of man, and man's attempt to create an ordered world around him. In another sense the fiction whose genesis we are bidden to observe is fiction itself, fiction in the abstract. Or, more profoundly, language, and its role in the multiplicity of private understandings, personal fictions, which co-exist in the social life of man.

The name *Defoe* is, of course, a fancy version of Defoe's own family name, Foe; this fact itself, and the reference to it in Coetzee's title, indicates something of the way in which this, the great-grandfather of all modern prose fiction-makers, is himself an invention, a 'naming', a self-made man. Coincidentally, the word *foe* has its own meaning, and Coetzee seizes on the fact as a punning felicity: the word suggests a combative relationship between the fiction-maker (himself a kind of fiction) and the fictions which he manipulates.

The claim which Defoe makes in his fictions is that he is recording and editing what somebody has told him, or written down for him:

> The editor believes the thing to be a just history of fact; neither is there any appearance of fiction in it.[8]

> The author is here supposed to be writing her own history . . . the style of this famous lady we here speak of is a little altered; particularly she is made to tell her own tale in modester words than she told it at first. . . . In a word, the whole relation is carefully garbled of all the levity and looseness that was in it.[9]

Defoe claims to be no more than middleman, and some of his original readers might have believed him. But *we* do not; we think we know what fiction is. In a more radical sense than Defoe used the word it is *garbling* (the word is a commercial one, derived ultimately from an Arabic word for sifting corn through a sieve; its current meaning is to do with mutilation, but its original one is to do with selection and discrimination). Whatever records or reminiscences of Moll Flanders's life Defoe had to hand, he picked over and used for purposes of his own, but whether as friend or Foe to the real Moll's memory is quite another matter.

The principal narrator in *Foe* is Susan Barton, and the first part of her narrative is an account of how she came to be shipwrecked on an island with 'Cruso' and Friday, and how the three escaped. The narrative differs from Defoe's in significant ways. First, it is not told either by Crusoe, or by Daniel Defoe affecting to 'garble' the words of a Crusoe that does not exist. It is told by Coetzee, pretending a communication from his invention Susan Barton to his invention, Foe. The narrative of Coetzee/Barton enters into a silent dialogue with that of Defoe/Crusoe, which confirms us in our sense of the insecurity of both narratives, indeed all narratives. When the captain who rescues them suggests publication of her story, Susan demurs:

> 'A liveliness is lost in the writing down which must be supplied by art, and I have no art.' 'As to art I cannot pronounce, being only a sailor,' said Captain Smith; 'but you may depend on it, the booksellers will hire a man to set your story to rights, and put in a dash of colour, too, here and there.' 'I will not have any lies told,' said I. The captain smiled. (*F* 40)[10]

Crucial facts differ in the two narratives, and the *différances* create a dialectic. The effect is somewhat like the new pattern which emerges if you superimpose two or more visual patterns or sounds, producing a new pattern. Such interference patterns in physics have a parallel in the process of language-learning, where the structures of the learner's first language 'interfere' with his competence in a second. Interference is a kind of garbling. But Coetzee's is an analytic garbling, a witty exploration of the unreliability of narrative and the treacheries of author and reader, speaker and listener, towards each other. There are somewhat analogous processes in the relationships between prime text and invented scholarly commentary in *The Dunciad* and in *Pale Fire*, but in *Foe* Susan Barton's narrative is given a free-standing status as independent narrative, unlike the parasitic status of Dr Bentley's or Dr Kinbote's interferences. This does not stop us being aware, as an implicit condition of our experience of the text, that there is not, and never has been, a Susan Barton. She is a fiction intervening (interfering) in the interconnected and mutually supportive experiences we call the reading of fiction.

So Cruso is a morose recluse, occupying his time in building fantastic and useless terraces around his island, more like Uncle Toby or Sisyphus than like the purposive, practical Crusoe of Defoe's *homo oeconomicus*. Indeed, he refuses to contemplate the salvage of tools from the wreck: 'We have a roof over our heads, made without saw or axe. We sleep, we eat, we live. We have no need of tools' (*F* 32). But, just as surely as Defoe's invention, he is a mirror of his culture, or to be more precise, he embodies a certain view of that culture. Both Crusoe and Cruso are figures of pride; both embody ways of seeing achievement; both are tropes for an idea of civilization. But Crusoe's pride is that of the trader who can shift for himself if need be. Cruso's is that of Cheops and Ozymandias and Pope's Timon, of NASA and Cecil Rhodes. It is the pride of monumental culture. 'The farther I journey from his terraces, the less they seem to me like fields waiting to be planted, the more like tombs: those tombs the emperors of Egypt erected for themselves in the desert' (*F* 83-4). It is a culture which denies the present in favour of an ever-delayed future. 'We have nothing to plant. . . . The planting is reserved for those who come after us and have the foresight to bring seed. I only clear the ground for them' (*F* 33).

Coetzee's Friday is not the natural innocent who serves Crusoe, learns his language and his religion well enough to ask awkward questions about God, a successor to Montaigne's Carib *cannibales* and Shakespeare's Caliban. He is a slave to that monumental culture, a black African torn from his *ethos* and rendered mute by the loss of his tongue. He becomes a figure of the African diaspora, stranded, robbed of his speech and culture, and put to work in furthering an incomprehensible construction of alien purpose. In an acid parody of eighteenth-century attitudes to the education of the poor and of slaves to a level adequate to their status in life, or, in twentieth-century South Africa, Bantu Education, he is not admitted to more than a meagre allowance of the English language. He is like a participant in one of Wittgenstein's language games;[11] when Susan orders 'Wood' for the fire, he does not move. Cruso explains: ' "*Firewood* is the word I have taught him. . . . *Wood* he does not know." . . . "How many words of English does Friday know?"

. . . "As many as he needs," replied Cruso' (*F* 21). Thus he might be seen as a figure for more than the transported slave; he suffers the deprivation of the culturally dispossessed at any time or anywhere.

There isn't anything in *Robinson Crusoe* to compare Susan Barton with directly, though there are some resemblances between her and Defoe's Moll and his Roxana. In the first place, of course, she serves the function of supplying the 'missing' parts of the palimpsest which the fiction would have us believe (or disbelieve) lies beneath the familiar *Robinson Crusoe*. But there's something more than this. Crusoe's kingdom is a male kingdom; so, even more so, is Cruso's. Crusoe's labours lead him to do much that is conventionally left to the woman, though he copes with persistence and energy which are by convention as masculine as may be. Cruso, on the other hand, does nothing but command and possess, slave, woman, and island, with an arrogant presumption of right which is the cultural heritage of a male.

The presence of Susan Barton adds another layer to the stratigraphy of the island metaphor. She is our principal witness to the crazed enterprise. And yet, in this society of three, she is subjugated in a way which is almost as complete as, though somewhat more subtle than, the subjugation of the slave:

> Cruso gave me his knife and warned me not to venture from his castle; for the apes, he said, would not be as wary of a woman as they were of him and Friday. I wondered at this: Was a woman, to an ape, a different species from a man? Nevertheless, I prudently obeyed, and stayed at home, and rested. (*F* 15)

The *différance* registered in Susan's narrative becomes a complex of questions about rule, authority, possession, and its critical part in a society which subordinates everything to the culture of the white male. The question, raised in Susan's narrative, is developed further in Part II, the letters written by her to Foe from her lodgings and subsequently from Foe's own lodgings, letters from a character to an absent author (and later, as Foe seems to disappear altogether, letters from an author to an absent character). Here, increasingly, it is the role of the teller in the tale that comes under scrutiny. It is linked with the theme of possession as the guarantee of substance in this society of arbitrary rule. Susan doubts her own narration:

> I seem to exist only as the one who came, the one who witnessed, the one who longed to be gone: a being without substance, a ghost beside the true body of Cruso. Is that the fate of all storytellers? . . . The island was Cruso's (yet by what right? by the law of islands? is there such a law?), but I lived there too. . . . Return to me the substance I have lost, Mr Foe: that is my entreaty. For though my story gives the truth, it does not give the substance of the truth. (*F* 51)

If Susan, who tells the tale, loses substance in the act of telling, and if we, who can find no Susan Barton in *Robinson Crusoe*, might reflect that even the prime informant of the fiction may disappear in the garbling, what about Friday? And what about Cruso? Susan reflects on the total loss of personal history in Friday:

> To tell my history and be silent on Friday's tongue is no better than offering a book for sale with pages in it quietly left empty. Yet the only tongue that can tell Friday's secret is the tongue he has lost! (*F* 67)

And she attempts, but fails, to discover the truth by showing Friday pictures of alternative versions of his mutilation, by Cruso and by an Arab slaver. There is a sense, of course, in which this is eloquent of the loss of an articulated history and culture in the African diaspora.

To cap it all, we have a version of Friday before us already, a version invented by Mr Defoe, that tradesman from Stoke Newington who began the European tradition of fiction. A Friday who can speak, and who readily submits to the superior culture, language, and ideology of Mr Crusoe. As for Crusoe (though Cruso is dead before he reaches England, and Susan's account of him is quite different), the grandfather of European fiction 'improves' his story. He does so much in the way that we Europeans have written history to 'improve' our sense of our own past, removing from it the voice of the woman, the mutilation of the slave, our failure not only to live up to an ideal, but to find an adequate one to live up to. The name 'Foe' is serendipitous in many ways, not least in suggesting that the way in which we tell our history may make us enemies of history and of ourselves.

One of the subjects which emerges from the fiction is the way in which the tale hurries ahead of the teller: 'Alas, my stories seem always to have more applications than I intend, so that I must go back and laboriously extract the right application and apologize for the wrong ones and efface them' (*F* 81). Coetzee is wry here. The whole tenor of the fiction is to subvert the claims to 'rightness', not only of our 'fictions' ('The editor believes the thing to be a just history of fact'), but also of our 'truths', our 'histories', to gesture to the way in which most of humanity is rendered inarticulate, edited out.

There are two more characters of significance in the fiction. The name of the first is also Susan Barton, and we might distinguish her from the Susan Barton who tells the story of Cruso's island by putting her in parentheses, thus: (Susan). (Susan) waits and watches outside the house where Susan is living and writing. She claims to be Susan's long-lost daughter. In this and certain other respects her role is reminiscent of the long-lost daughter in *Roxana*, but her role in *Foe* is not quite the same.

Susan denies (Susan)'s story, tells her that Foe is her real father:

> 'what you know of your parentage comes to you in the form of stories, and the stories have but a single source.'
>   'Who is my true mother then?' she says.
>   'You are father-born. You have no mother. . . . What you hope to regain in my person you have in truth never had.' (*F* 91)

If 'the stories have but a single source', then that source must be the story-teller. In the narrative fiction of *Foe*, the story-teller (in all but a few pages) is Susan Barton. If that fiction were 'the truth', then, in a manner of speaking, Susan Barton is 'the mother' of everything in the fiction so far, including (Susan Barton) and Susan Barton. Susan, in denying her mother-hood of (Susan), and making her father-born of Foe (and/or Coetzee), is subverting the claim of her authorship (and authority), which has sustained the narrative so far. Subsequently, in Part III, there seems to be a confirmation of Foe's authorship, particularly in the matter of the 'daughter' (Susan), since Foe tells Susan his version of Susan's own story, seeking more detail from Susan herself (*F* 116-17). It is a narrative which differs widely from Susan's, not least in the centrality of (Susan) and her search for her mother. But Susan Barton does not demur. Foe dominates the telling of the story as Cruso dominates the island.

Of course we know that the narrative is not written by 'Susan Barton', a substantial historical individual. Equally we know that it is not written by 'Daniel Foe', or 'Daniel Defoe'. The introspection of the fiction-writer Coetzee takes him into territories which have so far, perhaps, been traversed only by that wizard of *ficciones*, Jorge Luis Borges, and, if Borges is right, by Shakespeare:

> No one has ever been so many men as this man who like the Egyptian Proteus could exhaust all the guises of reality. . . . Richard affirms that in his person he plays the part of many and Iago claims with curious words 'I am not what I am'. The fundamental identity of existing, dreaming and acting inspired famous passages of his.[12]

This is a fiction which permits interpretation, to a degree. By that I do not mean that any set of interpretations may be guaranteed 'right' or 'wrong' by any verifiable standard. The best hope I have for my own comments, for instance, is that they hang together, more or less, and that the way they hang together illuminates something in Coetzee's enterprises. But Coetzee deliberately tests interpretation to its limits (as, in industry, materials are tested to destruction). For instance, in Part III, after Susan has been introduced to persons who are ambiguously fictions or reality, characters from Susan's or Foe's (lives?) (fictions?), including (Susan), Amy (from *Roxana*), Jack (who strolls in from Defoe's novel *Colonel Jack*), Susan and Foe speak of the ghostliness of everything in the mutual fiction they inhabit. Foe then asks Susan why she haunts him, and she answers 'For your blood. Is that not why ghosts return: to drink the blood of the living?'

> Instead of answering, Foe kissed me again, and in kissing gave me such a sharp bite to my lip that I cried out and drew away. But he held me close and I felt him suck the wound. 'This is my manner of preying on the living,' he murmured. (*F* 139)

The episode, and Foe's body, reminds her powerfully of Cruso. We have the elements of a series of interpretations, concerned with the insubstantiality of the world presented, the interdependence of the fictional personae, Foe's role in the novel, Cruso's role on the island, truth and its masculine distortions, the vampirism of Foe/Cruso, and Susan's sharing in all this ghostly intercourse. But one thing upsets the ensemble: Susan's assumption that she is ghostly is defeated by Foe's bite, and her pain. Similarly, in taking the superior role in their sexual intercourse, Susan whispers 'This is the manner of the Muse when she visits her poets.' The insecurity of the relation between 'ghost' and 'real' defies any stable interpretation, as I suppose it might be said to do in any story or life.

There is, as I have said, a section of the fiction in which the narrator is not Susan Barton, Part IV. It begins with the first words of Part III, and contains the first words of Part I. We are not told the name of the narrator, who calls him- or herself simply 'I'. It is set first in the room where Foe has entertained Susan, but then in the sea, in the wreck which Cruso escaped from. It is three hundred years later, and only one person still lives: Friday. It is some restitution for his enforced silence over the centuries. 'I' speaks to Friday. 'But this is not a place of words. . . . It is the home of Friday. . . . His mouth opens. From inside him comes a slow stream, without breath, without interruption' (*F* 157). I suppose we are promised the true story at last. It is not a chronicle of darkness.

Notes

1   Chronicles of darkness

1 Doris Lessing, 'Desert child', *New Statesman*, 15 Nov. 1958, 700.
2 ibid.
3 Chinua Achebe, *Arrow of God*, rev. edn, London, 1974, 46.
4 Stephen Gray, 'Introduction' to *The Penguin Book of Southern African Stories*, ed. Stephen Gray, Harmondsworth, 1985, 7-12.
5 Chinua Achebe, *Morning Yet On Creation Day*, London, 1975, 50.
6 Very few black African writers are made readily available to readers outside Africa in regular editions stocked in ordinary bookshops. Series like the Heinemann 'African Writers Series' and Longman's 'Drumbeat' are excellent in their way, providing good and cheap editions for the prime market. But there is a sense in which they form a kind of publishing ghetto which makes it less likely that the common reader in Britain or America will read them.
7 Nadine Gordimer, 'The English novel in South Africa', in *The Novel and the Nation*, NUSAS, Cape Town, 1960, 16.
8 Dan Jacobson, 'Introduction' to Olive Schreiner, *The Story of an African Farm*, Harmondsworth, 1971.
9 'The writer in the Commonwealth', in *Time of Arrival, and Other Essays*, London, 1963, 1967, 161.
10 Steve Biko, *I Write What I Like*, London, 1979, 64.
11 ibid., 24.

2   Joseph Conrad: *Heart of Darkness*

1 I allude to J. L. Austin's insight that some speech acts are not sayings, but actions of another kind (as for instance promising, bequeathing, warning). 'Other minds', *Proceedings of the Aristotelian Society*, supp. vol., 1964, reprinted in J. L. Austin, *Philosophical Papers*, Oxford, 1961; and J. L. Austin, *How to Do Things with Words*, Oxford, 1962. See also John R. Searle, *Speech Acts: An Essay in the Philosophy of Language*, Cambridge, 1969. I want to extend the idea to suggest that what Marlow utters, while it narrates a set of fictional events, is also, itself, a *deed* and is at least as important for what it does as what it says.
2 References to *Heart of Darkness* (abbreviated *HD*) are to the Uniform Edition of the Works of Joseph Conrad, *Youth: a Narrative, and Two Other Stories*, Dent, London, 1923.

3 John McClure, in *The Black Presence in English Literature*, ed. David Dabydeen, Manchester, 1986, 160.

4 '*Mise en abyme* is a term in heraldry meaning a shield which has in its centre (abyme) a smaller image of the same shield, and so, by implication, ad infinitum, with ever smaller and smaller shields receding toward the central point.' J. Hillis Miller, 'Steven's rock and criticism as cure', *Georgia Review*, 30 (1976), 11. See Edward W. Said: 'The problem of textuality: two exemplary positions', *Critical Enquiry*, 4 (1978), 673-714. I am grateful to Dr K. M. Newton for this note.

5 I follow John Willett, in *Brecht on Theatre*, tr. John Willett, London, 1964, in using 'gest' to convey the meaning of Brecht's word '*Gestus*'. Willett's note (p. 42) explains: ' "*Gestus*", of which "*gestisch*" is the adjective, means both gist and gesture; an attitude or a single aspect of an attitude, expressible in words or actions. . . . The translator has chosen the obsolete English word "gest", meaning, "bearing, carriage, mien" (*Shorter Oxford Dictionary*) as the nearest manageable equivalent, together with its adjective "gestic".' The word conveys a function of linguistic behaviour which goes beyond lexical definition; its action isolates an aspect of performative, as opposed to constative, uses of language.

6 F. R. Leavis, *The Great Tradition*, London, 1948, 177.

7 Ian Watt, *Conrad in the Nineteenth Century*, London, 1980, 138.

8 It is remarkable how some critics still rely uncritically on nineteenth-century sources for their reconstruction of the Africa which Marlow hints at. Stephen A. Reid, 'The "unspeakable rites" in *Heart of Darkness*', *Modern Fiction Studies*, IX, 4 (Winter, 1963-4), 347-56, assembles his version of African ritual behaviour from Sir James G. Frazer's *The Golden Bough*. The first edition of this appeared in 1890, the extended edition in 1911-15. As far as Africa is concerned, it is an anthology of traveller's tales dating from the three decades after the scramble for Africa, selected in such a way as to ratify preconceptions gleaned from readings of Classical myths. Reid's argument might be justified in this sense, that Frazer retailed the stories which visitors like Conrad or Marlow may well have brought back from the heart of their darkness, but to say that Marlow 'has reported accurately enough what he did see, and we can reconstruct the rest' is a bit odd. It is very difficult to prove or disprove some of the assumptions which are still current among Europeans about the civilizations which Europe scrambled. For instance it is very difficult to find hard evidence for customary cannibalism in Africa or any other continent.

9 Edward Garnett, unsigned review of *Heart of Darkness*, *Academy and Literature*, 6 Dec. 1902, 606. Reprinted in Norman Sherry (ed.), *Conrad: the Critical Heritage*, London, 1973, 131-3.

10 Joseph Conrad, *Lord Jim, A Tale*, London, 1923, 416.

11 *Youth: a Narrative, and Two Other Stories*, ix.

12 ibid., xi.

13 Joseph Conrad, *Letters to William Blackwood and David S. Meldrum*, ed. William Blackburn, Durham, NC, 154.

14 Behind the curtain in the temple, some said, was the *shekinah*, the glorious dwelling of the Divinity. Others argued that it was only present in the first temple, and therefore absent in Herod's. Either way the rending of the veil would show it wasn't there. My thanks are due to J. C. Q. Stewart for this point.

15 Watt, op. cit., 248.

16 Jacques Derrida, 'Structure, sign and play in the discourse of the human sciences', in *The Structuralist Controversy: The Languages of Criticism and the Sciences of Man*, ed, Richard Macksey and Eugenio Donato, Baltimore, 1972, 248.
17 J. Hillis Miller, *Fiction and Repetition*, Oxford, 1982, 26.

3 Olive Schreiner: *The Story of an African Farm*

1 Norman Sherry, *Conrad's Eastern World*, Cambridge, 1977; *Conrad's Western World*, Cambridge, 1980.
2 Elaine Showalter, *A Literature of Their Own*, rev. edn, London, 1978, 198.
3 All references to *The Story of an African Farm* (abbreviated *AF*) are to the Penguin edition, Harmondsworth, 1982.
4 Stephen R. Clingman, *The Novels of Nadine Gordimer: History from the Inside*, London, 1986, 4.
5 Ian Watt, *The Rise of the Novel*, London, 1957. See ch. 3, '*Robinson Crusoe*, individualism, and the novel'.
6 Showalter makes much the same point, op. cit., 199.
7 Ruth First and Ann Scott, *Olive Schreiner*, London, 1980, 97.
8 *Transvaal Leader*, 22 Dec. 1908, reprinted in *Closer Union*, Constitutional Reform Association, Cape Town. Cited in First and Scott, op. cit., 257-8.
9 Showalter, op. cit., 198.
10 Laurens van der Post, 'Introduction' to William Plomer, *Turbott Wolfe*, 1965, cited from the Oxford University Press edition, 1985.
11 References to *From Man to Man* (abbreviated *FMM*) are to the Virago edition, London, 1982.
12 Letter to Havelock Ellis, 2 Feb. 1889, *The Letters of Olive Schreiner*, ed. S. C. Cronwright-Schreiner, 1924, 153. Cited by First and Scott, op. cit., 175.
13 Showalter, op. cit., 201.

4 William Plomer: *Turbott Wolfe*

1 Mohandas K. Gandhi, *Satyagraha in South Africa*, Madras, 1928.
2 See Jack Simons and Ray Simons, *Class and Colour in South Africa, 1850-1950*, London, 1983, 132-8.
3 ibid., 140-1.
4 ibid., 252-5.
5 An excellent account of labour relations and the early years of socialism in South Africa is to be found in E. R. Roux, *Time Longer than Rope*, London, 1948.
6 Simons and Simons, op. cit., 386-415.; S. P. Bunting,. *Red Revolt and the Rand Strike*, Johannesburg, 1922.
7 References to *Turbott Wolfe* (abbreviated *TW*) are to the Oxford University Press edition, London, 1985.
8 David Rabkin, 'Race and fiction: *God's Stepchildren* and *Turbott Wolfe*', in *The South African Novel in English: Essays in Criticism and Society*, ed. Kenneth Parker, London, 1978, 77-94.
9 William Plomer, *Double Lives*, London, 1943, 186.

5 Laurens van der Post: *In a Province*

1 Jack Simons and Ray Simons, *Class and Colour in South Africa, 1850-1950*, London, 1983, 353.
2 André Brink, 'Mahatma Gandhi today', in *Mapmakers*, London, 1983, 58.
3 Simons and Simons, op. cit., 354.
4 ibid., 411-19.
5 References to *In a Province* (abbreviated *IP*) are to the Penguin edition, Harmondsworth, 1984.
6 Simons and Simons, op. cit., 419.
7 ibid., 423.
8 Marcello Caetano, *Os Nativos na Economia Africa*, Coimbra, 1954, 16, cited B. Davidson, *Africa in Modern History*, Harmondsworth, 1978.

6 Karen Blixen ('Isak Dinesen'): *Out of Africa*

1 References to *Out of Africa* (abbreviated *OA*) are to the Penguin edition, Harmondsworth, 1954.
2 Jacques Derrida, *Margins of Philosophy*, tr. Alan Bass, Chicago, 1982, 95.
3 Ngũgĩ wa Thiong'o, *Detained: a Writer's Prison Diary*, London, 1981, 36.
4 G. H. Mungeam, *British Rule in Kenya, 1895-1912*, Oxford, 1966, 84.
5 Basil Davidson, *Africa in Modern History*, Harmondsworth, 1978, 87.

7 Evelyn Waugh: *Scoop* and Joyce Cary: *Mister Johnson*

1 References to *Scoop* (abbreviated *S*) are to the Penguin edition, Harmondsworth, 1951.
2 In his discussion of the semantic complexities of *pharmakon* and *pharmakos* Jacques Derrida notes that *pharmakos* may carry the sense of 'magician', 'wizard', 'poisoner', and 'the one sacrificed in expiation for the sins of a city' (*Dissemination*, tr. Barbara Johnson, London, 1981, 132n.). Derrida argues the scapegoat role of writing in a literate society, and Waugh, expelling journalism from his Republic with a truly Platonic energy, seems to confirm Derrida's argument. As with Pope in *The Dunciad* or Nabokov in *Pale Fire* the rejection of scribblers by the scribe has an irony which is comprehended in the writing. I suspect that Plato, too, relished the situation of the writer praising the primacy of orality with his pen, the philosophical myth-maker rejecting the myth-makers as unphilosophical.
3 References to *Mister Johnson* (abbreviated *MJ*) are to the Penguin edition, Harmondsworth, 1962.
4 M. M. Mahood, *Joyce Cary's Africa*, London, 1964, 170.
5 Malcolm Forster, *Joyce Cary, A Biography*, London, 1969, 329.
6 Not all black writers condemn *Mister Johnson*. Ezekiel (Es'kia) Mphahlele writes about how he changed his mind about the book, and eventually found the characterization of the eponymous character 'a splendid success' (*African Image*, rev. edn, London, 1974, 187). There's a strange blandness in Mphahlele's critical work which isn't entirely a matter of tolerating diversity.
7 Mahood, op. cit., 183.
8 ibid., 186.

8   Elspeth Huxley: *The Flame Trees of Thika*

1 Elspeth Huxley, *The Mottled Lizard*, Harmondsworth, 1981, 185.
2 Colin Turnbull, *The Mountain People*, London, 1973, 235.
3 References to *The Flame Trees of Thika* (abbreviated *FTT*) are to the Penguin edition, Harmondsworth, 1962.

9   Graham Greene: *The Heart of the Matter* **and** *A Burnt-Out Case*

1 David Lodge, *Graham Greene*, New York, 1966, 32.
2 Kenneth Allott and Miriam Farris, *The Art of Graham Greene*, New York, 1951, 218.
3 M. M. Mahood, *Colonial Encounter*, London, 1977, 119.
4 T. S Eliot, *Selected Essays*, London, 1951, 422. Cited in Allott and Farris, op. cit., 12.
5 Eliot, op. cit., 421.
6 References to *The Heart of the Matter* (abbreviated *HM*) are to the Penguin edition, Harmondsworth, 1962.
7 Basil Davidson, *Africa in Modern History*, Harmondsworth, 1978, 273.
8 ibid., 274.
9 Mahood, op. cit., 120.
10 ibid.
11 References to *A Burnt-Out Case (abbreviated BOC)* are to the Penguin edition, Harmondsworth, 1963.
12 Amos Tutuola, *The Palm-wine Drinkard, and his Dead Palm-wine Tapster in the Dead's Town*, London, 1952 and *My Life in the Bush of Ghosts*, London, 1954 were the works which had received most attention. In the *Observer* Dylan Thomas led the chorus of praise for the former 'tall, devilish story'.

10   Alan Paton: *Cry, the Beloved Country*

1 Ngũgĩ wa Thiong'o, *Homecoming*, London, 1981, 43.
2 Circumstances have prevented me from checking the citation. It is quoted on the cover of early Penguin editions of *Cry, the Beloved Country*.
3 Jane P. Tompkins, 'Sentimental power: *Uncle Tom's Cabin* and the politics of literary history', in *The New Feminist Criticism: Essays on Women, Literature and Theory*, ed. Elaine Showalter, New York, 1985, 81-104.
4 Harriet Beecher Stowe, *Uncle Tom's Cabin*, cited by Tompkins, op. cit., 90.
5 Wilbur Smith, *When the Lion Feeds*, London, 1966, 109.
6 Ezekiel (Es'kia) Mphahlele, *African Image*, rev. edn, London, 1974, 157.
7 References to *Cry, the Beloved Country* (abbreviated *CBC*) are to the Penguin edition, Harmondsworth, 1958.
8 Jack Simons and Ray Simons, *Class and Colour in South Africa, 1850-1950*, London, 1983, 574.
9 I allude here to Derrida's use of *pharmakon* and *pharmakos*, with their semantic complexity. See above, ch. 7, n. 2.

11   Doris Lessing

1 References to Lessing's short stories are to the Triad/Granada edition of *Collected African Stories*, London, 1979: vol. 1, *This was the Old Chief's Country* (abbreviated *OCC*); vol. 2, *The Sun Between their Feet* (abbreviated *SBF*).

2 Joseph Conrad, 'Author's Note' to *Youth, a Narrative, and Two Other Stories*, xi.

3 There may be a memory of *Four Quartets* here:

> I met one walking, loitering and hurried
> As if blown towards me like the metal leaves
> Before the urban dawn wind unresisting.
> (T. S. Eliot, *Four Quartets*, 'Little Gidding', II, 33-5)

4 Inta Ezergailis, *Women Writers: The Divided Self*, Bonn, 1982, 15.

5 John Milton, *Paradise Lost*, IX, 432-3.

6 Sydney Janet Kaplan, in 'The limits of consciousness in the novels of Doris Lessing', *Contemporary Literature*, 14, 536-49, comments on the 'abundance of organic imagery in *The Golden Notebook*, and its relationship to the reproductive role of woman'.

7 Jerzy Grotowski, *Towards a Poor Theatre*, ed. Eugenio Barba, London, 1968, 23.

8 References to *The Grass is Singing* (abbreviated *GS*) are to the Triad/Granada edition, London, 1980.

9 *The Cocktail Party* was first performed in London in 1949, and in it, of course, Celia Coplestone is made to die, off-stage, on an ant-heap. It would be gratifying to demonstrate another allusion, but the date makes that unlikely.

10 Ezekiel (Es'kia) Mphahlele remarks, 'It would seem that when a white writer is still groping to define a black man's character which he or she is not sure how to present in dramatic terms, the writer finds it best to portray the character as a symbol. Moses is the epitome of the destructive forces that make up the African landscape as viewed by Mary' (*African Image*, rev. edn, London, 1974, 166). That may be part of it, but I think it a bit more tricky than that. You might reverse the proposition: Moses is the epitome of the destructive forces that make up Mary in the African landscape. Either way a conventional post-romantic view of character gives way under soteriological pressures.

11 References to *Going Home* (abbreviated *GH*) are to the Triad/Granada edition, London, 1980.

12 Lessing was co-signatory, with E. P. Thompson, Eric Hobsbawm, Christopher Hill and others, to a letter which appeared in both the *Tribune* and *New Statesman*, protesting against Soviet intervention in Hungary.

13 Margaret Drabble, 'Doris Lessing: Cassandra in a world under siege', *Ramparts*, X (Feb. 1972), 50-4.

14 Jenny Taylor (ed.), *Notebooks, Memoirs, Archives: Reading and Rereading Doris Lessing*, London, 1982, 7.

15 J. W. von Goethe, *Poetry and Truth: From my own Life*, tr. Minna Steele Smith, London, 1913, xxxvii-xxxviii.

16 G. W. F. Hegel, *Aesthetics*, tr. T. M. Knox, 2 vols, Oxford, 1975, vol. 1, 593.

17 Doris Lessing, 'Desert child', *New Statesman*, 15 Nov. 1958, 700.

18 References to *The Golden Notebook* (abbreviated *GN*) are to the Penguin edition, Harmondsworth, 1964.

19 Interview with Alan Yentob, *Arena*, BBC2, 30 January 1987.

20 Taylor, op. cit., 9.
21 From Idries Shah, *The Way of the Sufi*.
22 Doris Lessing, 'The small personal voice', in *Declaration*, ed. Tom Maschler, London, 1957, 24.

12   Nadine Gordimer: The short stories

1 John Cooke, *The Novels of Nadine Gordimer*, Baton Rouge, 1985, 26.
2 In a personal communication.
3 References to *The Soft Voice of the Serpent* (abbreviated *SVS*) are to the Penguin edition, Harmondsworth, 1962.
4 Dennis Brutus, 'Protest against apartheid', in Cosmo Pieterse and Donald Munro (eds), *Protest and Conflict in African Literature*, London, 1969, 97.
5 Cooke, op. cit., 11.
6 References to *No Place Like: Selected Stories* (abbreviated *NPL*) are to the Penguin edition, Harmondsworth, 1978. (Later editions published with the title *Selected Stories*.)
7 Sigmund Freud, *The Complete Psychological Works*, tr. and ed. James Strachey in collaboration with Anna Freud, vol. XVIII, London, 1955, 23.
8 References to *A Soldier's Embrace* (abbreviated *SE*) are to the Penguin edition, Harmondsworth, 1982.
9 Cooke, op. cit., 123.
10 Nadine Gordimer and David Goldblatt, *Lifetimes Under Apartheid*, London, 1986; *On the Mines*, Cape Town, 1973.
11 Gordimer and Goldblatt, *Lifetimes Under Apartheid*, unnumbered prefatory page.
12 'Love among the madness', an interview with Anthony Sampson, *Observer*, 29 Mar. 1987.
13 Nadine Gordimer, 'A South African childhood: allusions in a landscape', *New Yorker*, 16 Oct. 1954, 143.
14 Eugène Marais, *The Soul of the Ape*, with an Introduction by Robert Ardrey, Harmondsworth, 1969. The precise date of writing is unknown, but his basic research seems to have been in the Waterberg area from 1903 onwards.
15 Robert Ardrey, 'Introduction' to Marais, op. cit., 29.
16 Marais, op. cit., 59.
17 References to *Something Out There* (abbreviated *SOT*) are to the Penguin edition, Harmondsworth, 1985.
18 Cooke, op. cit., 123. Gordimer, *SOT*, 118.

13   Nadine Gordimer: The novels

1 There are two early unfinished novels in typescript. I have not been able to consult them, but there is an account by Stephen R. Clingman in *The Novels of Nadine Gordimer: History from the Inside*, London, 1986, 24-7. Clingman's account of the interfiliations between history and literature in Gordimer's novels is so good that I have felt able to deal with these matters very lightly in my own account.

2   Where dost thou careless lie
       Buried in ease and sloth?
     Knowledge, that sleeps, doth die;
       And this security.
       It is the common moth,
     That eats on wits, and arts, and oft destroys them both.
     (Ben Jonson, 'An Ode. To Himself')

3 Sigmund Freud, *Civilization and Its Discontents*, 1929, 1930, in *Complete Psychological Works*, tr. and ed. James Strachey in collaboration with Anna Freud, vol. XXI, London, 1961, 122.

4 John Cooke, *The Novels of Nadine Gordimer,* Baton Rouge, 1985, 64; see also Freud, op. cit., 69-72. References to *Occasion for Loving* (abbreviated *OL*) are to the Virago edition, London, 1983.

5 Freud, op. cit., 72.

6 References to *The Lying Days* (abbreviated *LD*) are to the Virago edition, 1983.

7 Clingman, op. cit., 39-44.

8 References to *A World of Strangers* (abbreviated *WS*) are to the Penguin edition, Harmondsworth, 1962.

9 Clingman notes (op. cit., 71): 'In Sophiatown the street marking the frontier between the black township and the white world of Johannesburg was called Toby Street, after the son of the township's original owner. Toby Hood therefore lives in a state of Toby-hood in the novel, or perhaps to-be-hood. . . . The destruction of Sophiatown had already begun. . . . And the street where the demolitions began was no other than Toby Street.' See also Trevor Huddlestone, *Naught For Your Comfort*, London, 1956. This happy explanation does not quite erase my own feeling that 'Hood' in an upper-class English outsider (even an outlaw) recalls the refugee of Sherwood Forest, while 'Toby' suggests, in multiple ways, the cosy self-congratulation of the English. But I concede the point.

10 Clingman, op. cit., 59.

11 'Towards a desk drawer literature', 71, cited by Clingman, op. cit., 96.

12 References to *The Late Bourgeois World* (abbreviated *LBW*) are to the Penguin edition, Harmondsworth, 1982.

13 References to *The Conservationist* (abbreviated *TC*) are to the Penguin edition, Harmondsworth, 1982.

14 Judie Newman, 'Gordimer's *The Conservationist*: "that book of unknown signs"', *Critique: Studies in Modern Fiction*, 22, 3 (April 1981), 81-99.

15 Clingman, op. cit., 161-2.

16 The Rev. Canon Henry Callaway, MD, *The Religious System of the Amazulu*, Springvale, Natal; Pietermaritzburg; Cape Town; London, 1868. Gordimer used the facsimile edition, Cape Town, 1970.

17 Clingman makes a similar point, op. cit., 141.

18 References to *Burger's Daughter* (abbreviated *BD*) are to the Penguin edition, Harmondsworth, 1982.

19 Athol Fugard, John Kani, and Winston Ntshona, *Sizwe Bansi is Dead*, London, 1974.

20 See also *BD* 83.

21 Steve Biko, *I Write What I Like*, London, 1979, 23.

22 'A game at which the liberals have become masters is that of deliberate evasiveness. The question often comes up "what can I do?" If you ask him to [deny] . . . all provisions that make him privileged, you always get the answer – "but that's unrealistic!" ' Biko, op. cit., 22-3.

23 The quotation contains the germ for the title of a remarkable novel by Hilda Bernstein, *Death is Part of the Process*, London, 1986. Bernstein's political career as a Communist in South Africa is part of history. The novel, very different from any of Gordimer's, is very revealing about the political process in South Africa.

24 Cited by Gordimer from *Selections from the Prison Notebooks of Antonio Gramsci*, tr. and ed. Quintin Hoare and Geoffrey Nowell Smith, London, 1971.

25 References to *July's People* (abbreviated *JP*) are to the Penguin edition, Harmondsworth, 1982.

26 References to *A Sport of Nature* (abbreviated *SN*) are to the Jonathan Cape edition, London, 1987.

27 Biko, op. cit., 24.

14 André Brink

1 In 1988 Janet Suzman directed a production of *Othello* at the Market Theatre in Johannesburg, with John Kani in the title role. The production was filmed, and presented on Channel 4 Television on 27 December 1988, too late to be taken into account in the text of this book. The circumstances of the production, and the performance of Kani, brought to light many aspects of the play which have been comparatively obscure in other productions.

2 Jerzy Grotowski, *Towards a Poor Theatre*, ed. Eugenio Barba, with a preface by Peter Brook, London, 1968. The work of Athol Fugard, especially the two plays in which he, John Kani, and Winston Ntshona co-operated, has had great influence on subsequent developments (*Sizwe Bansi is Dead* and *The Island*).

3 Antonin Artaud, *The Theatre and Its Double*, tr. Victor Corti, London, 1970, 64-87 and *passim*.

4 *Looking on Darkness*, London, 1974, translated from the Afrikaans, *Kennis van der Aand*, Cape Town, 1973. References (abbreviated *LD*) are to the Fontana edition, London, 1984.

5 *Argus*, 27 Aug. 1984, cited by Roger Omond, *The Apartheid Handbook*, Harmondsworth, 1985, 25. Omond also cites Hans Heese, *Groep Sonder Grense* ('Groups without Boundaries') and his argument that the forebears of many leading Afrikaner families had married or had relationships with Asian slaves. Heese argues that at least eighteen of the 'white' members of the racially exclusive House of Assembly have surnames indicating a mixed genealogy (*Guardian*, 5 Mar. 1985). The ensuing row led to Dr Christiaan Barnard challenging Dr Andries Treurnicht (leader of the right-wing Conservative Party) to submit to medical tests, sixteen people threatening to sue the *Sunday Times* for publishing Heese's findings, and punch-ups between members of the Pretoria City Council.

6 The Population Registration Amendment Act, Number 64 of 1967, cited by Omond, op. cit., 22.

7 André Brink, *The Ambassador*, rev. edn, Faber & Faber, London, 1985, 9.

8 André Brink, 'Writers and writing in the world' (1969), in *Mapmakers*, London, 1983, 45.

9 Once again, I borrow the word from Austin and Searle, to suggest that the force of such art lies in what it does rather than what it says.

10 Brink, *The Ambassador*, 9.

11 References to *An Instant in the Wind* (abbreviated *IW*) are to the Fontana edition, London, 1983.

12 References to *Rumours of Rain* (abbreviated *RR*) are to the Fontana edition, London, 1978.

13 André Brink, 'Mahatama Gandhi today' (1970), in *Mapmakers*, 55.

14 Helen Joseph, *Side by Side: The Autobiography of Helen Joseph*, London, 1986, 177.

15 See Donald Woods, *Biko*, London, 1978, 261.

16 John D. Jackson, *Justice in South Africa*, Harmondsworth, 1980, 69. One of the most revealing trial accounts is Lionel Forman and E. S. (Solly) Sachs. *The South African Treason Trial*, New York, 1958.

17 References to *A Dry White Season* (abbreviated *DWS*) are to the Fontana edition, London, 1979.

18 See, for instance, Genesis 12:16; Exodus 20:10, 17; 21:2, 5, 7, 8, 16; Deuteronomy 23:15ff; 24:7; Mark 12:2, 4; Matthew 24:45; John 8:25, etc. Paul's repeated dictum that in the kingdom of heaven there shall be neither bond nor free (1 Corinthians 12:13; Galatians 3:28; Colossians 3:11) has no implications for the practice of slavery in this world.

19 References to *A Chain of Voices* (abbreviated *CV*) are to the Fontana edition, London, 1983.

20 Among the many para-texts which surround the title, the uses Sophocles, Boccaccio, Defoe, Camus, and Artaud make of the plague are prominent.

21 References to *The Wall of the Plague* (abbreviated *WP*) are to the Fontana edition, London, 1985.

15   J. M. Coetzee

1 References to *Dusklands* (abbreviated *D*) are to the Penguin edition, Harmondsworth, 1983.

2 References to *In the Heart of the Country* (abbreviated *HC*) are to the Penguin edition, Harmondsworth, 1982.

3 References to *Waiting for the Barbarians* (abbreviated *WB*) are to the Penguin edition, Harmondsworth, 1982.

4 R. D. Laing, *The Divided Self*, Harmondsworth, 1965, 76-7.

5 Lionel Trilling, *The Opposing Self*, London, 1955, 39.

6 Of course Coetzee has read Derrida. Whether he is enjoying a pun here, recalling Derrida's use of *pharmakon* and *pharmakos* (see above, ch. 7, n. 2), I do not know. But it's a cap that fits well.

7 References to *Life & Times of Michael K* (abbreviated *MK*) are to the Secker & Warburg edition, London, 1983.

8 Daniel Defoe, 'Author's Preface' to *The Life and Strange Surprising Adventures of Robinson Crusoe*, Everyman's Library, London, 1945, 1.

9 Daniel Defoe, 'Author's Preface' to *The Fortunes and Misfortunes of the Famous Moll Flanders*, Everyman's Library, London, 1930, 1, 3.

10 References to *Foe* (abbreviated *F*) are to the Secker & Warburg edition, London, 1986.

11 Ludwig Wittgenstein, *Philosophical Investigations*, tr. G. E. M. Anscombe, Oxford, 1963.

12 'Everything and nothing', tr. James E. Irby, in Jorge Luis Borges, *Labyrinths*, ed. Donald A. Yates and James E. Irby, Harmondsworth, 1970, 285.

Index